LEE COUNTY LIBRARY
SANFORD, N. C.

THE POET AND HER BOOK

Other books by Jean Gould

MODERN AMERICAN PLAYWRIGHTS

ROBERT FROST: THE AIM WAS SONG

WINSLOW HOMER

A GOOD FIGHT

THAT DUNBAR BOY

YOUNG MARINER MELVILLE

LEE COUNTY LIBRARY
SANFORD, N. C.

THE POET
AND HER BOOK

A BIOGRAPHY OF

Edna St. Vincent Millay

By JEAN GOULD

ILLUSTRATED

DODD, MEAD & COMPANY

NEW YORK

The poetry of Edna St. Vincent Millay to which reference is made throughout the text appears in *Collected Poems* by Edna St. Vincent Millay, published in 1956 by Harper & Brothers, which became Harper & Row in 1962.

Copyright © 1969 by Jean Gould

All rights reserved

No part of this book may be reproduced in any form without permission in writing from the publisher

Library of Congress Catalog Card Number: 69-17603

Printed in the United States of America
by The Cornwall Press, Inc., Cornwall, N. Y.

With love
to
Dorothy and Hugh
who keep the candle burning brightly at both ends

Acknowledgments

This book about Edna St. Vincent Millay could not have been written without considerable aid from a number of sources. I wish to thank Gladys Ficke for permission to consult the Ficke Collection at Yale University, which includes material that she plans to use in her projected biography of her husband, Arthur Davison Ficke. My thanks go as well to Mr. Donald Gallup, Curator of the Yale Collection of American Literature, and to Mrs. Dorothy W. Bridgewater, Acting Head of the Reference Department during Mr. Gallup's absence while on a Guggenheim Fellowship; to them and to other members of the staff at the Beinecke Rare Book Library I am most grateful for assistance in consulting the Millay files of the Ficke Collection.

My thanks go to the staff at Vassar College Library, particularly to Miss Frances Goudy, Special Collections Librarian in charge of the Millay Collection, who provided a cubicle and desk for my research in the Library files concerning Edna St. Vincent Millay's years at Vassar College; to Miss Rogers and other staff members who gave prompt assistance with photographs. The New York Public Library granted me desk and shelf space in the Wertheim Study for special research over a period of several months, which was of invaluable help in preparing notes.

I am grateful to Edmund Wilson for suggesting certain additions to the quotation from his remarks on the Millay translation of Baudelaire poems in his literary chronicle of two decades, *The Shores of Light,* and to the people who furnished personal reminiscences of Edna Millay and her friends. Among the latter are Mrs. Winifred Fuller Byrd, and her sister, writer Maud (Fuller) Petersham, both Vassar graduates who had known the poet at college and in Greenwich Village. Mrs. Byrd was one of the four participants in the famous motoring trip which nearly caused Vincent to lose her graduation privileges, so she was able to supply authentic details of the incident that caused the "splendid row" at Vassar in June of 1917. Both sisters furnished fresh anecdotal material of Millay's madcap Village days, as did the British sculptress, Lu Duble, and the painter, Andrew Dasberg, who was sharing a studio apartment with Robert Edmond Jones at the time and knew most of the Provincetowners. I am also indebted to Mr. Dasberg, and to the newspaper writer and columnist, "Spud" Johnson, for reminiscences of Witter Bynner. Both of them had known him for many years, Mr. Johnson having served as his secretary for a time, and Mr. Dasberg having seen both Bynner and Ficke in the East and in Santa Fe.

Finally, I am deeply grateful to those who provided the place and peaceful atmosphere necessary to the concentrated work of writing: to Mr. and Mrs. Clifford West, Directors of the Ossabaw Island Project, Savannah, Georgia, for a period of residence during which the book was begun; to Georgina Klitgaard, painter and good friend, who gave me a summer's stay and a studio in which to work at her home near Woodstock; and to Dr. Henry A. Sauerwein, Director of the Helene Wurlitzer Foundation of New Mexico, where the manuscript was completed during a five months' residence grant, February to July, 1968.

JEAN GOULD

New York City

Contents

LEE COUNTY LIBRARY
SANFORD, N. C.

Illustrations

xi

CHAPTER I

They Called Her "Vincent"

ONE DAY around the turn of the century in a small town in Maine, a spindly-legged little girl with elfin eyes was standing on a mossy hillock, straining to see as far as she could across the cranberry swamp below. She stood perfectly still, silent and still, a small, inscrutable sphinx: only the green-flecked eyes, alive and alert, would have betrayed the agile, singing mobility of her being; but within was the invisible heart, vibrating like a tightly strung harp.

She was watching the figure of her father, suitcase in hand, grow smaller and smaller as he strode through the cranberry bog, taking the shortcut to the railroad station. Her parents had been arguing again; this time her mother had told her father to leave and not come back. Or maybe, the little girl thought, she said that he might come back if he would "do" better. Although he was a staid man in many ways, the girl's father could not resist gambling, but her mother could not abide the habit. She would no longer put up with his irresponsible mishandling of the family's only income, his meager salary as combined high school teacher and superintendent of schools.

The seven-year-old girl, her long red-gold hair ruffling in the sea breeze, sensed with the sure intuition of a precocious child that her father would never come back. Not to stay. As her eyes saw his figure dwindle across the cranberry swamp, she somehow knew that he would never again live in their house in Union,

Maine, or in any other town. There was an air of finality about the scene that sent the chill of eternal loneliness through her veins, a feeling never quite dispelled by warm, demonstrative affection from her mother and younger sisters. In spite of their high spirits and the sunny insouciance of their bookish, bohemian household, humming with intellectual activity in days to come, and despite the girl's passionate love for mankind, for the wondrous earth she inhabited, she was destined always to be in some measure a solitary soul.

An unusually perceptive child, she was instinctively aware of the somber portent in the sight of her father's receding figure; and she stood like Peter Pan in never-never land, somewhere between the worlds of childhood and adulthood, in her own sphere. Here part of her would always dwell—"an exile far out upon the world's forsaken rim, her wild feet forever seeking Beauty"—as one of her lovers, a fellow poet, was to write.

A sudden, excited twittering of warblers in a tamarisk grove on the edge of the swamp quickly diverted the child in her, bringing her body to life in one of her mercurial changes of mood: there must be a nest close by! Where? Were there babies in it? She swung swiftly around and, like some spirited wood sprite, nimbly climbed the gnarled branches of an old apple tree on the knoll, ignoring her full skirts. She brushed past an empty wren house, recently vacated by a noisy family amid much coaxing and calling of the young. The robins, too, had abandoned their house of twigs, straws, and strings. This commotion must be caused by some variety of songbird she didn't know yet. Brimming with curiosity, she began to search for a nest in the thicket from her vantage point atop the apple tree. At that moment she heard her singular boy's name sung out below in her mother's crisp, yet melodic tones: "Vin-n-cent!" But she was so intent on her quest she did not answer. She felt a strong tie of kinship with winged creatures who could soar at will or pour forth a fine trill whenever they pleased.

Her mother's next call was more insistent, so she climbed down, promising herself as she dropped from the lowest branch to the ground that she would come back the next day. She started out for home on the run, but stopped to gather a handful of delicate field daisies and sturdy stalks of burdock for her mother. What did it matter if her mother did despise the burs because they "stuck so" to children's socks and drawers? Then she ran on with the airy speed of a spinney elf.

Her face lit up with happiness when her mother, giving her a hard hug, said "Oh, what a fine bouquet!" Later in the summer she heard her mother remark to a neighbor, "She's always dragging in those weeds!" and it nearly broke her heart; but the slur only made her love wildflowers the more, a feeling she was to keep all her life. She clung to her mother's neck, returning her almost too-hard embrace in an unconscious effort to offer comfort because of the latest family quarrel. She was breathless from running, and her freckled nose quivered in high excitement as she reported the discovery of the new bird's nest, whispering the words dramatically into her mother's ear. But she said nothing about having witnessed her father's departure. She knew that her forthright mother—who bore the Celtic surname of Buzzelle before she married Henry Tolman Millay—would reveal soon enough whether Papa had gone for good or would be coming back before long.

Cora Millay was a mixture of common sense, droll wit spiced with earthy humor, honest and open affection, more than a dash of musical talent, and a touch of the poet. She had developed a strong sense of responsibility and independence "early on," when she had had to look after five younger children following the untimely death of her mother. She had managed to study piano and voice and had learned enough about music to rehearse the town orchestra, a practice she kept up for many years. As a young girl she had longed to be a singer or a writer, but had little time to realize her dreams, and she determined on her wedding day that if she was lucky enough to bear a child with even a spark of talent she would fan it into flame. She gave her daughters their first music lessons, along with her lively appreciation of the arts.

Shortly before her first child was born, when she and her husband were living in Rockland, Maine, Mrs. Millay received word that her youngest brother, a sailor who had been seriously injured during a storm at sea, was recovering well under the excellent care he had been given at St. Vincent's Hospital. Deeply grateful, Cora Millay, confident that her baby would be a boy, decided to name him after St. Vincent, patron saint of the sick and, according to an earlier legend, protector of wine growers. When the baby turned out to be a girl, Cora included "St. Vincent" as a middle name, a sign of her fervent appreciation of the hospital. Mr. Millay had also hoped for a boy, and they called the child "Vincent" in the family circle. For the first name they chose "Edna," akin to an old Norse word for poetry, whose Greek and Hebrew meaning was "rejuvenation."

"Vincent" was born on Washington's Birthday, February 22, 1892. She was born with "Beauty's kiss," and with the unmistakable imprint of the Irish leprechaun. Except for the anguished howl with which she came rushing into the world, she seemed a child born with love and laughter on her lips, and a foreknowledge of life's sorrow as well as its joy. Almost from infancy she revealed, in her knowing ways and quicksilver responses to life and the varying moods of others, a capacity far beyond that of an ordinary child. In her wonder at each new discovery in the world around her, from her own tiny perfect hands to the first flowers and birds her eyes beheld, she seemed transfixed with joy and awesome delight. Yet her expression changed to one of sadness when her mother's face was troubled, and her sympathy flowed intuitively. In her astonishing ability to learn by heart the nursery rhymes and songs her mother sang at bedtime and the first poems and lessons in school, and in her immediate grasp and love of music, she early showed the signs of the rarely gifted, a spark more glowing than her mother's fondest dreams had imagined.

Shortly after Vincent's birth, the Millays moved to Union, Maine, where a second daughter, Norma, was born in December, 1893, and a third, Kathleen, in May, 1896. Each child had her own brand of charm. Kathleen, the "baby," was perhaps the prettiest, a dark-Irish beauty. Norma, who was blonde and eventually the most voluptuous, inherited her mother's talent as a singer. Vincent, the brightest and most winsome, was the least pretty in the conventional sense, but she possessed the greatest potential for real beauty: a small but perfectly formed, fine-boned body; a transparent skin faintly freckled in summer; carroty hair that took on glints of gold in the sunlight; and gray-green bewitching eyes, by turns mischievous, mysterious, and dreamy.

If Cora Millay had a favorite, it was her firstborn, and during the disruptive years of her marriage she found both comfort and diversion in fostering the growth of the seeds of grace disclosed day by day in the daughter she had presented with such a symbolic and rhythmical name. Small Vincent seemed indeed to be the embodiment of the poetic and the saintly, combined with a pantheistic joy in being alive. When she was nearly five she composed her first poem: three rhymed couplets on the theme of "One Bird." It was a child's poem, the simplest of songs. But the lines showed an observant eye, a sense of meter so necessary in a poet; and they brought the fond encouragement of her mother, her lifelong inspiration.

CHAPTER II

St. Nicholas Leaguer and
Nomad of Mount Megunticook

A FTER MRS. MILLAY had told her husband to leave forever unless he could "do" better it did not take her long to make up her mind to get a divorce, despite the taboos of the time and the unfriendly criticism she would have to face. Aside from Henry's gambling, particularly his poker-playing, Cora and her husband viewed life so differently and had such divergent interests that Cora was convinced both they and their daughters would benefit if they dissolved their marriage. And she had the courage to act on her convictions, a quality that Vincent was to admire and emulate as she grew older.

The Millays parted on friendly terms, with the understanding that Henry could visit the girls whenever he wished, although no binding terms of alimony or regular contributions were set by the court. Henry offered no resistance to the proceedings, feeling relieved perhaps that he could pursue his own pastimes without having to listen to his wife's objections; and strong-minded, sturdy little Cora Millay stood ready to assume the responsibility of the household and the upbringing of the children. If she had any misgivings, she kept them to herself; she was cheerful and matter of fact about the divorce and the enormous task before her, and the girls unconsciously absorbed and reflected their mother's sanguine outlook.

Nevertheless, there was bound to be a certain amount of up-heaval as a result of the family breakup. Vincent, who had turned eight by the time the decree was granted, and whose high-keyed sensibilities rang with responsive chords at the slightest ripple of human emotions, experienced a bewilderment and a feeling of abandonment which was to become outright skepticism toward the concept of enduring love between man and woman. The theme, based on the fleeting beauty of love, was to run like a dis-sonant leitmotif through most of her work.

Soon after the separation, Cora packed up the family belong-ings and with her three little girls went to "live around with" her three sisters. It was a jumpy sort of existence. They went first to Rockport, where the girls attended school. Vincent made a giant leap in literary taste from *Mother Goose* to Shakespeare. She had always wanted to get her hands on the big illustrated volume so highly prized by her mother, and the opportunity came when Mrs. Millay had to be away frequently. Left to her own devices she lost no time in reading books considered too old for a child of her age. The eight-year-old girl found herself enthralled by the Elizabethan lines, which she read with amazing ease. The language of poetry seemed natural to her, and the comedy or drama unfolded in the play became part of her own experience. She read with mounting excitement, with an almost sensual pleasure, just as she sang for sensual pleasure and played the piano for the thrill of the sound. She had a good voice, though her talent was never as marked as Norma's. At choir practice, which she began attending in Rockport, her voice swelled out above the other children's in an ecstasy of joy.

The inner turmoil caused by her father's apparent alacrity to give up his place as head of the family came to the surface in odd ways in this exceptional oldest child of the Millays. She had the redhead's quickly fired temper, flareups that came and passed at the slightest provocation during this period, and from this time on, whenever she was crossed, harassed, or troubled by deep emotion. She could be contrary to the point of being utterly ex-asperating. Her Aunt Susie, Mrs. Frank L. Ricker, with whom the family stayed for a while, said that "Vincent was just *plain impish*" when she cut the fringe on the damask tablecloth because

her aunt told her not to, one of many pranks she would pull unexpectedly. On the other hand, she could be as sweet and tract-
able as her elders could wish, and most of the time she tried to
be helpful, especially to her mother.

Mrs. Millay decided to become a practical nurse as a means
of livelihood, and while she was in training out of town, her eight-
year-old daughter kept her informed of the state of affairs in
Rockport. She wrote her mother that Kathleen's cold was better;
that Norma and she were doing "all right" in school; that she
went to "practice" and a boy called her a "chamipion" and when
she asked what he "ment" he said "because she was the best
singer" and she thanked him. She also included the comment
that her teacher "blused red as a June rose" at the mention of her
mother's cousin, George Keller, who had "gone around with" the
teacher, a precocious observation in a child, and one that brought
an appreciative chuckle from her mother. The letter was signed,
"Lots of love to you, your loving daughter, Vincent"; it was the
first of many intimate and deeply affectionate records of daily
life and thought that the daughter was to send her mother whenever they were apart.

A year or so later, when she was nearly ten, and the family
was living in Salisbury for the moment, the embryo poet sent a
"business-like letter" to the firm that was, unknown to her then,
to be her principal publisher, enclosing, with a concise note in
a child's round hand, two dollars for her subscription to *Harper's
Young People*. The note was signed, "Respectfully yours, E. Vincent Millay." This was the version of her name she chose to fix
to most of her early poems, giving a touch of mystery to the
identity of the author and an expression of the tomboy in her.

During her childhood she sometimes seemed more boy than
girl. She much preferred outdoor pursuits to dolls or playing
house, even as a very small child; and at nine she scorned such
pastimes when Norma or Kathleen, who occasionally enjoyed
them, wanted her to join in. Then she would wander off by herself, "lonely as a cloud," feeling a vague, indefinable melancholy
of unknown origin, filled with childhood's mystic imaginings of
unknown regions in the great cosmos of the heavens. Although
she became very close to her sisters, especially Norma, next to her

in age, the already budding poet often found herself wandering alone, particularly in periods of flux, when life seemed totally transient.

A few months after her tenth birthday, when the family was staying at Ring's Island, Massachusetts, Vincent set off one early summer day in search of wildflowers, though she had little hope of finding any since the soil was sandy, yellow, and barren. She no longer presented her mother or any of the elders with these bouquets, for wildflowers would never be "weeds" to her, as they evidently were considered by most grownups. It would be years before the gentle ironic humor of the difference in viewpoint found expression in a series of brief, nostalgic poems, entitled "A Very Little Sphinx," which was lighter in key than most of her lyrics at that time.

She ambled for an hour or more, listening for birds as well as watching for wildflowers. By now she could recognize many of the calls. She knew the bobolink's chuckle, the meadowlark's limpid song, and the whippoorwill's twilight whistle. She could spot the golden-yellow flash from the underwing of the flicker in flight and tell the difference between his hard hammering and the staccato drilling of the downy woodpecker. She had learned the names of many more wildflowers in previous summers, from early hepatica to the late autumn gentian, but there were still some she could not identify, and she was always looking for new finds, rare forms and colors combined with a sweet or spicy fragrance, like the minty leaves of bergamot. Today the search seemed idle in such a patchy green landscape, but she kept on doggedly. Perhaps she wanted to prove to herself that wildflowers were more beautiful than the cultivated kind, which never held as much interest for her. Perhaps she was still resentful of the word "weeds," and that was why she had pulled up "all the flowers in the front border" at her Aunt Susie's, right after her aunt expressly told her not to: sometimes the "imp" in her became an outright devil.

She was about to give up when she arrived at a "barren naked stretch of ground not far from the sea," and a tall plant with large purple trumpet-shaped flowers leaped into view from quite a long way off. She ran toward it with all the eagerness of a treasure-seeker, her melancholy dispelled, her senses excited to a high pitch: what a beauty! She bent over one of the purple trumpets, happily taking a deep whiff before plucking it, and was nearly overcome by a rank, nauseating odor. She turned and fled from the evil smell in horror, somehow feeling as if she had been betrayed and reviled. She was ill for a few moments and finally went back to the house, pale and shaken, unable to tell anyone what had happened. Many years later, in England, she learned the name of the "rank-smelling" plant with the beautiful blossom, called by the English "thorn-apple," by Americans "Jimson weed," and whose botanical name [1] signified that it was very poisonous, of the deadly nightshade family. Years more passed before she could bring herself to relate the revolting incident to anyone; and the story came to light then only because she included the "thorn-apple" in her elegiac poem, "In the Grave No Flower," one of a sequence written after her mother died.

The next stay was in Newburyport, Mrs. Millay's home town, but she found it was a mistake to return as a divorcee with three little girls; and she finally decided to try an entirely different sort of place, the seacoast town of Camden, Maine, not far from Union, where the Millays had lived before the divorce. To Vincent, it was like coming home after nearly three years of wandering.

Camden was a delightful resort and shipbuilding center, set between the mountains and Penobscot Bay, its snug harbor dotted with fishing boats, shining yachts, and tall-masted schooners. When a ship built at the yards was ready for launching, the whole town turned out for the event. As the craft went down the ways—occasionally it was a schooner with as many as six masts—a rousing cheer went up from the watchers, and the children jumped in the air, laughing and shouting. The beaches furnished a never ending source of fascinating enterprises: digging for clams and mussels; gathering shells and oddly shaped pieces of driftwood twisted and worn smooth by time and the waves; running barefoot along the sand and clambering across the barnacled hulls of shipwrecks slowly rotting away on the shore. Sometimes Vincent liked to sit on the rocks by herself, watching

[1] *Datura tatula.*

the seagulls circle for food, soaring and swooping, winging their way across the water and back, while the little sandpipers scurried along the edge, looking as if they were propelled by rollers. On gray days and during winter storms the fog bells sounded their eerie warnings day and night and the surf crashed high against the rocks, forbidding to all but the hardiest of sailors and fishermen. Yet Vincent Millay somehow loved the mournful sound and the severe aspect of the angry, endlessly pounding sea, washing in white foam over the rocky coast. It appealed to her strong sense of the dramatic, evoking in her poet's eye a vision of the mysterious deep, and the wild lonely reaches of the universe.

The town was quiet and peaceful, with tree-lined streets, houses set in wide lawns, and back yards ample enough for vegetable gardens. It resembled a country village, shady and green in summer, starkly white in winter. The three long mountains headed by Megunticook rose straight up from the shore beside the town in a protective wall of high cliffs, topped by tall pines that sighed in the wind summer and winter. The wood was hallowed ground for hikers and nature lovers, the special haven of a wildflower seeker like Vincent.

In 1903, the family of three little girls and their mother moved into a house at 40 Chestnut Street, their permanent home as long as they lived in Camden. Here the poet passed, in her words, "an extraordinarily happy childhood," though it was never a pampered one. As the oldest child, Vincent had to shoulder the household duties, taking the lead for the younger girls when her mother was away on a case. At first Mrs. Millay tended patients only in the evening after the children were asleep, but from the time Vincent was eleven or twelve, they were often left on their own day and night, sometimes for several weeks. Not that Vincent ever allowed housekeeping tasks to become a burden: she let them lag as long as possible and then sailed into cleaning up with whirlwind energy, a merry captain of her small crew. Norma and Kathleen were quick to fall in step; all three regarded their premature independence as something of a lark. Mealtimes, especially supper, was set by appetite, and might take place any time from right after school to some hour long after dark if the children were absorbed in playing outdoors.

Meals in general took on the air of the ever tardy Mad Hatter's tea party. Sometimes Vincent sent her sisters to the corner bakery for pastry treats, which they enjoyed with milk; this was their favorite menu. Sometimes the grocery money had been spent on such items as crayons or sheet music, or, when they were older, a play or concert, and they would settle for odds and ends, cleaning out the larder: leftover beans and stale cake, perked up by pickles. If the cupboard was completely bare, they often fixed and consumed a pan of fudge for supper, to the astonishment of a schoolmate who was once invited to stay. In summer, like all New England children, the girls went berry-picking and could usually count on blueberries or wild blackberries and milk for supper.

Dishes were allowed to pile up; when the sink was full, the girls would pitch in, with Vincent washing while her sisters dried. She made up a ditty to cheer them on one day: delightful doggerel about "pots and pans galore . . . always some more . . . a dozen . . . a score," ending with a royal flourish, "I'm queen of the dishpan—hooray!" which inspired her helpers to toss their towels in the air. They all went to the parlor organ, which was replaced by a piano as soon as Mrs. Millay could afford it, where Vincent pumped out a wheezy tune for her jingle, and they all joined in singing the words with the gusto of the Anvil Chorus.

On Saturdays and during summer vacation, Vincent conscientiously set up a schedule of fifteen-minute periods: "Wash dishes," "Study," "Write," "Prepare lunch," "Go into garden"; but it was only followed if they felt like it. The young poet was apt to concentrate on the single item, "Write," forsaking the others while she wrestled with words and rhythms. The first time Mrs. Millay took a live-in case for a week, the girls did no housecleaning till the day before their mother returned. They decided to clean the house from top to bottom as a surprise welcome home for her, and Vincent devised a game to make the job easier. When she shouted, "Corner!" each of the girls dashed to a different corner of the room and started cleaning; from there they moved to the middle; when they met, they all cleaned the last corner together. They went from one room to another in a frenzy of scrubbing; Vincent had a towel tied around her head like the best of New

England housekeepers, presenting a funny sight to her sisters. But they finished the task in no time at all.

Their mother's astonished delight over the immaculate house was ample reward for the girls, though they knew she would not have scolded them if they had let the housework go in favor of schoolwork, music, painting, reading, or writing. Mrs. Millay, a person of boundless energy, usually did the washing, ironing, and mending when she was off duty. She might "run up" a pretty blouse for one of her daughters, and she customarily baked a week's loaves of bread besides a batch of beans on Saturday night; in summer she put up jams and jellies and canned vegetables, so the girls would have something on hand when she was away. But practical though she was, Cora Millay valued the things of the spirit, especially the arts, above all else in the world. No daughter of hers would ever be told to pick up her room if a poem was in the process of creation. Instead, she would goad the project along, suggesting words if asked, or urging, "Look it up, look it up!" when unknown classical allusions arose in one of the girls' reading. For one of her birthdays, Cora gave Vincent an expensive twenty-volume encyclopedia, which proved invaluable to her during her school years and long afterward. It was said, with asperity by some of the townsfolk, that though Mrs. Millay earned hardly enough to pay the grocer or the coal company, she managed to provide her girls with the finest collection of books in Camden. And she made it clear that she did not buy them for decoration!

Vincent appreciated her mother's warm, active desire to shape the girls' careers along artistic lines. A year or two after they settled in Camden, she started keeping a notebook of her completed poems, on the cover of which she printed a rather pretentious title, "Poetical Works of E. Vincent Millay"; and on the first page, the ardent dedication, "To my mother, Whose interest and understanding have been the life of many of These Works, and the Inspiration of many more, I lovingly dedicate this volume." On the following page was her first poem, "One Bird." As new "poetical works" were created and polished, often with the help and encouragement of her mother, she copied them in successive pages in the round, neat handwriting of her school years.

And as the pages of her notebook began to fill up, the budding poet became more confident of her ability until she had enough self-assurance to start submitting them for publication to her favorite magazine, the *St. Nicholas.*

Like other young readers from the 1890's until well into the 1920's, the Millay girls were dedicated subscribers to this remarkable magazine, which served to inspire more than one young genius who later became famous in American letters. When the new issue came in the mail every month, there was always a merry scramble as each girl tried to get her hands on it first. Just to tear off the wrapper and dive into the latest installment of one of the serials was a rich experience. Sometimes a squabble ensued; Vincent always emerged victorious, but she was generous enough to compromise with the others by giving her solemn pledge to turn it over to Norma or Kathleen as soon as she had taken a look at the *St. Nicholas* League section, pages in the back of each issue devoted to contributions from readers considered worthy of publication. To further the "expression of artistic ability through competitive striving" on the part of its young readers, the magazine awarded silver and gold badges to the writers of the best manuscripts submitted; and it was among "E. Vincent Millay's" fondest dreams that one of her poems would be an award-winning contribution.

She was fourteen years old before that early dream was realized, and by then two of her pieces, one prose and the other poetry, had appeared in the high school paper, *The Megunticook.* But the thrill of seeing her first poem, "Forest Trees," in the October, 1906, issue of the *St. Nicholas* was even more electrifying—to think that E. Vincent Millay was listed as a *St. Nicholas* Leaguer! In the weeks that followed she trembled with happy excitement every time she thought about it, whether she was hiking in the autumn woods or fixing a cup of tea or hurrying to church with her sisters on Sunday morning. Her Sunday School teacher and friend, Abbie Huston Evans, had published a number of poems in New England periodicals, and had been a ready source of encouragement for her gifted pupil. Abbie must have been almost as pleased as Mrs. Millay when Vincent's poems appeared in print.

The following year three more were accepted by the *St. Nicholas;* one of these, "The Land of Romance," was awarded the coveted Gold Badge. More important, it was reprinted later in *Curent Literature* with the significant remark, "The poem that follows seems to us phenomenal. . . . Its author (whether boy or girl, we do not know) is but fourteen years of age." The future poet was already on her way to wide acclaim, although for several years she was to waver between the equally alluring paths of poetry and music.

As soon as Mrs. Millay bought a piano, all the girls took lessons, but it was Vincent who showed the most talent. Norma, who preferred singing, and eventually studied voice, developed a capacity for opera as well as concert performance. When she was at the piano, Vincent lost track of time almost as easily as she did in trying to perfect a poem. She seemed to be a born musician, possessing a knack for composition as well as a true gift for playing. She probably picked up a basic knowledge of harmony and counterpoint from her mother, who often copied parts for orchestras in addition to playing and rehearsing; music indeed was as much a part of the Millays' unusual household as literature. The feeling and fine shading she instinctively gave to simple pieces, along with a certain power of touch rare in children, struck her mother as extraordinary. Never one to miss an opportunity, Mrs. Millay asked a patient of hers, John Tufts, who was a retired piano teacher of some note, if he would listen to her daughter play. One day shortly before Vincent's twelfth birthday, he listened and was so impressed that he decided to teach her himself. His lessons were one of her mother's presents for which Vincent was always deeply grateful. Like poetry, her first great love, music became a passion with her, and she spent many hours practicing the piano with concentration and zeal. At thirteen she composed an operatic version of "Little Boy Blue" for a school production, and to entertain her sisters she set the girls' favorite Mother Goose rhymes to music. All three had naturally good voices and sang for pleasure, often repeating Vincent's roundelays over and over. On summer evenings they sang them walking along country roads; and on winter nights they gathered around the piano, sometimes with school friends, but more often just by themselves until their high school years.

At school Vincent's chameleon-like nature caused her to take on a many-sided role. She was by turns a wiry, daredevil tomboy, skeptical and more than ready to accept a challenge; a quick, bright student in all but arithmetic; and an imaginative, dreamy child of the arts. That she was also a child of nature, a half-ephemeral creature of the outdoors, her classmates could only glimpse occasionally. Lean and agile, she could outrun most of the boys as well as outwit them in games. She pooh-poohed idle superstitions passed around the playgrounds and once set off to disprove the old wives' tale that stolen apples would give the thief a terrible stomach-ache. She climbed a tall Hesperides apple tree by moonlight, stole a skirtful of the golden fruit, and ate them all without suffering a single pain. For good measure, she declared that they had the most delicious flavor of any apples she had ever tasted.

In class, she was almost too vociferous, too eager and enthusiastic. In most subjects, especially languages and literature, she was a brilliant student, although arithmetic was her anathema, and she made no secret of her struggle or her failure to solve complicated problems from fourth-grade long division on to higher mathematics like algebra. The time-honored McGuffey readers did not seem dull to her. She loved the excerpts of Latin poetry, delighting particularly in the sounds of lines from Catullus that had to be memorized and recited in class. From those first exercises on, she was a devoted reader of the Roman poet of love. At a much later time, whenever she was on tour, she always took along a tiny leather copy of Catullus to read or parse for pleasure, relaxation, and comfort.

With Shakespeare and Catullus as the base of her reading, Vincent read omnivorously, perhaps indiscriminately, but not superficially. She retained a surprising amount of all she devoured. In English class her small hand shot up before the teacher's questions were quite finished; as an inquisitive, curious, and enthusiastic student, she asked innumerable questions of the teacher, who probably wished occasionally that she were less articulate. On the other hand, it was most unusual to find a pupil so eager for knowledge that there was no need for the teacher to inquire if she had done her homework. One summer, at the age of fourteen, she spent a good part of the vacation reading Caesar's *Gallic Wars* on her own, because she wanted to take up Cicero's orations in the fall in order to be able to read Vergil's *Aeneid* sooner. When Cora Millay saw her oldest daughter lying in the hammock with a book, she understood that the girl was not being lazy, but was being extremely diligent in her scholarly pursuits.

To Vincent, summer was a time to be treasured, not only because she could spend all day long outdoors, or because everyone who lived in the rugged Maine climate prized the brief span of mild weather, but because her mother was apt to be at home more often, since there was usually less sickness in the summer. Of course this meant that there was less household money, and the grocer might get impatient about his bill, but they could always get along on bread and tea and fresh vegetables from the garden.

Early in May, Mrs. Millay would let the girls help her set out the flower and vegetable garden: they put in radishes, onions, lettuce, peas (it was always a treat to gather, shell, and eat the first green peas of the season), potatoes, beans, and perhaps a few rows of corn. In the flower plot, they planted phlox, larkspur, marigolds, and lemon verbena, varying annuals from summer to summer, except for the huge climbing nasturtiums that covered the trellis beside the porch every year that Vincent could remember. Her mother was very proud of them and would not let anyone plant those seeds but herself, though any child of seven could easily have stuck them in the ground. But no amount of teasing by the girls could change Cora's possessive attitude toward her climbing nasturtiums.

And she was almost as particular about the herb garden planted just outside the kitchen door: here they grew parsley, thyme, tansy, rosemary, and fennel. Later these names were liberally sprinkled through the verse of Edna St. Vincent Millay; her second volume of poetry, *Second April*, was originally entitled *A Stalk of Fennel*, which appears in the lines, "I have stolen breath/ In a stalk of fennel" from her notable plea for immortality, "The Poet and His Book," in the same volume. In the fall, her mother would dry the herbs for winter use, and there would be a piquant, almost pungent fragrance from the bunches of seasonings hung up to dry on the porch, mixed with the scent of autumn apples and pine branches gathered for the winter. Here was part of the earth lore the poet learned from her mother that gave her lyrics the sweet, strange aroma so characteristic of her song.

Vincent usually began the gardening with a will, but she was so taken up with other things that she forgot all about cultivating if her mother wasn't there; or she might remember in time to do a little at odd hours. The Millays' garden-stuff was apt to lag way behind the neighbors', who looked askance at the peculiar schedule. When she wrote, in "Portrait by a Neighbor," the thumbnail sketch of herself, "She digs in her garden / With a shovel and a spoon, / She weeds her lazy lettuce / By the light of the moon," Edna Millay was hardly exaggerating. She was never afraid of the dark and would often stay in the garden after her sisters had gone to bed, if not to weed then to meditate until moonset, when even the rose was blackened by night. She felt at peace and at the same time a-quiver, as if she were on the verge of some deep philosophic revelation.

The truth was that though she made a valiant effort at gardening to please her mother, Vincent much preferred to roam the woods or comb the beach or climb the mountains during those childhood and adolescent summers in Camden. Often a group of friends would ask the girls to go for birdwalks, beginning before dawn. They usually took food for breakfast, and, starting up the mountainside in the dark, would stop to fix it just as the faint rays of the sun began to light up the ledges of Mounts Battie or Magunticook, dotted with other parties of townspeople or vacationers enjoying the fresh mountain air and the superb view of the sea circling out below. Although she entered into the gay camaraderie of these summer-resort pastimes—in a few years there would be sailing parties, all-day excursions that included picnics on one of the islands in Penobscot Bay—the poet found greater excitement and romantic adventure in going off by herself, all of nature her province. A miracle unfolded in the woods one day when she first caught sight of a small faun emerging from a fernbrake. She scarcely dared to breathe as she watched him "walk /

Among the ferns, not breaking back / One frond, not bruising one fern black." He came into the clearing, and she saw him lift his delicately modeled head, "unhurt and new," his newborn eyes appraising the world "with mild, attracted, wondering gaze." The poet-child felt a wild delight so deep within it made her dizzy, a shock of ecstasy that held her captive to the spot as the pristine beauty of the moment was revealed.

So it would always be, no matter how many times her eyes beheld "such marvels," no matter how touched by time or tragedy her life became. Like an earlier New England poet, Emily Dickinson, who died just six years before she was born, young Vincent Millay went "reeling through endless summer days / From inns of molten blue." There was a marked similarity of personality between these two, perhaps merely the emotional intensity of the poet in both, different as the form of self-expression of each might be. Both had extraordinary verve, a brimming curiosity, an eagerness and eye for detail, combined with a spirit that transcended human love of life to the point of mysticism.

Only when she was by herself did Vincent experience the throb of nature's pulse with such a quivering sensation. The planned birdwalks, pleasant as they were, robbed her of the moment of joy in nature. She could stand lost in rapture listening to the variations of song among the warblers, trying to identify by call birds that she could not see clearly as they flashed through the trees. Often she was able to get close enough to see them plainly. She liked to make her own private discoveries of nests and share them with friends afterward. And when, one spring, she happened upon a whole field of mayflowers during a solitary ramble on top of Mount Battie, she felt an exultation she would not have sensed in a jolly group of chattering friends. Later she led them to the spot to feast their eyes, and they came to count on her for woodland lore.

If Vincent and her sisters missed their father, they hardly had time to dwell on it. In the early years at Camden, he came to visit them frequently, usually when their mother was home; and the two parents chatted amiably, exchanging bits of news like a pair of old acquaintances. Mr. Millay sent Christmas presents to the girls and remembered their birthdays. Occasionally, if their mother couldn't afford something they wanted, they would write to their father for it; he seldom refused such requests, provided he had the money. But he expected a note of thanks for his generosity and complained if he didn't receive it promptly. He was proud of their triumphs, particularly Vincent's published poems, but his was more the interest of a friendly relative than the concern of a father, and the girls never thought of turning to him for advice.

Since their mother often was not at home to advise them, they relied on each other most of the time. Kathleen especially looked to Vincent for help until she was old enough to hold her own against Norma in an argument; there were bound to be more than a few disputes among the three bright girls. But in the main there was more love than animosity among them; they called each other by homely and even ugly nicknames, to them a form of intimate affection, though meaningless to anyone else. Each of them learned to be self-sufficient, yet they needed to lean on each other in order to reach that state. Sparked by Vincent's imagination and verve, they accepted material deprivations with gaiety and courage and overcame occasional catastrophes with the spontaneous, cheerful practicality of children. During one dreadfully cold winter, when the coal ran out and there was no money, the pipes burst, flooding the kitchen floor with water that soon turned to ice. To Vincent it looked just like a frozen pond, so they put on their ice skates and gleefully skimmed back and forth across the floor, forgetting the frigid house and the fact that they couldn't buy any more coal unless the weekly money order from Mrs. Millay came the next day. If nothing else, they always had kindling wood for a fire in the cookstove, and could huddle together in back of it to keep warm. Small wonder that their neighbors considered the Millays' a harum-scarum, gypsy household, run by that strange redheaded elder daughter with the tomboy name. As the poet put it long afterward, the Millays "usually had all the luxuries of life, but sometimes few of the necessities."

Naturally enough, the madcap element frowned upon by the town elders attracted many young people to the Millays. By the time the girls were in high school they had scores of friends, though Vincent, who entered during midyear, found the students cliquish and cool at first. But she soon overcame their indifference. In an early display of the amazing objectivity toward personal experience that marked her poetry, she wrote an endearing auto-biographical piece called, "The Newest Freshman." It was printed in the *Megunticook* and was followed by some of the poems that resulted from her woodland walks. Before long she was not only sought out but was assuming leadership in the literary life of the school. She joined the staff of the paper and then became its editor-in-chief. She was invited to become a member of a reading group, the Huckleberry-Finners, who met to read the works of Mark Twain aloud, an entertainment for which Vincent proved to have surprising skill.

Now the theater, a third potential artistic career, came to the fore, as the young poet showed interest and marked talent in both playwriting and acting. She wrote a Halloween play and took part in several school productions. Acting became another source of exhilaration in life. The students, who saw her move across the stage and heard her low voice surcharged with emotion, declared she was a "born actress." Their applause gave her courage to try out for bit parts in the productions of touring companies that came to Camden. Sometimes she and Norma appeared as extras in mob scenes; more often Vincent received minor character parts to play as an old woman or a young boy. She was particularly well suited for the latter role at this point, being still more a tom-boy than the dainty, feminine creature she was to personify in a few years.

In high school, as in grammar school, academic studies offered no trouble except for algebra; her closest friend, Stella Derry, happened to be a "whiz" at math, so they exchanged help, Vincent providing assistance in Latin and French. She displayed a true flair for language, whether classical or modern, foreign or her native tongue. Her sensitive ear, combined with her quickness of mind and facility of speech allowed her to grasp the fine nuances of other languages as well as English.

And always, no matter what else occupied her time, Vincent Millay had her mind on poetry. In school she read romantic poets: Coleridge, whose mystical "Rime of the Ancient Mariner" stirred her own strange imaginings of the deep; Wordsworth, the philosophic worshiper of nature; Tennyson, Browning, and Arnold; the flamboyantly romantic Lord Byron; and those two tragic sufferers, Keats and Shelley. From the last two she memorized long passages for pure pleasure, and they were to loom large in various ways throughout her life. But she had to write her own lines, her own rhythms; she found the time, even if it was at the dark of the moon when Camden slept and the only sound was the surf. In wintertime she often wrote at dawn, after she had fed the birds that came hopping to the doorsill for breadcrumbs. She had formed the habit of rising before sun-up to feed the birds.

The *St. Nicholas* published poems by "E. Vincent Millay" in 1908 and 1909. One of these, "Young Mother Hubbard," received the Silver Badge in 1909, the year she graduated from high school. And the folowing year, she won the coveted cash prize of five dollars, the top award granted to Leaguers, for her poem, "Friends." It was a proud achievement, but her elation was lessened by the fact that this had to be her last contribution, for she had turned eighteen, the age limit for League authorship. In her farewell letter, thanking "Dear *St. Nicholas*" for the award, she informed the editors that she was going to use her prize money to buy a copy of Browning, because it would give her "more pleasure in that form than in any other." She ended, "I am sorry to grow up and leave you," and signed it tenderly, "Your loving graduate," spelling out her first name instead of putting in just the mystifying initial, thereby revealing her sex at last: "Edna Vincent Millay." It would be a number of years before she used her full name, including "Saint" before "Vincent," and she was known mainly by the latter alone until she finished college.

Now Vincent was on the verge of an important decision, in her choice of career. The conflict between poetry and music had been growing in her conscious seeking for self-expression. In the spring of her junior year, shortly after her seventeenth birthday, she had been presented in a public recital, in which she played Bach, Haydn, Mendelssohn, Godard, and Chaminade. She wanted to give a perfect performance and practiced long and arduously. Her hands were so small she could barely reach a full octave, a serious drawback to a concert pianist, but her love for music was so

strong that she struggled to overcome it. She was startled when
Mr. Tufts suggested that she have surgery to extend her reach.
She had not been able to decide on the matter by the night of
the concert, the peak of her musical career.

The date of the crucial event, long anticipated by all, finally
arrived. As if by magic, her mother produced a costly new dress
for the grand occasion; it was a creation of yellow chiffon which
set off Vincent's red-gold hair. She cherished the memory of the
dress for years. She played well; the recital was an unqualified
success in Camden; but Vincent wondered whether her ability
would measure up to artistic standards in the world outside. Her
poetry had already been accepted by publications with wide audiences as well as high standards. She was sure her love of music
would not diminish, but she was not sure she wanted to risk the
judgment of the general public, and she was not at all certain
that she wanted to undergo surgery in the cause of a career.
Moreover, an operation meant an additional expense to her
mother, who had already borne so much. So Vincent had been
torn between her two loves; but with the final award from the
League in 1910 she began to tend more toward poetry.

She had also won a prize of ten dollars for her high school
graduation poem, significantly entitled, "La Joie de Vivre," which
she read aloud at the exercises in June, 1909. She had worked
on it for months, directly following her recital. The response of
the audience to her poem seemed more enthusiastic and was
more heart-warming to her than the applause for her piano performance had been. The class prophecy in her high school year-
book cited her many gifts and the possibilities that lay before
her; but it was not until a year after graduation that she knew
the music of words would probably strike the decisive chord in
her life. And then she knew intuitively that no matter how many
loves she might have, human or divine, poetry would always be
her overpowering passion.

CHAPTER III

Death and Rebirth,
the Remarkable Story of "Renaissance"

NOW THERE CAME a kind of "strange interlude" in the career
of the budding bard of Camden who was also housekeeper
pro tem until her sisters, both still in high school, had graduated.
Always an odd mixture of the mundane and the divine, Vincent
continued to invest her household chores with elements of imagination and humor, but she was restive, at a loss to know which
way to turn. Although she had finished high school and had decided with her mother's approval, to be a poet, she felt a need
for further academic knowledge, for a broader background of
classical learning to substantiate her flights of fancy. However,
there was no money for college, and, since she had "graduated"
from the *St. Nicholas*, there was no publishing outlet for her
poems.

She seems not to have considered other young people's magazines, like the *Youth's Companion*, one mainstay of Robert Frost
who was eighteen years her senior and who wrote poetry between
his stints of haphazard farming and part-time teaching in the
nearby state of New Hampshire during these years. And she apparently had no interest in submitting her work to some of the
New England periodicals which her friend Abbie Huston Evans
and other regional poets relied upon for publication. Perhaps Vincent was waiting, as she had written at fifteen in a poem she did

not send to the *St. Nicholas* until she had composed a message which would "pierce a way into the world's great heart."

Certainly there was little social life in Camden suitable to the needs of an ardent and brilliant young poet. Except for Abbie, whose gift for poetry was not particularly original, there was no one interested in discussing the birth pangs of a poem or technicalities of form and meter. Vincent was not inspired to experiment with free verse, just then making its entrance in Europe and soon to invade America, perhaps because her mother had imbued her with a love for the time-honored forms from the start. Indeed, as Floyd Dell was to phrase it, "Her mother put more emphasis on her respecting the conventions of art than the conventions of behavior. She never did learn to respect the conventions of behavior; though sometimes she played at observing them, in a not very convincing, grand-lady style, exaggerating them as a gypsy-child would." Even Abbie had little time for poetry talk. She was occupied with Sunday School teaching and other church activities; at her suggestion, Vincent joined the Genethod, a girls' group which met in the parlor of the church chapel to sing songs, play games, and toast marshmallows—hardly enthralling pastimes for a young poet yearning for rich experience!

She still belonged to the Huckleberry-Finners and no doubt enjoyed the brash, bristling, often acid humor of such books as *Roughing It* and *Innocents Abroad*. She was also a member of a hiking club, composed of six girls who wound up a long walk every Saturday afternoon with tea at a different member's home. But such pale, harmless pursuits could not fail to pall on a girl like Vincent Millay, though she entered into them wholeheartedly, and her friends probably did not suspect that she was bored, spiritually stifled.

The local swains of Camden held little interest for her, nor she for them, for that matter. At this point in her life, she was rather plain, except for the red-gold aura of her hair and the sudden animation of her face in moments of excitement. Her high school graduation picture, for which she wore the traditional hairbows on top of the head and back of the neck, shows a thoughtful, almost prim countenance, a touch of the New England spinster that unexpectedly reared up at odd moments through-

out her life. In high school, as in grade school, the boys had resented Vincent's tendency to run things, her superior ability in
literature and language, her quickness of mind and body. Few
of them really saw the poetic and solitary side of her makeup.

There was only one among all of them, a boy named Jim, whom
she "truly loved," and with whom she apparently experienced a
sweet romance, in the course of which he gave her a rather un-
romantic present, a Corona portable typewriter. Their adolescent
idyll ended abruptly and mysteriously in what might have been
disaster, but Vincent treasured the little Corona typewriter for
years. She used it constantly for preparing manuscripts, among
them no doubt some of her incomparable early poems. A decade
later, when she was in Europe, she was still using her Corona,
and when she wrote to her mother on the portable machine, recalled its youthful donor with soft, sweet memories devoid of
rancor.

Except for Jim, she had no other suitors in Camden. Both
Norma and Kathleen attracted numbers of beaux among their
classmates; and the boys who now flocked to the Millay home on
Saturday nights regarded Vincent as the "oldest sister," at times
pleasant, intelligent, and hilariously funny; at others, remote, removed from them all. Only five feet tall, she was shorter than
either of her sisters, and weighed scarcely a hundred pounds. She
was full of grace and lightness, almost birdlike in her swift, dart-
ing movement when inspired to sudden action.

If she was in a clowning and satiric mood, she could be most
amusing on those Saturday nights. She would take short, furious
puffs on her cigarette and deftly show their friends how to blow
smoke rings. The Millay women, including Cora, were probably
among the first females to take up the habit; in 1910 few women
outside New York had the temerity to try it. And sooner or later
Vincent would lead the way to the piano, where stacks of sheet
music and books of opera scores would be piled on the floor or
on top of the piano as well as in the rack. With Vincent at the
keyboard the girls would sing trios, sometimes comic ballads they
concocted together. One of these was a "Song to Men," playful,
but synical and satiric. Kathleen sang soprano; Norma, tenor; and

Vincent, baritone. The chorus began with the baritone, which Vincent sang in a deep, mocking voice:

"Oh, darling men!/ Oh, men, men, men,/ Oh, men alluring,/ Waste not the hours—"

Then the tenor came in: "Sweet idle hours/ In vain assuring/ For love, though sweet/ .... / Is not enduring./ Ta de da! . . .

Shall we have a smoke? We can—
Oh, a man is just a man/ But a little old Fatima/Burns so snug.

Here baritone Vincent might puff on her cigarette before booming out:

"She burns so snug.
Should we have another drink/ Do you think? (Spoken) Oh, let's not think!/ Pour another/ From the little/earthen jug—
(Sound of cork) "gug-gug-gug. . . ."

After several more "gugs" the chorus began again, "Oh, darling men . . ." and the jibing jingle ended abruptly: "So there you are."

Once started, the girls might keep on entertaining all evening; they coordinated parts very well. Frequently they would perform the entire score of some opera, preferably *Aida*, their favorite of all operas. If Mrs. Millay happened to be at home, she might conduct, using a makeshift baton. She always shared the girls' antics as well as their enterprises and ambitions.

During the hours of the day that Vincent was alone, she spent a good deal of time at the piano, keeping up her music for the joy it gave her. She preferred Bach and Beethoven closely followed by Mozart and Brahms. Throughout her life she was to find peace and comfort as well as pleasure in playing and in listening to music. Toward the end she declared that of all the senses she would rather keep her hearing than any other, even more than the precious sense of sight, because of her love of music.

So she divided her intellectual energies between music and poetry. As for her household duties, she learned to cook fairly well, to bake beans, bread, and pastries, so she could report to her mother, "we are living almost wholly from home cooking," but she never developed a real love for culinary art. She did not have the patience for it, except for certain dishes on special occasions, like the "Shrimp wiggle" the group of girls prepared on an island picnic excursion in the summer of 1911. Vincent took along her chafing dish—a present from her mother, to which she had given a boy's name, "James"—and it was a sport to cook up a mess of shrimp for twelve people; but she was too restless a soul to be content with day-to-day domestic triumphs. In addition to her chores, she did part-time typing for summer visitors. On the surface, to most of her friends in Camden at this time Vincent seemed to be an exceptionally quick, enthusiastic, even ebullient personality, in whose nature one of them said "the spirit of happiness . . . burned brightly." But in the dark recesses of her mind she was a seething, searching, throbbing soul, trembling with wonder and great expectations of life. Pacing hand in hand with sexual passion as yet unrecognized were hidden chambers in which tragedy and the sense of sorrow stalked like ghosts of the past from her readings of Vergil, Shakespeare, Milton, Tennyson, Shelley, Tolstoi, and, among the moderns, certainly Housman and Hardy.

More and more frequently during her free time in the summer she took to going off by herself, climbing the rocks to sit and stare out over the ocean. Often, especially toward the end of the season when the vacationers began to thin out, she would awake before dawn, the sense of wonder full upon her, as if she had been roused from sleep by some insistent force calling to her to climb the mountain. Quickly, quietly, she would dress in the dark and dash out of the house, snatching an apple from the barrel on the back porch on the way, and go running through the "sleeping town," a wraith, still so light of foot her ghostly gallop did not "arouse even a dog." Out of some mysterious impulse, like the sudden flight of birds, she pursued her way up the stony, steep mountain path, all alone in the dark. The surge of exultant youth pushed her on, even though she might slip on rotting leaves wet with dew or scratch her legs on thorny shrubs. The wonderful smell of bark was like wine to her giddy senses; the secret joy of being the only one awake "in all the world" was an added elixir. On top of Megunticook she would stretch out in an "earth-ecstatic" state of mind, waiting for the first golden banners of light to streak above the horizon. For joyous moments without end she would "lie on a high cliff" until her elbows ached, in order "to see the sun come up over Penobscot Bay." Thus it was that she vividly recalled her sensations near the end of her life; but at the time of occurrence those moments of solitary rapture must have been mingled with untold longing and impatience.

Wild and beautiful as the scene around her was, Vincent Millay was filled with vague yearnings to extend the horizons of her life physically as well as artistically. She was impatient at seeing no farther than Megunticook and its twin mountains on either side in one direction, and triple, green-dotted Penobscot Bay in the other. She had made only one journey by herself, directly after graduation. She had used the ten dollars of prize money for her poem, plus two dollars from her father, to visit Mrs. Curtis J. Holt, her Aunt Georgia, in Chelmsford, Massachusetts. It had been a jolly sojourn, and Vincent's first ride on a roller coaster made an indelible impression on her. The record of it, which she sent to her sisters was a gem of animated, realistic descriptive writing. But such a jaunt inside the family circle could hardly be called travel and afforded Vincent no real adventure. She longed to see strange sights, to sail to India and the Far East on one of the Oriental merchant ships that occasionally brought their wares into port at Camden. Much as she loved the wildflowers of Maine woods, she wished to "smell the Carthaginian rose" just once, to be sure of her choice. She did not want to miss possible deeper sensual experiences that might be waiting over the horizon.

The longing preyed upon her, causing private periods of depression and melancholy, as it had before when she was in a state of transition. In spite of her beloved family and her many friends in Camden, she could never hear a train whistle without wanting to follow the trail no matter where it led. In spite of her deep attachment to the mountains and the sea, she felt shut away from the rest of the world, because she could see no farther than "three long mountains and a wood" and "three islands in a bay," which became symbols of the emotionally and spiritually confining boundaries of the small-town community. Realizing, with her penetrating mind and extraordinary objectivity, that her attitude was the result of a philosophic shortcoming on her part, she began to analyze her feelings in a long poem, on which she concentrated for months. It was a narrative, allegorical poem, so she chose iambic tetrameter, the meter of "The Rime of the Ancient Mariner," and, like Coleridge, she used simple language to create an eloquent masterpiece of storytelling and spiritual truth.

Within the framework of octosyllabic couplets, the poet pictured her imaginary supernatural experience, based, she asserted some years later, on a similar vision that came to her during one of her predawn watches on the mountaintop. She "reached up her hand to try, and screamed to feel it touch the sky—to feel Infinity settling over her, forcing her to look through a glass until she saw Immensity made manifold; and whispering a word which brought to her ears the ticking of Eternity." With the awesome sight and sound, the girl in the poem "knew at last / The How and Why of all things, past, / And present, and forevermore." But for that knowledge she must pay a fearful toll: the burden of all human sin and suffering, human guilt, "every greed, every lust," every tragedy and sorrow, fell upon her with unbearable weight. The oppression was so great that she felt herself sink under it, inch by inch, until she was "full six feet under the ground."

The terrible weight has rolled away; in the grave all is stillness, a grim, solitary, silence unrelieved by human face or warmth, by the smallest flower or lowliest weed. Then she hears the "friendly sound" of the "pitying rain"; she imagines the beauty of "a drenched and dripping apple tree" in its fragrant freshness after a rain, but she realizes that she is dead and can no longer behold the beauties of the earth. She prays to God to let the "heavy rain" wash away the grave; her prayer has hardly ceased when the wild whistling and crash of a terrible storm sends the "big rain" pouring down to release her from the ground pressing around and over her. She smells the wondrous fragrant breath of the orchard and springs up with such a cry as was never heard before—a cry of wild joy and happiness; she hugs the trees, she hugs the ground. She has learned the miracle of life through death and rebirth. She celebrates the joys of being alive and able to share in the beauties of the earth once more, hailing the source of life and strength: "God, I can push the grass apart / And lay my finger on Thy heart."

The final section could be called the coda to this symphonic poem: the young poet's ardent conviction that the human spirit is capable of encompassing the universe, that the world is "no wider than the heart is wide," and the sky "no higher than the soul is high"; but she warns with the words of an oracle that "East and West will pinch the heart / That cannot keep them pushed apart"; and let that man beware whose soul is flat, for "the sky will cave in on him by and by."

Among the myriad phrases this remarkable poem was to evoke from readers and reviewers was Floyd Dell's comment that the second part of the work was a "suicide fantasy," a drastic surmise that may or may not have been correct. The poet did have a narrow escape from death, however, an experience which undoubtedly had a strong impact on her creative expression. At about the time Vincent began to write the poem, she and Norma learned to swim in the depths beyond the shallow waters of the harbor. As usual, Vincent's enthusiasm knew no bounds and, after she had given her mother a glowing account of mastering a seventy-five-foot swim, she felt ready to attempt any distance.

One soft summer day when she had wandered off alone to a neighboring but unfamiliar beach to swim in the bay, she saw what appeared to be a lovely green islet shimmering in the sunlight. It was very far out, but the lure of the silvery green was so great that she started for it with vigorous strokes, hoping to make this extra distance by speeding her tempo. As a result she tired quickly, and her self-confidence began to wane. But she kept going and with stupendous effort reached the spot, only to find it was not an island but a mass of floating seaweed! There was no foothold, nothing solid enough to stand on; she tried, but felt herself sink in the marshy mass. Panicky, her strength all gone, she started to swim back, and only the courage of despair kept her afloat. She had not yet learned to relax and rest in the water as she did in later days, and every stroke was agonizing, but her strong will drove her on; more than once she began to sink with fatigue, but struggled to the surface again. She would not allow her courage to ebb, and it carried her safely to the shore, where she must have hugged the sand as she "hugged the ground" in her poem. And it can hardly have been entirely happenstance that she chose to employ the image of sinking six feet under the ground in depicting her imaginery death and grave.

She encountered the eternal evils of human suffering and injustice in her varied and omnivorous reading, and undoubtedly she brooded on them. The verses of Milton, Shelley, and Wordsworth planted the first seeds of social consciousness, which was to flourish and grow so strong it almost strangled her gift of poetry; yet it gave her work greater stature and depth. And the realistic novels of Hardy and Tolstoi must have haunted her sensitive mind during those solitary hours on the mountaintop. However, her love of life was too all-pervading to permit suicide tendencies to take hold; it is more likely that her narrow escape from death induced the fantasy of the grave and the miracle of resurrection, with its accompanying paeons in praise of life through the beauty and joy of nature, its reaffirmation of the value of the human spirit in relation to God.

The poem was begun while Vincent was eighteen, and she was still working on it when she turned nineteen. She had made a number of changes during the course of writing and had put it aside altogether for a time after completing the first part. She often consulted her mother, who was also writing verses in her spare time and sending them to New England newspapers. The whole family knew Vincent was concentrating on the most serious work she had ever attempted. About a month after her nineteenth birthday, word unexpectedly came from Kingman, Maine, that her father was seriously ill in the hospital, and had expressed a wish to have his oldest daughter near him. The request came as something of a surprise to Vincent, but she decided it was her duty to go, and, packing her manuscript along with her clothes, she took the first train for Kingman.

On March 4, she sent her mother a rather matter-of-fact report on her father's condition: he had had a severe attack of pneumo-

nia complicated by asthma and a weak heart. She stated that
"Papa" was better and the doctor thought he would get well.
She stayed in Kingman for a while, however, doing little things
for him during the hours she spent at the hospital and, between
visits, polishing and reworking the lines of her poem. She was
still there when she received an excited letter from her mother
urging her to come home.

Mrs. Millay had been leafing through a magazine one night
while sitting at the bedside of a sleeping patient, when she came
across the announcement of a poetry anthology, *The Lyric Year*.
It was to be published as soon as the hundred best poems written
by American poets during the year had been selected by the
judges. Prizes were being offered to the top three poems among
those chosen. The first prize was five hundred dollars; second and
third prize were each two hundred and fifty dollars. The competition, open to all American poets, had been first announced the
previous fall, but there was still time to submit manuscripts. To
Mrs. Millay, who knew enough about poetry to realize that her
daughter's talent far exceeded her own, and that the long poem
might very well be a prize winner, this meant that Vincent had
no time to lose! She had better come home immediately and get
some of her work ready to submit.

Acting on her mother's advice, Vincent hurried back to Camden. Her father was probably out of danger by then, but neither
she nor her mother seem to have hesitated to leave him alone in
the hospital. She completed the second part of her long poem,
changed two lines that joined the first and second parts together,
and decided to give her work the French title, "Renaissance,"
perhaps unconsciously hoping to duplicate the success she had
had with her prize-winning poem, "La Joie de Vivre." She included "La Joie de Vivre" and several others along with "Renaissance" and mailed the package with a high heart. She was beside
herself with mingled hope and fear for her poetry. Her friend
Abbie could not help feeling that the young poet was in for a
damaging letdown when Vincent, confiding to her that the poems
had been submitted, cried out, "Oh, Abbie, think how wonderful
it would be if I should get in that volume!" Abbie, who no doubt
had entered dozens of competitions without any luck, thought

privately, "You poor child." The odds were staggeringly against her: more than ten thousand poems had already piled up in the publisher's office, many from more established poets than "E. Vincent Millay."

One of the judges, Ferdinand Earle, was also the editor of the projected book of poems. He and his assistant, Professor Donner, had plowed halfway through a pile of manuscripts one weekend without turning up a single manuscript of note. They had come to the point of eliminating an entry if it didn't strike a responsive chord in either of them in the opening lines, and the "discard" wastebasket was filling up rapidly. Donner laughed as he tossed in some pages he had been glancing through. Earle, who felt the need of diversion, asked, "What's so funny?"

The assistant fished the manuscript out of the discards, and read the first two rhymed couplets of "Renaissance" aloud. Shaking his head and chuckling, he was about to consign it to oblivion again, but Earle caught his arm. The utter simplicity of the opening lines had captured his interest. "Wait a minute," he objected. "That sounds good! Read some more of it." Donner skimmed through the pages and read from the finale, with its ringing symphonic tones and intuitive wisdom. Now he too had caught the music of the lines and turned back to the beginning, and then, without prompting from Earle, he read it through again. Both men came under its spell. As Earle later wrote, after all "the insipid and drivelling nonsense" he had been forced to consider, "Renaissance" seemed a virtual revelation. In a burst of enthusiasm, he sent a letter to the poet immediately, addressing her confidently, "E. St. Vincent Millay, Esq., Dear Sir." He praised the poem and rashly said if his high rating meant anything, it would probably win the first prize of five hundred dollars. He added that his only suggestion would be that, since this was to be a volume of American poetry, the French title should be changed to "Renascence."

The day the letter arrived at 40 Chestnut Street, Vincent was out picking blueberries in the nearby field. When she came back from the pasture carrying her pailful, her mother was waiting for her on the doorstep, waving the envelope. Vincent tore it open with trembling fingers and read the astonishing news aloud in joyous amazement; her mother stood in the doorway beaming with satisfaction, as if she had arranged the whole matter. With the warm bond of affection between them, they must have hugged each other in triumph. Five hundred dollars represented a fortune to them, and was to seem a fortune to Vincent again, nearly a lifetime later. After supper, she hurried to tell Abbie the good news: "Just think, Abbie, I'm going to be in that book!" As the words rushed out, it was evident that her greatest happiness lay in the fact that her work was to appear in a publication of national importance, among recognized poets.

Nevertheless, contemplation of the prize money was more than pleasant. It was the source of dreams, plans for college education, and Vincent was unprepared for the blow which shortly befell her star-crossed poem. Ferdinand Earle, in virtually promising the first prize to the author of "Renascence," had reckoned without the opinions of the other two judges, who had not even seen "Mr. Millay's" entry when the letter was written. Perhaps Earle thought his post as Editor would carry enough weight to sway them if they disagreed with him about his first-prize choice. But neither one agreed with him, and neither was to be shaken in his belief that, although "Renascence" was an excellent poem, it was not of prize-winning caliber. The poem placed fourth in the list of the hundred selected for publication.

Vincent was crushed for a time after Earle had broken the embarrassing finals of the contest to her. She felt as if someone had stuck a pin in the golden bubble of her dreams just as it was in her grasp. But with her Irish practicality and her unerring sense of values, she realized that it was a mark of recognition to have been considered for first prize and to finish among the five at the top of those accepted. Her native optimism asserted itself, and she began to look forward to publication.

In that fateful summer of 1912 Robert Frost sailed to England to win his initial fame; Amy Lowell was converting to the imagist movement of the expatriate poet, Ezra Pound, and was preparing to launch it in America as her own; and perhaps it was inevitable that so highly individual a poem as "Renascence" should unexpectedly win a private medal of literary honor on its own.

The immediate signs were not auspicious. Norma invited Vincent to be her guest at the annual "ball for the waitresses" sponsored by the Whitehall Inn, the principal resort hotel in Camden. The ball was to honor daughters of the local families, who worked at the Inn as Norma did during the summer. Vincent almost did not go; the girls were supposed to perform, if they had any talents to display, and although Vincent was not shy, she felt that this evening should be Norma's. But her sister persuaded her, feeling that it would be good for Vincent to get out, and hoping privately that she would be called upon to read from her latest work.

The evening worked out as Norma had planned. After she and some of the others had performed, singing songs or playing the piano, Norma coaxed Vincent to play a few of the ballads she had composed, which they performed together. After that it was natural to suggest that Vincent recite verses she had written. She hesitated, but finally decided to see whether she could present a poem as much a part of herself as "Renascence" in front of an audience. Like Robert Frost, she had almost total recall of her poetry and rarely read from any of her volumes, which might be on the podium merely for reference. In her musical, deeply dramatic voice, with its varying range of tone from low to mid-tenor, she recited her long poem gravely and simply, forgetting her audience entirely. Both the townsfolk who had heard her before and the "resort people" were enthralled by the lyrical lines, which she delivered with such pristine eloquence; those who were present never forgot the moving experience. One of them, Miss Caroline B. Dow, head of the National Training School of the YWCA in New York, a summer visitor in Camden, was so touched by the poem and its youthful author that she sought Vincent out when the party was over. She learned that the girl had finished high school and was more or less in limbo at the moment, but was hoping for an opportunity to continue her education. Miss Dow, a genteel woman originally from the South, whose soft accent belied an energetic, efficient administrator, offered to help raise the necessary funds, arrange interviews, look into academic requirements of various colleges, and so on. She knew many influential people who would be interested in giving assistance to a talented poet in need of finances. Making specific plans to start at once with a letter that Vincent was to write to Miss Dow outlining her academic and literary background, they talked until late that night.

The poet went to bed full of renewed expectations; she was on the threshold of that wide domain beyond the "thin, fine line" of the horizon.

CHAPTER IV

First Laurels
for a Newfound Lyricist

O N OCTOBER 23, 1912, Vincent Millay wrote her own letter of recommendation to the head of the YWCA Training School (soon humorously referred to in her letters as "Aunt Calline"). It was a simple, naïve, unaffected account of her scholastic achievements and her heterogeneous reading in English and American literature. Of the latter she commented that the list must seem "awfully crazy" to Miss Dow, but she had read so much she hardly knew what to pick out.

Less than a month later, in November, when *The Lyric Year* came off the press, the young poet who had written so artlessly of her literary background found herself catapulted into fame because of the judges' failure to award "Renascence" a prize. She was at the vortex of a public and professional storm of protest, which was as remarkable as the early fate of the poem in so narrowly escaping oblivion. The outraged objections were extraordinary; they did more honor to the poem in that they were shouted at a time when new trends were reshaping the forms and ideas of poetry. Besides the imagist movement marshaled by Amy Lowell, there were various experimental groups including the realists and impressionists clamoring for recognition. They had sprung from the era of new thought ushered in by Charles Darwin, Karl Marx, and Sigmund Freud, particularly the latter, whose theory concerning the significance of sexual repression in human behavior gave rise to the revolt against Victorian standards in art as well as in society. Out of this massive rebellion came cubism and varied types of abstraction in painting as well as new tonal systems in music; and, beginning more or less officially in 1912, modern poetry emerged as an unmistakable force in literature. The "traditionalists," who rushed to the defense of time-honored forms, produced in an excited spurt of activity more poems than they had in several decades. Such a welter of creativity demanded a unified voice, and in 1912 Harriet Monroe in Chicago founded *Poetry: A Magazine of Verse* as a mouthpiece for American poetry, regardless of form or theme. The purpose of the magazine was to provide an outlet for the surging wellsprings of artistic souls. The main qualification was excellence. And, although inevitable controversies arose between groups, and among various factions within groups, all were united in an outpouring of poems that flooded the offices of the magazine, and had inundated the competition for *The Lyric Year* with ten thousand entries, exactly a hundred times more than could be chosen. Small wonder that 1912 was hailed as "the dawn of the poetic renaissance" in America as well as England. And in spite of the loyalty of the traditionalist groups, modern poetry was in the ascendancy.

The universal outburst in recognition of the merit of "E. Vincent Millay's" allegory, so fortuitously entitled "Renascence," was, therefore, nothing short of astonishing, especially to the poet herself. Readers from all camps, struck by the poem's freshness and originality, berated the judges for not awarding it first prize without hesitation. Despite its conventional form, "Renascence" was considered by the majority of readers the finest poem in the volume, and the fact that it had won no prize at all was "poetry's scandal of the century."

To the chagrin of the judges and what must have been the utter frustration of Ferdinand Earle as Editor, letters poured in from all over the country. Some were addressed to Earle and to the publisher, Mitchell Kennerly; a great many more were sent to the author herself, her sex and age having been cleared up in response to Earle's request for biographical data before publication. One critic observed tartly, "The young girl from Camden, Maine, became famous through *not* receiving the prize."

The prize winners themselves and their poetry were the direct targets of angry criticism. The barrage was so heavy they began to feel that their entries did not merit the awards; indeed, as poets they probably recognized in "Renascence" a true achievement in poetic art. Orrick Johns, whose "Second Avenue Girl" won first place, wrote in a forthright statement that his prize was "as much an embarrassment to me as a triumph . . . . The outstanding poem in that book was 'Renascence.'" But he continued to receive insulting letters, newspaper clippings, and magazine articles inveighing against the award until in the end he refused to appear at the presentation dinner. "I didn't want to be the center of a literary dog-fight," he explained ruefully. Feeling ran so high that one of the lesser prize winners sent a letter to the author of "Renascence" confirming the public acclaim with his offer, "I have $250 that belongs to you, any time you ask for it."

In Camden, the cause of this literary maelstrom must have experienced increasing astonishment and delight. The neighborhood postman may have complained, but Vincent and her sisters no doubt hailed his armloads with shouts of joyful anticipation. One letter in particular brought a surge of gratitude from the poet and sounded a note of friendship that would heighten into love, echoing undiminished down the years. The unforgettable missive came from two professional contributors to the anthology, H. Witter Bynner [1] and Arthur Davison Ficke, both of whom had already won recognition through steady publication in periodicals. Ficke had two volumes to his credit in print, and a third, poems inspired by the Ukioye school of oriental art, *Twelve Japanese Painters,* was soon to appear in a finely printed limited edition. Bynner was writing criticism as well as poetry. They had formed a close friendship at Harvard, where they had been classmates a few years earlier. According to Bynner's account, he had gone to spend the November holiday with Ficke, who had married and was practicing law in his home town, Davenport, Iowa. Arthur had just received a copy of *The Lyric Year,* and on Thanksgiving Day in 1912 as they walked home from his law office, Bynner was

[1] The initial, which stood for his first name, Harold, was later dropped.

leafing through the volume for the second time, hoping to find an interesting new poem. Suddenly the title "Renascence" caught his eye; after glancing at the first few lines, he sat down with Ficke at the base of the Soldier's Monument and read the entire poem aloud.

Both of them were carried away. As they wrote later to Earle, the caliber of the selections they had seen until then had made them feel "somewhat disheartened . . . . And suddenly we stumbled on this one, which really lights up the whole book. It seems to both of us a real vision, such as Coleridge might have seen . . . ." As soon as they got home, they read "Renascence" to Arthur's wife, and the three of them immediately wrote a letter of appreciation to the author, beginning, "This is Thanksgiving Day and we thank you . . . ."

Their tribute, sent through the editor's office, reached Camden on December 5. Vincent was deeply moved by the generous and spontaneous praise and answered at once with a brief but telling note, written in a forward flowing hand over an inch high: "You are three dear people. This is Thanksgiving Day, too, and I thank you." That was all. After "Very truly yours," she signed her full name, Edna St. Vincent Millay.

In their letter to Earle the two poets had voiced their suspicions in regard to both the name, which they felt positive was a pseudonym, and the biographical note, which they considered "a marvel of humor." It was not possible, Ficke and Bynner asserted, for a "sweet young thing of twenty" to write a poem with the depth and vision of "Renascence." ". . . it takes a brawny male of forty-five to do that."

The editor passed their remarks along to the poet in Camden, who was quick to defend her "reputation." She simply would not be a "brawny male!" She went on to give them a glimpse of her personal life, purposely picturing herself not so much as the girl-mystic they might expect, but as a down-to-earth creature who had formed her own philosophy of living and was "now a frivolous young woman with a new pair of dancing slippers and a mouth like a Valentine," to cite Floyd Dell's often misquoted image of Edna Millay. As final proof she included a photograph of herself with a postscript informing them that the "brawny male" sent his picture: she "*had* to laugh." The imp in her could not resist the jibe.

The exchange marked the beginning of a correspondence among the three poets. It was also the beginning of lasting friendships that were to take on by turns an amusing, dramatic, complex, and, in regard to Arthur Ficke and Edna St. Vincent Millay, a mysterious aspect, an undying love quite apart from all other relationships either one would experience. At this point, however, she regarded both Bynner and Ficke as mentors and advisers as well as colleagues.

Here again, the spirit of Vincent's letters recalls Emily Dickinson, who looked upon her friends, Ben Newton and Leonard Humphrey, as her "teachers" and spiritual guides. Both women poets were inclined to idolize their close friends, male or female; both loved passionately. If Emily had lived in a later era, or had not been so sheltered by an overprotective father, she might have been more venturesome in living her love. Conversely, if Edna Millay had known greater stability in her father, she might have been less profligate in giving hers and less likely to withdraw at its height because of mistrust. Both poets poured their passion into their poetry. Emily found her freedom in unconventional forms; her uneven, subtle rhyme schemes and economy of words antedate modern poetry. Edna Millay found security in classical form: the sonnet was the golden scepter with which she ruled her poetic passions. Late in life she wrote, "I will put Chaos into fourteen lines," the opening of a sonnet celebrating "this sweet Order," published posthumously in *Mine the Harvest*.

From the beginning, there was a continuous flow of artistic give and take, of professional shop talk, in the three-way correspondence, particularly between Arthur Ficke and Vincent. Ficke was a poet's poet, one more appreciated by those in the profession than by the general public. His songs did not find in the average reader "a heart that loved them" as the eager poet in Camden did. She received and promptly devoured copies of Ficke's *The Happy Princess* and *The Earth Passion* less than a month after their literary introduction in December, 1912. They discussed the poems by mail and soon established the fact that both felt a profound "earth passion." He was the only person, she told him, whose lines about flowers, birds, and skies, which were filled with his "so evident Earth Ecstasy," could quite satisfy her "Earth-Ecstatic" soul. He was to be her "Spiritual Advisor" long before he became her "beloved," but she asserted her strong individuality in regard to her work. In analyzing "Renascence" Arthur asked if one of the lines had its source in "a book," hardly expecting her firecracker response by return mail: "I'll slap your face." She went on to assure him in no uncertain terms that she never got anything from a book. She saw things with her own eyes "just as if they were the first eyes that ever saw . . . ." Then, she continued, she set about telling, as best she could, just what she saw. Yet she could accept specific criticism or suggestion with grace and humor, as she did some months later in agreeing with him that "The Little Bush," a poem she had recently sent him, needed "pruning." She respected his advice, his scholarly, analytic viewpoint and broad literary background, both oriental and occidental. In one of his packets, he included a small pocket edition of Blake's *Songs of Innocence,* which she treasured all her life.

Vincent's youthful thoughts on poetry and the poetic spirit, her hopes and dreams for the future were expressed in those early letters to Arthur Ficke. She told him of the arrangements that were being made for her to attend either Smith or Vassar, which she hoped would improve her poetry. She preferred Vassar; with its foreign students it was a more cosmopolitan school than Smith; it was also more progressive, in the forefront of movements like the emancipation of women. But, she added with an awareness of her own bent for social justice, wouldn't it be dreadful if she came back a suffragette instead of a poet?

Early in January, 1913, word came from Caroline Dow that sufficient funds had been raised for at least the first year, and arrangements had been made for Vincent to attend Vassar, although she would have to take some preliminary courses at Barnard starting in February in order to qualify for the Vassar entrance examinations at the end of the summer. There was a great flurry of activity in the Millay household as the three sisters rushed around preparing for Vincent's adventure in New York. She would be twenty-one in a few weeks and was the first one in the family even to visit the metropolis, let alone be provided with the means for a prolonged stay!

She arrived in New York the first week in February and found it something of a magnificent monstrosity, at once more enthralling and more appalling than she had expected it to be. The solid concrete phalanx formed by street after street of buildings anywhere from seven or eight stories to a "million and billion stories" seemed far more formidable than the mountains which had walled her in at Camden. On every side buildings shut away the view of the sea. It was hard to believe, from the Residence of the YWCA National Training School on East 52nd Street, where she was comfortably installed and cared for by the staff under Miss Dow, that Manhattan was an island and that huge ships put into port or steamed out through the Narrows into the Atlantic every day. Occasionally at night you could hear the great ships blow their long blasts of arrival or departure, but mostly that sound blended into or was lost in the enormous amount of noise in the city. In New York the multiplicity of sounds—raucous honking of auto horns, screeching of brakes, clanging of streetcars, the occasional clop of horse-drawn vehicles, and the rumble of subways, in addition to the voices of machinery and men—was so tremendous you could "*see* the noise." In the first hours after arrival, Vincent wondered if she could stand the constant din, but found that she could "sleep better for it." Her courses at Barnard began immediately, and she was soon absorbed into the intellectual, artistic, and social life of New York City, so that such hazards as crossing streets became a kind of challenge. She learned to glare with a "wild hunted expression all about" her at corners, and, in running to grab a streetcar, to "elbow fiercely those fellow creatures whom I love as myself." Although she was probably uneasy, she appears to have managed remarkably well by herself; and it hardly seems likely that she "wouldn't cross a street alone," as Edmund Wilson has stated. She wrote vivid, detailed accounts of her impressions to her mother and sisters, and in one of them she mentioned that you "couldn't go across the street alone at night in New York," but otherwise, evidence indicates that she got around rather well by herself.

Before she left Camden, Vincent had received a number of

invitations from notables who wanted to meet the author of "Renascence." One of these was Louis Untermeyer, who had been among the first to praise the poem in a review in the Chicago *Post*. Soon after she was settled in New York, Vincent called on the Untermeyers in their uptown apartment late one Saturday afternoon. With her red-gold hair ringed by a "nimbus" of lamplight, delicate features, dainty figure, and breathless way of greeting them, Edna St. Vincent Millay seemed to the Untermeyers the embodiment of a poet. But she felt more like "a scared little girl from Maine." At first her host, with his beady eyes, hawk nose, and crooked grin, seemed to be leering at her; but his enthusiasm for poetry in general, and "Renascence" in particular, was so infectious that she lost her self-consciousness and found herself reciting her verses: not only her long poem, but shorter ones she had recently written, including "Journey," "God's World," and a stanza or two from poems still in a formative stage.

Jean Untermeyer, who had not yet begun to write poetry, relates in her memoirs that from the moment Vincent started to read the lines in her "lovely, low, expressive voice," she was so moved that she had to leave the room several times to hide her tears. And after the younger poet had left with Louis, who escorted her back to the YWCA Training School, Jean, inspired by the enchantment of the verses she had just heard and by the emotions still welling up within her, set down her own initial attempts at poetry in stanzas that seemed to gush forth fully formed.

When Miss Jessie B. Rittenhouse, Secretary of the recently founded Poetry Society of America, gave a party for the express purpose of introducing Edna Millay to some of the most illustrious members, however, Vincent was so overwhelmed by the number of celebrities that she could not shed her shyness long enough to recite her poetry. Among the guests were Mr. and Mrs. Edwin Markham, Mr. and Mrs. Louis Ledoux, Sara Teasdale, and Anna Hempstead Branch. And, to her suprise, she met Witter Bynner, whom she had come to know well by correspondence. He was kind and courtly and made her feel as if he were an old friend who would look after her in the company of strangers. He even asked, to her amusement, whether his cigarette bothered her! Soon she was calling him "Hal," as he was familiarly known. She felt enough at home with him to request that he read "Rena-scence" aloud to the guests while she sat on the sofa listening quietly. She was pleased with the reading, pleased at the sound of the syllables coming from another voice.

She had never heard poetry read by someone else, and she found the experience curiously rewarding. It was even more grati-fying when her English teacher at Barnard, Professor William Tenney Brewster, known for the ironic, sometimes mocking tone he used in his delivery of student work, read her poem, "Interim," aloud to the class. To her amazement, he read the poem, a dra-matic monologue of a widower in the throes of grief over the recent death of his wife, with complete seriousness, giving the lines full/dramatic impact, and afterward praising the concept and technique of the poem. Vincent had feared the professor would deride the treatment of such a subject by a young poet. During the same session, the usually acid-mouthed professor praised the first draft of a short story she had written, "Barbara on the Beach," which was published the following year in the November issue of *Smart Set*.

After the Rittenhouse party, the starry-eyed poet from Maine was caught up in a whirl of invitations from people in New York literary circles. It was a thrill to be asked to tea, and then to dinner by a noted poet whose work she admired, Sara Teasdale. The two had much to talk about, and found each other's company so congenial that these visits were shortly followed by a long ride on one of the double-decker buses that lumbered up Fifth Avenue and across town to Riverside Drive. As they took in the sights of the city, they chatted about poets and poetry. Both women wrote of love in their poems, but Edna St. Vincent Millay's lines were to attain the fire of passion, while Sara Teasdale's flame never waxed greater than the soft warmth of exquisite sentiment which occasionally waned into sorrowful sentimentality and self-pity. Shortly before her death in 1933, at a time when she was tor-mented by the illness, stress, and strain that led to suicide, Sara wrote to Edna Millay, "I like to think that when I first read you, long ago, I knew you and named a star."

Vincent had another, more frequent companion and colleague with whom she took rides on the top deck of Fifth Avenue buses, a young Nicaraguan poet, Salomón de la Selva, who was giving a course on modern Spanish poetry at Columbia University. As a Barnard student, she attended one of his early lectures. He was captivated at once by the combination of her intelligence, live-wire wit, feminine charm, and intense poetic spirit as well as by her creative ability; and before long they were exploring New York together as two novitiates to life in the big city. Another of their favorite rides was on the foredeck of a Staten Island ferryboat, along with all the rest of New York's less than affluent young people who took full advantage of the five-cent fare, and the fact that one could ride back and forth all night on the same nickel. Sometimes they got off and roamed the wild stretches of beach or hilly shoreline on Staten Island, munching fruit they had bought from a vendor along the way. The delightful "Recuerdo," not published until 1922, in *A Few Figs from Thistles,* was probably the record of such a spree. Allen Churchill has attributed the source of this poem to a similar night that Edna St. Vincent Millay spent in the company of John Reed and Floyd Dell toward the end of World War I; but the latter circumstances were quite different, and, since the title is Spanish, it is likely that the "remembrance" describes one of the many "merry" times that Vincent enjoyed with her friend Salomón during those early months in New York.

They took in the famous 1913 International Art Exhibit held at the Armory in March. Vincent, writing home after her return from the show on Sunday afternoon, March 13, was apparently more entertained than startled or shocked by the mad impudence of dadaism or the radical experiment of cubism which, to her provincial eyes used to Maine lumber yards, resembled "piles of shingles." There were free lectures and concerts that young people could attend besides taking venturesome trips to various sections of the city, including Chinatown, with its oriental flavor and its hints of mysterious smoking orgies in opium dens. Vincent, who was determined, not to miss anything that was offered in the stimulating environment, was away from the Training School so much that Miss Dow must have wondered when her poet-prodigy had time to study, let alone do creative work. But Vincent could have assured "Aunt Calline" that there was no cause for worry.

In her bare little room at the "Y" she wrote as she had at home, late at night or early in the morning before going to class. Less than a month after her courses at Barnard began she sent two new poems to the editor of *Forum* magazine, put out by Mitchell Kennerly, publisher of *The Lyric Year*. Kennerly had offered to publish "Renascence" in book form as soon as she had enough poems to go with it to make a volume; in the meantime, he suggested, *Forum* might accept some of the new work. And on April 8, when Vincent opened a letter from the magazine, a "pinky-lavender slip" fell out; it was a check for twenty-five dollars! She was so excited she could scarcely read the figures. She sat down and wrote the grand news at once to her "Dearest Darlings" in Camden: she had finally broken the "hoo-doo of all praise and no profit" for the product of the labor that represented the very core of her being. It was characteristic of her not to think of spending her first check on herself, but to apologize for not sending it to her mother immediately: she wanted to keep it a few days, just to look at it. Three days later, when she did mail the slender pastel slip of paper, she urged her mother to do something with part of the money to "make things easier," such as buying new shoes or having her glasses fixed. She added tenderly, almost shyly, that she would like it if Norma and Kathleen as well as her mother "would get some little tiny silly thing that she could always keep."

Between studies, writing, New York's diversions, and social engagements, the weeks of her college preparatory semester at Barnard sped by, and suddenly it was May; her stay in New York was almost over. As if to cap the newly discovered thrills of the months just past, she reported breathlessly ("Oh, Girls . . .") to her sisters in Camden that she had just seen "*Sarah Bernhardt in Camille!*" and was "all gone to pieces." Actually, the unforgettable performance was only the last act of *Camille*: Bernhardt appeared in vaudeville as the headliner on a variety bill, but twenty-one-year-old Edna St. Vincent Millay was transported by the great tragedienne to the realm of theater immortals.

By late June she was back in Camden, her "native heath," as she called it in a letter to Arthur Ficke. During the summer she had to bone up for Vassar by herself in math and history. In Latin composition, for which she did not qualify in spite of her great love for the classical language, she was tutored through the mails by Vassar professor Elizabeth Hazelton Haight, who offered her services when she heard that a "poor young poetess from Camden, Maine, was coming to Vassar." A rapport developed between the two even before they met; Miss Haight found her poet-pupil's wide reading in Latin provided an invaluable background and that she was "diligent, eager, accurate in getting hold of syntax, word-order, style . . . ." By the time Vincent entered Vassar in the fall she felt well acquainted with her tutor, and after Elizabeth Haight had been her Latin teacher only a few weeks, they became close friends, were soon on a first-name footing outside of class, and formed a lifelong relationship.

Vincent was glad to be in Camden with her beloved family during these summertime weeks of preparation for Poughkeepsie. Now that the doors of the wide world had been opened to her, the "three long mountains" no longer seemed to wall her in, but served as a bulwark against confusion in the life she had entered, and the life she had committed herself to lead in the future. New York was no longer a far-off mirage, but an experienced reality. As she lay in the hammock reading American history, it was good to be able to visualize the Fifth Avenue bus and the Staten Island ferry, just over the doorstep from 40 Chestnut Street "in everything but distance."

CHAPTER V

"Vincent at Vassar"

U NEXPECTEDLY, college life had countless drawbacks, irritating and exasperating limitations. During most of the fall term, the poet acted like a caged bird beating its wings in angry resentment against the bars of rules and regulations. Free and independent when growing up, she could not understand the insistence on regular attendance at chapel, classes, and meals; the complicated system of cuts and absences seemed silly to her. That she *had* to attend classes was ridiculous in her eyes. Even more ludicrous was the heavy chaperoning if a man appeared on campus: the girls were trusted with everything but a man. A man was "forbidden as if he were an apple," whether he was a cadet from West Point across the Hudson, a Yale student, or any other species of male. To Vincent Millay, who was twenty-one years old—the age of most seniors—and had spent a winter in New York more or less on her own, Vassar was more like an "orphan asylum" than the sophisticated college she had been anticipating so eagerly. The entire code of conduct seemed utter nonsense to her, and for at least five months she rebelled, disregarding or circumventing the rules as often as she could.

Even before the term began Vincent created a stir by presenting the views of an iconoclast and thoroughly original thinker on her entrance examinations, particularly in history. She started by stating that she had prepared for American history at her home in Camden, "in the hammock, on the roof, and behind the stove."

She had spent two months studying Barnes's *Brief History of the United States,* and her corollary reading consisted of Young's *Night Thoughts* and Emerson's *Essay on Compensation.* She also stated that five years before, in high school, she had "read, studied and understood" Burke's "Speech on Conciliation with America." Among other things, Vincent concluded her discussion of England's treatment of the colonies by saying that it was "not a policy at all, just a habit." She closed her paper with a touch of the Irish blarney she probably inherited from her mother, stating that although she knew "a great deal more about American History, the pleasing lady in an Alice blue coat, who she wished might be her instructor in History," had requested them to turn in their papers. She was "sorry, but obedient." The startled history teacher, Miss Mildred Thompson, grew more and more puzzled as she went over the extraordinary examination paper. Here was an applicant with little or no understanding of history who wrote "grand epithets." From a history academic marker's point of view, the paper was a failure, but it was so remarkable that Miss Thompson felt she should report the results to her superior. She was not at all familiar with the student's name, but on the way to the Dean's office she happened to meet President Taylor. She described the contents of the remarkable examination paper she was carrying and showed him the first page of the yellow second sheets on which Vincent had scrawled her answers. Seeing the name, he exclaimed, "Oh, our poet!" and the mystery was cleared up.

As it turned out, Miss Thompson *was* her instructor, but in the matter of attending history class or any other class whose subject didn't interest her, Vincent Millay was not obedient. She cut classes regularly, especially her "eight o'clocks," and would have skipped early morning chapel entirely if she hadn't been obliged to appear now and then. Almost everyone tried to get out of chapel whenever possible, so Vincent's frequent omissions were not nearly as reprehensible as her flagrant disregard of class-attendance rules.

When the alarm went off at an early hour, Vincent's congenial but quite conformist roommate, Harriett "Harry" Wiefenbach from Denver, Colorado, would jump out of bed to get dressed for chapel, but Vincent would usually turn over and sleep another hour or two. She had most likely stayed up until the wee hours working on a poem, and needed more sleep. Poetry-writing was her most frequent excuse for missing chapel or class. Occasionally, she pleaded illness, but was unabashed if found out, even by so important a professor as the new president, Henry Noble Mac-Cracken, with whom she studied English drama. One morning she sent him a note saying she was not feeling well; later in the day, while she was trying to prove to the gate warden that she could hit the gate light with a high kick, the noted educator came up the walk. He commented rather coldly on her rapid recovery, and she retorted with equal coolness, "At the time of your class I was in pain with a poem!" Afterward she told the warden, "A poem is like a child, you know: when it's time for it to be born it has to have attention."

The poet had many private sessions in the President's office because of her refraction of rules, sometimes inadvertent. She did not think twice about going outdoors at three o'clock in the morning to enjoy a stroll on Vassar's beautiful wooded campus, its autumn colors scarcely dulled by the soft glow of moonlight; and she could not understand why taking such a walk, which to her seemed perfectly natural, should arouse the horrified protests of the faculty. Miss Thompson, who was fond of Vincent in spite of the poet's incorrigibility, once scolded her, "Well why *didn't* you think, you naughty little thing?" when she absent-mindedly overlooked one of the rules. Smoking was banned on campus, and Vincent simply avoided this restriction by having the pleasure of her cigarettes in the open air, sitting on the low wall of the cemetery across the road from the campus. But Vincent's constant cutting and tardiness, plus the fact that she usually turned in brilliant term papers and exams, infuriated most faculty members, who complained to the President about her highhanded ways. He would feel obliged to send for her, and a stormy scene would follow, accompanied by Vincent's angry tears.

Henry Noble MacCracken, who was one of the most progressive college administrators of his time and proved to be one of Vassar's outstanding presidents, was inclined to be sympathetic toward untamed poetic spirits, especially one like Edna St. Vincent Millay, whose creative gifts he recognized. Yet he felt constrained, as a newly inducted president, to be firm though not unfeeling in dealing with students of a rebellious nature. He was patient, but unmoved by tears. He reasoned with Vincent, trying to show her that the many college rules were necessary. He finally told her that he would never expel her: "I know all about poets at college," he said, "and I don't want a banished Shelley on my doorstep!"

Vincent stared out of the window, angrily considering his words for several minutes. Then, still defiant, she said hotly, "On those terms, I think I can continue to live in this hell-hole!"

And before the semester was quite over, she found herself in the center of a dozen activities, bubbling with school spirit, beginning to love the "pink and gray college" she thought she hated. Her mind was too quick and keen, her intellectual curiosity too intense not to respond to the stimulating atmosphere.

She gained a new awareness of social issues like the suffragist movement and women's rights in general, then coming to the fore in the changing world of the early twentieth century. She had had a vague knowledge of these questions in Camden, but did not realize their full significance until President MacCracken came out publicly in support of the suffragist movement. The college sponsored a series of lectures on the subject. One of the most stirring lectures was delivered by Inez Milholland, a brilliant, glamorous, and prominent Vassar alumna of 1909, in the spring of Vincent's sophomore year. Inez, called the "Amazon Beauty" of the suffragist movement, made an eloquent appeal for understanding of the cause and the poet was moved to join in the fervor that swept over the college in favor of the voting franchise for women. Inez Milholland became one of her idols. She paid tribute to her in the dedication of a sonnet on leading suffragist figures long after the speaker's sudden, tragic death in 1916, less than a year after her Vassar appearance. Another significant note sounded by this lecture was the poet's first encounter with Eugen Boissevain, then married to Inez Milholland. Like the suggestion in a line in a classical ode that later develops into a central theme,

their meeting was without any consciousness on either side that
he was to become an important part of her life.

Vincent's spontaneous spirit, essentially earnest and profound,
surcharged with emotional excitement and a keen sense of humor,
soon won her a following of friends among the students at Vassar.
Her capers and her clashes with the faculty caused no end of
entertainment for the girls, and not a little resentment by a few
who considered her merely an exhibitionist. There was much
speculation about her background, particularly about her religious
training, because she cut chapel so often and did not seem in the
least concerned about the salvation of her soul. Except for her
roommate and a small circle of friends during her freshman year,
few of the students knew the serious, meditative side of her
nature, or that she spent long hours writing poetry, which had a
marked, if highly unorthodox, religious aspect. The matter came
to a head one evening after dinner in the beginning of the second
semester, when Vincent, "Harry," and two other girls, "Kim" and
"Bee," were sitting around talking. In a particularly "scoffy" and
"skeptic" mood, they had been poking fun at Kim, a sweet,
southern girl who was devoutly religious, because she never
missed chapel and would stay up to study on Saturday night so
she would not have to open any books on Sunday execpt the
prayer book in Sunday morning chapel. Vincent jokingly called
her a "missionary," and she surprisingly shot back, "Heathen!"
which the poet hotly denied. Harry and Bee staunchly supported
her, and "somehow the thing grew" until the four girls found
themselves in Harry's room, holding a prayer meeting! Kim led,
reading three short psalms, Vincent read a couple of religious
calendar quotations, and they all said the Lord's Prayer to close
the service. They decided to meet every night in Harry's room
at ten o'clock; anyone who cared could come, but strictly for
prayer, which was to be short and sensible. One girl who came
with a novel in case things got dull was sent away at once, to her
surprise. Vincent sent home for her mother's Bible, which she
wanted to keep in her room, perhaps for moral support, she said
somewhat apologetically. It was not that she had suddenly "got
religion," for she had always had her own personal beliefs, the

inner faith that had been renewed and expressed in "Renascence," but she needed something as a counter to the skepticism it was fashionable to display at college. And, she added, she was old enough to appreciate the beauty of the Bible as literature.

Whatever the forces at play, Vincent Millay struck a balance before her freshman year was over and showed both intellectual and creative growth from then on. After an unsuccessful "expedition in untrameled verse," as she called it, entitled "Why did I Ever Come to this Place?" and published in "At Random, A Department of Nonsense" in an early issue of the Vassar *Miscellany*, the poet stopped her attempts at free verse, nonsensical or otherwise. She had to pursue her own path at her own pace. She made some final revisions on "Interim," the blank verse monologue Professor Brewster had praised, and, possibly at his suggestion, added a stage direction: "(*A Man Speaks*)." [1] With some trepidation, she submitted the poem to an intercollegiate competition in which it placed among the prize winners; it was published in the Vassar *Miscellany* for July, 1914. In September, Mitchell Kennerly published it in the *Forum*, and later in Vincent's first volume, *Renascence and Other Poems*. She had been composing a new work, begun in somber moments during the hysterical period of her adjustment to college life; and her next venture was to enter it in the Association of Northern College Magazines Competition, or rather, to submit it to the committee selecting the entries from Vassar; but here she ran into an unexpected stumbling block.

The poem, patterned after the Eclogues of Vergil she had been studying in Elizabeth Haight's Latin class, was called "The Suicide," and was a dramatic dialogue between a young girl who takes her own life and her heavenly Father, revealing her lofty but lonely fate in the afterworld. The committee members, so shocked by the title they did not bother to read the poem, were afraid it would harm Vassar's reputation. Vincent was sent for, and she read her lines before the faculty committee in firm, quiet, only dimly defiant tones. She knew it was a good poem, artistically and morally, and that the questioning was unwarranted; but the committee remained unconvinced until she read the last line, in which the Lord admonishes the sorrowful suicide who is

[1] Later omitted from the *Collected Poems*.

tired of languishing alone, and begs her Father for some small stint or duty: "Thou *hadst* thy task, and laidst it by. . . ." Then they allowed the poem to be submitted as a Vassar entry. Happily, it won the "cup" for verse, to Vincent's vast, triumphant joy. One of the judges in the competition was Robert Frost, then just coming into long overdue recognition because of his best-selling volume, *North of Boston,* which he had almost called American Eclogues. His fondness for the eclogue form, besides his ability to recognize a true poet when he saw one, no doubt influenced his vote.

"The Suicide," like "Interim," was published in the *Miscellany,* and both were included in a volume called *Vassar Verse,* which the college brought out in 1916. In *Renascence* and the subsequent *Collected Poems,* "The Suicide" is third, following the title poem and "Interim."

By the end of her freshman year Vincent had established a reputation as one of the outstanding students in her class, though hardly as a scholar. In French, she had already been promoted into a sophomore course and accepted by the French Club. She also wrote some poems in French, one of them a charming verse to the tune of "Au Clair de la Lune," of which the French teacher, M. Bracq, said, "C'est exquis!" But she was afraid she would flunk everything else. As it turned out, she received an "A" or "B" in all her language courses, including German, which she had never studied before but had grasped so quickly she was at the head of the class by Thanksgiving. Her only "C's" were in history and math. She excelled in Old English and Latin, and she enjoyed her fine friendship with Elizabeth Haight. Vincent often confided her dreams and innermost thoughts on all manner of things to the Latin teacher as they went for long walks in the country around Poughkeepsie. She had made many friends among the girls and was indeed "crazy about the college," as she wrote to her beloved family.

For all her popularity and success, she was just as "crazy to get home" for summer vacation. She had missed her mother and sisters keenly. She was already trying to find ways to get Kathleen into Vassar on a scholarship. She treasured every vacation and the brief visits her mother made to Vassar a few times during her college years. The strong affection Vincent had felt for her family from childhood was never weakened by separation, but rather increased, so that she was determined not to be away from her mother and sisters for any indefinite period.

In her second year Vincent Millay became the literary lion of Vassar and gave signs of emerging as one of its idols because of her broad activity in both creative writing and drama. Her interest in the theater, which had begun in high school, had remained fallow during the years in between because there was no outlet for her talents. But Vassar offered a veritable ocean of opportunity for self-expression in the arts. As MacCracken has related in *The Hickory Limb*, the school had an invigorating atmosphere of "creative gaiety" about it in those days. The girls spent much time singing and acting. There were "step-sings" on campus; student songs were sung at meals and parties; songbooks were compiled by each class; and the climax came with the annual song contest on Founder's Day, one of the biggest events of the year. Emphasis on acting and all phases of the theater was perhaps even greater. Any girl with a glimmer of talent or desire to act could find a part in some play, pageant, or dramatic reading that took place during the school year. There were Class plays; four "Hall" plays, productions that originated with the Philalethean Society in the mid-1880's, when they were put on in Society Hall, and later extended to the different student dormitories, or Halls; language and fine arts department plays; and major offerings presented to the public by the play production classes.

Vincent's participation in every facet of the performing and creative arts at Vassar began in the fall of 1914, when she played "Princess Daisy" in a skit written for the sophomore class party on October 26; she received a favorable notice in the weekly *Miscellany* for her acting in this minor production. Her appearance in a "classical soiree," arranged by the language department students a few weeks later, however, brought an outpouring of admiration and praise from students and teachers alike. The poet had been chosen to recite in Latin Catullus' "Passer Mortuus est"; and, with her usual ingenuity and flair for the dramatic, she had borrowed a stuffed song sparrow from the Museum of Natural

History which she held tenderly in her hands during the recitation. With her vivid imagination, her affinity for birds, and her deep emotional responses, she probably experienced a sense of mourning evoked by the thought of the inevitability of death in the poem; for out of this came such lines of her own as, "Death devours all lovely things, / Lesbia and her sparrow."

On February 27, 1915, in a presentation by the French Club, Vincent played Sylvette in Rostand's *Les Romanesques;* less than a week later, on March 5, she made a stunning appearance as the poet Marchbanks in Shaw's *Candida,* a role that won her plaudits from Poughkeepsie and New York newspapers as well as the school paper. From then on Vincent Millay was in demand for both performing and creative contributions to Vassar's varied cultural activities. Perhaps her most significant work came in the spring of 1915, when she wrote and took part in the entire Sophomore Tree program for 1915. The traditional ceremonies, which included a marching song and an outdoor pageant enacted just before the planting of a tree marked with the year of the class—in this instance, "1917"—were among the most memorable of each year's academic events. Vincent wrote and designed the printed program, which was distributed to the student body before the ceremonies began. She designed the stylized sketch of a tree on the cover and wrote a chant set in the ancient Druid context of tree-worship as "the symbolic expression of class unity." The leaflet "marks her first appearance in print outside of periodicals," according to an article in *Publishers' Weekly* for November 30, 1940, by John S. V. Kohn, and should rank as Item no. 1 in the Millay bibliography according to Kohn; but it was apparently omitted from Karl Yost's otherwise authoritative *Bibliography,* which came out in 1937.

The theme of the pageant foretells the poet's pacifism, her hope for love and unity among nations, here exemplified by "Egyptians, Greeks, Celts and Norse," and provides an intimation of the anti-war feeling that culminated in *Aria da Capo.* The "Song of the Nations" and the "Druid's Chant" which accompany it, as well as the basic concept of the pageant, may have been evoked by the war in Europe, which, though still distant, was disturbing to Americans by 1915. Both the "Druid's Chant" and the "Song of the Nations" were included in the *Collected Poems* published posthumously in 1956. After the ceremonies, which were "the best they ever had here," Vincent wrote home happily, the girls walked around for hours singing their marching song, which Vincent also composed, though her authorship of this was later contested.

In sharp contrast was her satiric ballad, "The Patient Periodical," which won the Class Song Contest on Founder's Day the following year. Beginning in October, 1915, her junior year, Vincent's career as actress and composer continued to blossom. She made a "spectacular appearance" as Marie de France in Hazel MacKaye's "Pageant of Athena," given in the Outdoor Theatre in celebration of Vassar's fiftieth anniversary. Dressed in white satin, she walked gracefully across the green, and in her resonant voice recited the tragic "Lay of Tristram and the Queen" in tones vibrant with feeling.

After midyear exams she began rehearsing for the role that won her the greatest public acclaim, Deirdre, in John M. Synge's *Deirdre of the Sorrows.* The New York *Tribune* as well as both Poughkeepsie newspapers, the *Eagle* and the *Enterprise,* praised her performance. The play was presented to a packed house on March 11, 1916, and the next day Vincent, surrounded by admiring students, read in the *Eagle:* "Dierdre, small and bewitching . . . lovely in her little Irish costume, clinched the attention of the audience and the whole play with the increasing intensity of her acting, building to a successful crisis." The Vassar *Miscellany* was equally enthusiastic. With such accolades, it is not surprising that she began to consider the stage as a secondary career and means of support, to augment the meager earnings she knew she would have to face as a poet.

Though she led a busy school life, she found time to write to Arthur Ficke, who commented on the change in her handwriting. And it is true that she had switched from a flowing, inch-high, forward-leaning style to a sprawling backhand. Although she made light of the question, answering that she didn't know if this meant a change in character or "simply an increase of it," the fact is that from her college years on, Edna Millay wrote a flat, twisted, straggling backhand that became increasingly illegible through the years as her life became more hectic.

Several notes to Dr. MacCracken in this scrawl concerned a scholarship for Kathleen, and, as she did everything else, Vincent pushed the plan with great intensity. Through Dean Ella Mc-Caleb at Vassar, she had managed to secure a grant for her little sister ("Wump" in her family letters) at the Hartridge preparatory school in Plainfield, New Jersey. Now she wrote the Vassar president that her heart was so set on having Kathleen there next year that if her sister didn't come back with her, she would not care if *she* didn't come back. Her family was never far from her concern, no matter how involved she became in other relationships or outside affairs. Hers was not a compulsive, but a spontaneous outpouring of love for those close to her; and although her letters seem almost embarrassingly affectionate at times, their ring of genuine feeling is unmistakable.

The same intensity and spontaneity carried over to her friendships with both men and women.

She was increasingly popular among the students at Vassar because of her acting, and in her junior and senior years formed friendships, a number of which were deeper and more lasting than those she made in the first two years. Most of the girls were much younger than she, since she was four years older than her own classmates to begin with; but she was so full of ready fun and zest for life, aside from her passionate inner drives toward artistic achievement, that even Isobel Simpson, a brilliant classical language major of the class of 1920, thought of Vincent Millay as about her own age. They studied Greek and Latin together and because of their love of Latin poetry felt a special love for each other. The poet adored Dorothy Coleman, a member of the class below Vincent's, because of her glorious singing voice, though she was generally popular for her wit and striking beauty, her pretty clothes and shoes. She had the air of the concert artist, but none of the pretensions that often accompany a performing vocalist. When she sang, her listeners, especially Vincent, were transported along with her, to the realm of beauty evoked by the purity of her tones. None of them could know that she would be taken tragically a few years later, a victim of the flu epidemic of 1918. The poet, heartbroken over her untimely death, was to immortalize her voice in the elegies she called "Memorial to D. C." published in *Second April.*

Two other girls, Frances Stout and Anne Gardner, were part of the small circle of Vincent's intimates at Vassar, with whom she kept up a warm correspondence for many years. But the closest friend among all the poet's classmates was Charlotte (Noyes) Babcock, from Bronxville, New York, a girl with a sweet, bright face, and lovely eyes that radiated intelligence and humor. The two were senior year roommates and were practically inseparable "sisters." They were "Charlie" and "Vince" to each other and spent long hours over innumerable cups of tea, talking, talking, talking their heads off, then dropping into silence—the "lovely, lovely silence" of unspoken communication between kindred spirits. They attended campus events together; they went ice-skating in the winter and motoring in the spring. And, although Charlotte became engaged during the last few months of college, Malcolm Sills, her fiancé, did not interfere with the intimate friendship of the beloved "sisters." Only after graduation, when "Charlie" was to be married, did Vincent feel a pang of resentment and loss. She hoped, almost desperately, that Charlie would not "forget her entirely because of that Mac Sills," and she begged her roommate to come to Camden during the honeymoon, or later by herself, and stay as long as she liked in the Millay's unconventional household. She did not go to the wedding, largely because of lack of funds, but sent as a present a *"tea-ball!"* an item they had often wanted to buy in college, along with a bit of doggerel, perhaps to disguise her deeper sentiments.

Vincent's New York companion, Salomón, was in 1916 teaching at Williams College, and sang her praises so extravagantly that Professor Rice, head of the Spanish Department, and his wife, invited her to spend a weekend with them in Williamstown. Salomón was eager to have her come; she made a special effort to go, and had "the most beautiful time." At the time of the invitation she was rehearsing for a performance of First Hall plays, a production of three one-act plays, in which she had the role of Vigdis in John Masefield's new play, *The Locked Chest,* and was also cramming for a Spanish exam. In Williamstown there was much fine music, and she could talk over her latest lyrics with the Nicaraguan poet, as well as pick up a little practice in speaking Spanish, which was still new to her (although she would be president of the Spanish Club before the year was over). She had just sent four of the poems to *Poetry Magazine:* "Kin to Sorrow," "Tavern," "Afternoon on a Hill," and "October-November." Miss Monroe had accepted for the sum of sixteen dollars all but the last, saying she would have to wait till the following November to print it! Salomón agreed with "Ednah" that this was an insult to "October-November," which he considered a "marvelous" title, and he "adored" the poem. It was obvious that he also adored the poet, the first of her many suitors to follow.

Vincent's performance as Vigdis in *The Locked Chest,* which she considered her most interesting and difficult role, took place right after her return from Williamstown, on December 9, 1916, bringing her fresh plaudits as an actress. She received a letter from Masefield himself, telling her that many of his friends had written him about her wonderful interpretation of the role, which she originated; he wished he had been there. He would send her a copy of the play as soon as it was published. Moreover, a good friend of Caroline Dow who saw the play told Vincent she had written Masefield that the talented actress also wrote poems, to which he had replied, "Tell Vigdis to send me some of her work." The poet-actress lost no time in mailing him a selection of her "very best"; and, although it was months before she had any word from him, he finally let her know that he liked her poetry very much, adding that she had a "quite rare personal gift."

Her reputation as both actress and poet was growing. A week after playing Vigdis, she appeared as Olga in Vassar's holiday offering, *The Christmas Guest,* by Selma Lagerlöf. And during the second semester of her senior year, the poet began to try her hand at playwriting. She was among the first to enroll in Vassar's new Workshop Theatre, patterned after Baker's 47 Workshop at Harvard and set up by Gertrude Buck of the Drama Department. Students acquired experience not only in writing, but in producing and acting in their own plays. With her usual ardor, Vincent wrote three plays during the course: *Two Slatterns and a King,* a clever, well-constructed morality play in blank verse; a prose play, *The Wall of Dominoes,* which won a prize in the competition held by the Association of Northern College Magazines, which had awarded her the poetry cup for "The Suicide" in her freshman year, and with its smart style was a forerunner of the *Distressing Dialogues* she later wrote under the pseudonym of Nancy Boyd; and finally, another verse play, *The Princess Marries the Page,* which, though light, she felt was "rather pretty." She played the part of the Princess in the production on May 12, 1917, in the Students Building.

Even before the presentation of her play, Vincent went to New York over the Easter vacation, ostensibly to spend the holidays with Miss Dow at the Training School, but actually to try to line up a place for herself with the Washington Square Players for the following year. As it happened, she did not even see her benefactress, who was out of town; she was just as glad, for "Aunt Calline" still objected to her going on the stage. Through Salomón, Vincent had met a member of the company who was arranging an interview with the manager; though it did not materialize into anything definite, the contact was one which she could follow up after graduation. She enjoyed being in New York again and was already making plans for Norma and eventually her mother and Kathleen to join her there the following year: they would take an apartment somewhere, if only a garret. Kathleen, who had not been able to enter Vassar that fall in spite of her sister's efforts, came up from the Hartridge school to see a performance of *Yellow Jacket* with Vincent. And then, just at the end of Easter vacation, Salomón invited the poet to hear Caruso in *Aida* at the Metropolitan! She was due back in Poughkeepsie the day before the performance, but the temptation to hear the great tenor in her favorite opera was irresistible and she remained in New York for the glowing event and had a glorious time. When she returned to college a day later she was "campused" as a penalty. This meant that she lost her overnight-absence "privileges" for the rest of the term.

The loss of privileges did not bother her too much because she had a great deal of class work and writing to do. Besides her play, she was composing a baccalaureate hymn, both words and music (the latter with the interesting direction, "to the tune of *St. Vincent*") to be sung at Commencement. The production of

The Princess Marries the Page, with its light touch and fairy-tale language and with her delicate, subtly satiric performance as the Princess, was a delightful success. Among other plaudits, it brought her the highly prized praise of the accomplished British actress, Edith Wynne Matthison, and her playwright husband, Charles Rann Kennedy. They were associated with the Bennett School at Millbrook, New York, and sometimes visited Vassar out of professional interest and, no doubt, in an advisory capacity when the Workshop Theatre was established. Vassar students often attended performances at Millbrook to study the acting technique of Edith Matthison, who was famous for her beauty and rich, warm voice, and who was the most eminent and glamorous of the poet's idols during the Vassar years. She worshiped the ravishing leading lady; the actress spoke in the best Shakespearean tradition, and Vincent hung on every syllable, and made her diction the model for her own clear delivery on stage and in her later poetry readings. She was moved to write a four-line tribute to Miss Matthison, claiming that if she lost her hearing, two senses would have pased beyond her reach: her own hearing and the other's speech. The Kennedys, who thought Vincent showed brilliant promise as actress and playwright, encouraged her to choose the theater as a career, and their influence was undoubtedly one of the forces then shaping her destiny.

They came back stage after the performance of *The Princess Marries the Page* to congratulate the young author-actress, radiant in her Princess costume. As Edith Matthison kissed her, Vincent was certain the older actress' feeling for her was akin to love; she was even more sure of it when the Kennedys invited her to visit them in their home during the summer. They also offered to send her letters of introduction to such prominent theatrical managers in New York as George C. Tyler, Winthrop Ames, and other important people in the theater world. Moreover, the Kennedys kept their word: Vincent received a generous supply of recommendations accompanied by a beautiful letter from Edith, full of tender concern for the poet's future.

From the beginning of May on, the students had to spend much of their time studying for final exams. Vincent, with her phenomenal memory, could "get a whole textbook by heart" in a night or two, and come out with a fairly high mark in spite of her class-cutting. There were some term papers, however, that had to be written, and she applied herself to these with the same earnest concentration she gave to every enterprise on which she set her heart. However, she could be diverted if the lure were great enough. One day early in May Elizabeth Haight asked her if she would like to try to get a look at the lunar sky-courting dance of the male woodcock that evening in a nearby swamp. The Latin teacher, like the poet, loved nature, especially the sea, hills, flowers, and birds. Vincent accepted on the spot.

They skipped dinner, and, taking sandwiches and small blankets, hiked out to the swamp, where they trod lightly and carefully on the tussocks of dry grass till they found a "camping place." They spread their blankets and sat down to wait until after sunset when the dusk began to deepen; for the most part they were silent and only whispered to each other now and then. Finally they heard "the woodcock's watery call" startlingly close to them, and as they leaned forward in excitement the huge bird rose straight up in front of their eyes and soared until he was out of sight in the evening sky. A moment later he suddenly fell wildly to the ground with a rhythmic beating of wings and a rhapsodic song, one of the most melodic mating cries of all birds. It was a thrilling experience, part of which would live forever in lines the poet was to write a few years later.

A different sort of diversion tempted Vincent Millay on a sparkling Saturday morning near the end of the term. She and "Charlie" had settled themselves for an entire weekend of study for finals, although it was the day the class picnic was held at Lake Mohonk across the Hudson and the weather was perfect for an outing. Before they had accomplished much, a friend of Charlie's, Gertrude Bruyn, who had graduated from Mount Holyoke the year before, and had been doing social work around Kingston, drove up with a Vassar graduate of 1915, Winifred Fuller. Both girls beckoned from the front seat of a "snappy little Saxon roadster," inviting Charlie and Vincent to go for a drive. There were not many sporty little cars in those days, and it was a treat they could not resist. All four were in high spirits, and, laughing and singing, they crossed the river and drove north. "We just yelled for joy,"

Charlie wrote to Mac Sills in giving her fiancé an account of the spree. Vincent, who felt as if she had been released from a cage, composed spontaneous verses about the blossoming orchards, fresh and fragrant.

They had lunch at an inn frequented by Vassar girls, and afterward, on impulse, Vincent signed the guestbook after a man's name. They left, laughing, and drove on north, "up hill and down dale." The social worker was eager to have them see the area she had been servicing; and, since it was not far from Kingston where both her and Winifred's parents lived, they decided to stop and say hello.

They had dinner at Winifred's home and stayed overnight at the Bruyn's. Winifred's father, who was a Baptist minister in Kingston, thought it was better for the girls not to drive back at night. Vincent thought vaguely that there must be some reason why she should not stay, but not wanting to spoil the fun for the others, she put it completely out of her mind. She and Charlie stayed at Gertrude's all night. The next day before returning they drove west of town to see the newly constructed Ashokan reservoir and went to the Fuller's for Sunday dinner. Afterward, Vincent played the piano and sang some of the songs she had composed, as she often did in the college lounge after dinner. They left toward evening and reached Vassar too late for much study, but, as Vincent said in a note to her family, she had had a "beautiful motor trip," and she would pass her exams somehow. She "sat up three whole nights getting her topics done."

Then unexpectedly, a terrible storm broke around her: one of the college wardens, who happened to lunch at the inn shortly after the girls were there saw Vincent's signature next to a man's and thought the worst. She reported the facts, stressing the point that Vincent had disregarded her last penalty. The faculty, probably persuaded by those who were annoyed with the poet's high-flying, flamboyant lack of respect for rules, voted to suspend her indefinitely! Since Commencement was only a week away, the faculty's rash vote virtually denied her graduation with the class. This was a harsh verdict indeed, for her creative contributions constituted the greater part of the ceremonies: the baccalaureate hymn, a repetition of the Tree Ceremonies, the marching song, and other songs. She would not be allowed to participate or attend any event, including the final awarding of degrees. Her diploma was to be shipped to her, as she told Elizabeth Haight tearfully, "like a codfish."

Vincent was stunned, outraged, and heartbroken. Her friends on the faculty and most of the student body were highly indignant. Dr. Elizabeth Thelberg, the college physician, invited Vincent to stay at her home in Poughkeepsie during the "rustication," which the doctor deemed totally unfair. "I wrote my name under Lord Kitchner's at Shepheard's Hotel in Cairo, and nobody thought the worse of me," she said hotly. Even though Vincent had proof that she had been on a perfectly innocent trip with three girls and had spent the night in the Bruyn home, the members of the faculty who voted against her were adamant. A petition signed by a hundred and eight seniors was sent to President MacCracken, requesting him to permit Vincent to attend all the events on the Commencement schedule. He also received individual letters from eighteen of her friends, including of course Elizabeth Haight, Dr. Thelberg, and other faculty members besides her circle of intimates, especially "Charlie," who was terribly upset. The whole school was in an uproar; and though Vincent called it "a splendid row," she shed "gallons" of tears, all over everyone. She sent two dramatic little notes to President MacCracken: one, bearing traces of sobs, begged him to see her that very evening; the other, evidently written after the interview, vows her undying gratitude for his "great gentleness" with her.

In spite of his sympathetic attitude, however, MacCracken could not seem to make up his mind to veto the verdict, and the controversy continued. In the midst of it, rehearsals for the baccalaureate hymn began, and since no one except Vincent knew the score well enough to conduct the chorus, she was allowed on campus for one hour a day to direct the singers. But she was kept away from the performance on Baccalaureate Sunday, which seemed to her the unkindest cut of all. Elizabeth Haight, visiting her at Dr. Thelberg's after the services, had never seen the poet so depressed; nor was she cheered by the Latin teacher's report that her hymn "to the tune of *St. Vincent*" had been beautifully sung, the most moving part of the program.

President MacCracken, meanwhile, had been communing with himself, and at the last minute sent the faculty a letter asking that suspension be ended the night before Commencement Day, so that "Miss Millay" could take her degree with the rest of the class. "I was ashamed not to have acted earlier," he wrote years later, "for there were few students who had done more for their college than this young poet." A rather feeble and tardy apology in view of the circumstances! And so it was that on Tuesday, June 12, 1917, a small but proud figure in cap and gown walked up the steps to the chapel platform, and with a radiant smile accepted from a smiling President the diploma of Vassar College, inscribed "Edna St. Vincent Millay, A.B."

CHAPTER VI

Summer of 'Seventeen

NOW THAT SHE was honorably graduated the poet became "Edna St. Vincent Millay" professionally, formally, and socially. Some of her intimates always called her "Vincent" or "Vincie," but for the most part she was known as "Edna," especially to her "suitors," as Edmund Wilson referred to the men who fell head over heels in love with her.

Directly after Commencement the poet went to New York to try to find a job in the theater or out of it. She needed to earn a good deal of money; like many artists she regarded material gain only as a means of furthering her art. Moreover, she had a conscientious desire to help her sisters get a start in life. She yearned to have her family with her wherever she was, and part of her plan to line up a job included bringing Norma to New York to live with her. Later her mother could come, too, and perhaps get an editing spot on a newspaper. Kathleen, whose scholarship at Vassar had been secured for the fall, including a room in the same Hall the poet had occupied during her freshman year, came up from Hartridge school to join her in New York while she was job-hunting. But June proved to be a poor month to seek any sort of work, and in the theater it was virtually impossible as all the managers were away for the summer. So the poet, accompanied by the docile Kathleen, who adored her elder sister and secretly longed to be a poet like " 'Sefe" instead of a mathematician, fled to Camden to get her clothes ready for the next attempt in a month or two. Actually, Vincent was dying to get home, to be back on the Maine coast with her family for the summer, or for part of it, at any rate.

She continued to write. She had to compose a number of poems in order to complete the volume Mitchell Kennerly planned to publish in the fall, and some poems still needed polishing. She had finally sold "October-November" to the *Yale Review;* before submitting it she had changed the title to the more descriptive, "When the Year Grows Old," so that it would not be considered a "seasonal" poem. She often revised her work, altering a word or line, even a punctuation mark as well as the name of a poem. If she was not satisfied with a poem, she would put it aside, sometimes for years, working on it from time to time until the whole gave her the gratification her poet's inner sense demanded. For example, "Cameo," which she wrote in first draft at this time, was not published until 1928, in *The Buck in the Snow.*

Most of the poems that eventually made up her first volume were written or begun at Vassar. The majority of them were concerned with sorrow, mourning for loved ones who have died, and the encroachment of death all during life. These themes were to persist throughout her poetry despite her joy in living and in the beauty of nature—or perhaps *because* of it. With the exception of "God's World" and "Afternoon on a Hill," the titles themselves sound a somber note: "The Suicide," "Sorrow," "Ashes of Life," "The Little Ghost," "Kin to Sorrow," and "Three Songs of Shattering." Yet there was slight indication in the madcap, rebellious antics of Vincent at Vassar—"Vince, the ne'erdo well of college days," as she called herself in a letter to "Charlie"—that she was in the process of creating dark, melancholy works during those years.

More than in most poets, there seems to have been a sharp cleavage in Edna St. Vincent Millay between her everyday living and her inner creative life. The poetic spirit radiated from her, enchanting those who met her without revealing its deep, powerful nature except to a few fellow poets who could perceive it. Indeed, hers was almost a dual personality, and her poetry often gives one the feeling that she was like a person possessed during

the hours of creativity—that she was enthralled by some supernatural vision, out of which she called forth her poems.

Edith Wynne Matthison had tried to get Vincent a place in
summer stock with a Broadway producer who was taking a company to Milwaukee, but she did not succeed. However, she hoped
that her friend would not forget her promise to invite Vincent
to visit them, and in the middle of July she received a letter from
the actress stating that Vincent must come to the Kennedy summer home near New Hartford, where she could work on her manuscript of poems while "Rann" was completing a new play. Edith
had written that the poet could at least "make a trial" of friendship
in this way; the casual remark seems to have aroused the poet
to an emotional protest of love for the actress, begging to be loved
in return. She was not, she said vehemently, a "tentative" person:
in whatever she did, she gave her whole self. Perhaps she realized this tendency in her behavior for the first time. In one of
the most revealing passages of her letters, Edna Millay exposed
her drives and her insatiable need to give and receive love, whoever might evoke such feeling. Not the least illuminating was her
comment that only among "tremendous things" did she feel
"happy and at ease."

She sent part of a sonnet sequence ahead, with some cogent
explanations of the liberties she allowed herself to take with the
form, because Edith was going to line up some readings for her,
as well as a production of *The Princess Marries the Page* at the
Bennett School in the fall, to be directed by the young playwright
herself. As soon as she had finished the typing and tutoring she
had taken on to earn a little money, Vincent set off for New
Hartford in a state of high anticipation.

She was not disappointed. The free and literary atmosphere of
the Kennedy house was a constant delight, perfectly congenial
to her poetic, bohemian background. The Kennedys provided
Vincent with a typewriter so she could prepare her manuscript
for Mitchell Kennerly, and during the day Rann and Edith went
about their own pursuits, he to a little house in the field to work
on his play, *The Army with Banners,* and the actress to her gardening. Meals were as casual as they had always been at the
Millays. In the evening the two writers discussed their manu-

scripts over a beer. Vincent once suggested a line of dialogue which Rann promptly put into his play.

At a gathering of a few friends one night the poet recited "Renascence," which received enthusiastic praise, particularly from Rann, who declared it to be one of the "great poems of all time in any language." One of the guests was Laura Hope Crews, the well-known actress, celebrated just then for her role in *Peter Ibbotson.* She was equally enthusiastic about Edna Millay's reading. She invited the poet to call on her at her nearby house and offered to arrange interviews with the Selwyns and other prominent producers. With the letters she had from the Kennedys, the promise of additional contacts raised the poet's hopes that there would surely be something *"somewhere"* for her in the theater. Surrounded by shoptalk of plays and players in the Kennedys' summertime circle of professionals, Vincent felt that she was already part of the Broadway scene. This was her initiation into the friendly, informal, even intimate, yet curiously disinterested world of theater people, and she was having a wonderful, "oh *wonderful!*" time, just watching and listening, learning to speak "English." The Kennedys, like Witter Bynner, Arthur Ficke, Elizabeth Haight, Caroline Dow, the Mitchell Kennerlys and several others, seem to have regarded Edna Millay as their special prodigy and wanted to do everything they could to help her. Edith not only arranged the production of her plays at the Bennett School, but saw to it that the poet would be paid for directing them and that she would give readings of her poetry there later on. The Vassar Latin teacher was equally solicitous about Vincent's welfare and success. Through Blanche Hooker, a wealthy friend of hers of Greenwich, Connecticut, more readings were arranged; and Caroline Dow was trying to secure part time work for her with one of the patrons who had donated funds for her scholarships at Vassar. For her part, the poet deeply appreciated all moves on her behalf, but she kept a firm hold on her individuality, her inner secret self which could not be swayed beyond a certain point by the economic requirements of society.

When her poems were all neatly typed and she was ready to take her manuscript to Mitchell Kennerly in New York, the Kennedys offered her the use of their apartment in the city, and

Vincent accepted gladly. She intended to see some of the theatrical managers if possible, and she didn't want Caroline Dow, who was still opposed to the idea of a stage career, to discover her. She no doubt would have if Vincent had stayed at the Training School, up till now her usual stopping place when she was in New York.

Now at last Edna St. Vincent Millay was able to visualize the forthcoming volume of her poetry. At one of her editorial conferences with Mitchell, he showed her the proof of the title page of the book, which was to be called *Renascence and Other Poems*. They talked about the typography of the book, the design, and the choice of paper; and when the editor-publisher told the poet that the whole book was to be printed on beautiful, rough, "torn-edgy" paper, she asked, wide-eyed, if it wasn't going to be "terribly expensive" to use such wonderful paper. Mitchell replied, smiling, "Oh, well—you *promised* me, Edna, it was to be a very small book!" And so it would be, a lovely thin volume, bound in black, with gold letters, perfect for a Christmas present. It seemed strange to be contemplating the business end of publishing; the poet mainly wanted her volume to be *read* much more than she cared about the "dirty, necessary money!"

Yet money was vital to Edna St. Vincent Millay if she was to continue her career, establish her name as poet, and at the same time look out for her sisters. Occasionally she sent Norma a dollar or two; and she wrote that if she received the $500 ("simoleons") Mitchell had predicted he would be able to remit when the book came out, she would bring her sister in Camden to New York at once. She managed to make appointments with George Tyler and Winthrop Ames and was promised an interview with the Selwyns; but before any of these engagements materialized, she went to Greenwich, Connecticut, to give a trial poetry reading before a group of Mrs. Hooker's friends. That lady, for all her wealth, was not willing to pay the poet for this preliminary engagement. She said, however, that it could lead to others that would probably bring a fee of fifty dollars, a fabulous amount, Vincent wrote to her old roommate, "Charlie," for sitting around reading her poems the way she used to do at Vassar!

The most notable feature of the poet's Greenwich appearance (which her parsimonious patron liked "*very much*") was that, quite by chance, it set the style of dress for which Edna St. Vincent Millay was famous, part of the legend of the public figure she was to become. Her trunk from Camden had not arrived in New York and she had nothing suitable to wear, so Mrs. Hooker decked her out in one of her own formal gowns. It was a creation made from three rainbow-colored scarves that trailed the floor about six inches all around, ending with a train in back. It was probably too large for the diminutive Edna Millay, but the feeling communicated by the floaty, trailing chiffon encircling her seemed to match the mood of evanescence in her poetry, the fleeting beauty of life, forever vanishing, forever renewing itself, only to vanish once again. Since the test appearance was so successful, Vincent was determined to wear long, trailing dresses for all future poetry readings, even if she had to buy scarves and make them herself. Like Emily Dickinson's pristine white dresses, which were for her the symbol of having taken the vow of true love, Edna Millay's long, sea-green or multicolored chiffon came to be the hallmark of her haunting, bittersweet, and flashingly brilliant attitude toward the transient quality of love, and the brevity of life itself.

She was in and out of New York a good deal during the next few weeks, seeing theatrical managers between her poetry readings. She stayed at her publisher's apartment after she left Edith and Rann Kennedy's, so she had no rent to pay, and since she had numerous dinner invitations her expenses were kept to a minimum. Salomón was in New York and took her out often, helping her "raise the devil." Mitchell Kennerly and his wife Helen were almost as solicitous for her welfare as were Edith and Rann. But one night she was seized with a fainting and sick spell after she and the Kennerlys had been to dinner and the theater. The strange seizure sent her to bed for five days, after which, she decided to take the soft job as social secretary to a Mrs. Thompson, one of her Vassar patrons. "Aunt Calline" had secured the position and was most anxious to have her accept it. Vincent had no desire for such a post. The mere idea of it went against her grain; her New England stubborn spirit of independence fought it. But she realized that her push to graduate and the harrowing, humiliating experience of her rustication before Commencement had left her physically and emotionally worn out. At "Sparkhill," the Thompson estate, she would have time to write, and she would receive a regular salary besides being in beautiful surroundings in the country.

As it turned out, the glamorous woman of fashion merely wanted the poet to rest and write poetry. She was free to do as she pleased, except that she had to confine her cigarette smoking to her own quarters, as Mrs. Thompson objected to the smell. Vincent's breakfast was brought to her room on a tray by a little Austrian maid every morning, a household custom. She lounged in bed till eleven o'clock and led the life of high society in general, driving to the theater in New York in the Thompson's Packard when she wished.

However, the novelty of easy living soon wore off for Vincent Millay; luckily her commitment to direct her plays at the Bennett School came up. In addition to *The Princess Marries the Page*, the school was presenting her morality piece, *Two Slatterns and a King*, and Vincent was to direct both productions. She went to Millbrook from the Thompson's and spent an exciting week pitching into rehearsals with renewed strength and enthusiasm. The productions were beautifully done by the cast she had coached and the audience "loved them." The poet-playwright stood in the wings listening to the applause, and her greatest gratification was the knowledge that some of the people she held dear at Vassar were out in front: Dr. and Mrs. MacCracken, Miss Haight, two other faculty members, Miss Yost and Miss Tholon, and Kathleen. They had been sent for in Miss Bennett's private limousine that night.

After the performance, Dr. MacCracken came up to her with both hands outstretched. They had not seen each other since he had "shied her sheepskin" at her a few months before, ending the whole tempestuous episode on a happy but rather restrained note. Now he was openly glad and exultant in his praise. "Oh, you're a wonder!" he exclaimed, clasping her hands warmly, and she knew his words came from the heart.

The next day Vincent visited Kathleen at Vassar and gave her five dollars from the fifty she received for directing the plays. She spent a very happy evening with the MacCrackens, talking with the President and his wife. They discussed the poet's future as if she were a contemporary; Dr. MacCracken was in fact only thirty-six years old and could see life as Vincent saw it: full of promise, despite the hazards and setbacks she might encounter. She came away feeling that he was "quite convinced she could do whatever she liked with the world"; his assurance was to be a source of happiness, vindication, and confidence for her in the coming struggle.

CHAPTER VII

The "Gamine of Greenwich Village"

B Y THE LATE FALL of 1917, as the streets of New York resounded with the marching feet of United States doughboys to the patriotic piping of "Over There," the poet was back in the city, staying at the YWCA Training Center, still "on the track of a job" in the theater and on the lookout for a room of her own. It was becoming difficult to remain under "Aunt Calline's" protective wing, much as she appreciated all that her benefactress had done and was still doing for her. Edna St. Vincent Millay was too wild and free a spirit to lead a restricted life under the surveillance of any eye, no matter how kindly and concerned it might be. She was made for romantic adventure, and could no more help running headlong into risk than she could writing poetry about everything that happened to her.

One night the poet and Miss Dow were returning on the train from Long Island, where they had attended a Red Cross Pageant in which Edith Matthison was playing. Vincent sat next to a man who turned out to be a young Polish musician from the Pageant Orchestra. With Aunt Calline only four seats in front of them— luckily it was in *front*, Vincent wrote later to Norma—she proceeded to become "very well acquainted" with the gentleman, a violinist with an interesting, international point of view, who was married and had a little girl named Edda, he told her. He invited her to a concert he was playing in the following week, and she went in secret, despite a pouring rain. The incident was harmless

77

enough, but the fact that Aunt Calline, Mrs. Thompson, or Elizabeth Haight, would disapprove of innocent behavior like making
friends with a stranger on a train was bound to become dispiriting
to someone like Edna Millay.

And she was determined to find a place for herself in the theater
despite Miss Dow's reproachful attitude toward her efforts. She
had to augment her poetry earnings; Mitchell Kennerly, for all
his promises and show of prosperity, had not sent her a single
dollar for her first volume, let alone a five hundred dollar advance.
He always took her to the best restaurants for dinner, and he cut
a dapper little figure walking along Fifth Avenue swinging his
silver-headed cane, but he was strangely vague on the subject of
royalties. The theater was not much more dependable than poetry
as a source of income, but the two seemed to go hand in hand:
the precedent had been established long ago by the Greeks, and
Shakespeare himself had acted on the stage of the Globe. There
was always a chance of sudden fame and fortune in a hit play.
But quite apart from any financial consideration, the theater
fascinated Edna Millay. She found a heady excitement in staging
her own plays particularly because it combined imagination with
the concrete reality of performance; it entailed working intently
with actors in rehearsal, building toward perfection; and it evoked
the expression of love she found in applause.

Furthermore, the Kennedys believed in her ability, and had
made her feel that she could be a successful actress and playwright; and they had been kind enough to give her letters of
introduction which she could not ignore. She felt gratitude and
obligated to them as well as to Miss Dow and probably did not
stop to ponder the merits of trying her skills in several directions
at once. After she had seen all of the big-name managers on
Broadway, she decided to go to Greenwich Village, where the
"little theaters" were coming into prominence. Perhaps the Washington Square Players would be interested in her now; and she
might apply for a job with the Provincetown Players, then in its
second successful season. Anybody could try out at the Provincetown, provided the aspiring individual's love for the theater was
so great that he was willing to work for nothing or practically
nothing: any remuneration was to be in the form of dividends,

depending on the future prosperity of the Players. At this time the prospects of such were still remote. Fortunately, few of the Provincetowners put money above art.

Under the inspiring if at times bombastic leadership of George Cram ("Jig") Cook, and his wife, Susan Glaspell, two dream-borne iconoclasts from Davenport, Iowa, the Players had started in Provincetown two years before in 1915. Few accounts of the famous group have drawn sufficient drama from the fact that communal living was the guiding concept of the Players. They believed in sharing material gains as well as artistic truths. They hoped to set the example of a perfect community, a visionary idea that had been tried by other American writers, but never in the realm of the theater.

They had come to Provincetown seeking a freer intellectual climate than they had known in Davenport, where the ideas that they and their friend, Floyd Dell, had tried to promulgate had been scorned. Dell, in Davenport a struggling young poet with socialist leanings who loved to vocalize on the ills of the existing order, and who in a few years was to become an influence in the life and thought of Edna Millay, drifted from Iowa to Chicago, where he joined the staff of the *Literary Review*. He became a Jack-of-all-trades: editor, critic, part-time poet, novelist, and playwright. When there was a vacancy on the *Review*, he found a spot for Jig Cook as alternate book and drama critic.

When the Irish Players came from the Abbey Theatre in Dublin to tour the country in 1910 and 1911, they created a considerable stir because of their revolutionary ideas. Cook reviewed several of their Chicago performances. He wrote in glowing terms and was immediately fired with a burning zeal to start a similar theater in the United States. "Quite possibly there would have been no Provincetown Players had there not been Irish Players," Susan Glaspell was to write some twelve years later in *The Road to the Temple*. There must be "no stage conventions in the way of projecting with true humility of feeling." Cook himself held that there could be "an American Renaissance of the twentieth century," wrought, like the Italian Renaissance, by a hundred creative artists, the core of which might well be the theater. The three friends decided that New York City was the most suitable place to try out their ideas; Floyd Dell immediately settled in Greenwich Village; Jig and Susan moved on to Provincetown during the summer, where, according to hearsay, there was a small circle of liberal-minded writers. They rented a tiny house at the tip end of the Cape, down the road from an old, crumbling fisherman's wharf.

The wharf was to become a landmark of theater history, for the dilapidated fishing shack at the end of it was soon to be converted into the original playhouse of the Provincetowners. The property belonged to Mary Heaton Vorse, the Cooks' nearest neighbor, and a veteran labor-journalist. She introduced them to the writers and artists who had followed her lead in getting away from New York, including Hutchins Hapgood and his wife, Neith Boyce; Max Eastman; John Reed (already famous for the workers' pageant he staged in connection with the Paterson silk strike of 1913); Wilbur Daniel Steele and his wife, Margaret, all of whom were interested in the new theater. This small circle was the nucleus of the Provincetown Players, who, on the inspiration of Jig Cook, eventually commandeered the old fishhouse, which Margaret Steele was using as her studio, transformed it into a makeshift theater, and presented their plays with great success. Only two "bills" were offered during the initial "season," and members of the audience had to bring their own chairs or camp-stools, placing them in among the oars, anchors, and nets, but their discomfort did not dim the applause. All too soon the summer was over.

During the winter, they all lived in New York City's bohemia, Greenwich Village, where the rents were cheaper and the tradespeople were more friendly to struggling artists than those uptown. This was "The Village" that Edna Millay first explored in 1913, when she haunted its shops with Salomón; she was soon to become one of its most prominent figures. The area was well known as a refuge for radical thinkers. There were the followers of Nietzsche, whose nihilistic philosophy fascinated Eugene O'Neill for a time; of Emma Goldman, famous for anarchistic ideals; of Henrietta Rodman, who set up the Liberal Club above "Polly's" restaurant, where one could get a good meal at low cost, afterward going upstairs to join in the discussions on the suffragist movement and other issues of the day, or watch a play presented by Liberal Club members. A casual meeting place was the Washington Square Bookshop, run by the brothers Charles and Albert Boni, and a hangout for anyone interested in the little theater movement. It was here that the Washington Square Players came into existence with a spontaneous performance of *Lord Dunsany* one afternoon; an impromptu set was created on the spot by Robert Edmond "Bobby" Jones. Then there were the numerous converts to Freudian theories: everyone in the Village seemed to be in the throes of psychoanalysis. "You could not go out to buy a bun," Susan Glaspell wrote, "without hearing of someone's complex."

That first season in Provincetown stimulated the imagination of visionary Jig Cook, who saw in it the means of realizing his dream of a Beloved Community; and the next spring they were back early to plan the foundation for a place of "true drama . . . born only of one feeling animating all the members of a clan . . . ."

It was a magical "season." At Jig's insistence, Susan wrote her first dramatic one-act play, *Trifles*, which has become a classic of its kind. Eugene O'Neill's *Bound East for Cardiff* was presented: his first play to appear on any stage. Other O'Neill plays were presented, and there were offerings by other members. It was a memorable summer for all concerned: they "swam from the wharf as well as rehearsed there . . . . would lie on the beach and talk about plays—everyone writing, or acting, or producing. Life was all of a piece, work not separated from play." And they were rewarded by the responsive audience composed of their associate members. The unqualified success inspired those two prime movers, Jig Cook and John Reed, to propose taking the company to New York for the winter. Under Jig's fervent guidance, they established the theater on MacDougal Street, first on the ground floor of an old brownstone at number 139; then, as their audience expanded, in another building a few doors away. Once a stable, it was large enough to be turned into a bona fide theater with a seating capacity of two hundred. Below, a roomy basement became workshop, dressing rooms, and storage area; above were clubrooms, even a "family" restaurant run by one of the members,

Christine Ell, where dinner could be had for sixty cents or less. An old hitching ring had been left in one of the walls of the converted stable, and around it a set designer painted the legend: "Here Pegasus was hitched."

And here it was that the poet Edna St. Vincent Millay, whose own Pegasus was to carry her worlds away from the Provincetown group, came to apply for a part in a play by Floyd Dell, little dreaming of the large part he was to play in her immediate future.

Floyd Dell, divorced after an unrewarding marriage began to affect his creative ability, had come to New York seeking the perfect mate through "free love" as much as an outlet for his ideas of social reform. He has called the Greenwich Village of this period "a moral health resort," where a young man could breathe the fresh air of an open love affair: he could live with a girl briefly, or as long as he liked, without having to fear the stifling bonds of matrimony unless he willingly chose to take them on. By a freak of circumstance, he arrived in New York just as the founders of the liberal magazine, *The Masses*, headed by Max Eastman, was in dire need of an associate editor. The policies of the publication, particularly its antiwar stand, appealed to Dell's idealism; and he could not resist the opportunity to air his views, although the salary was almost as low as that of the Provincetown Players. He was not closely associated with the actual formation of the group on the Cape because at that time he was producing and writing plays for the Liberal Club.

But when Jig Cook established the experimental theater on MacDougal Street, Floyd Dell immediately joined in the effort to modernize American drama, and their first bill in New York included his one-act play, "King Arthur's Socks," a satiric comedy of married life. Probably as a result of the failure of his own marriage in Chicago, Dell wrote a series of one-act plays dealing with the husband-and-wife relationship and with the suitability, or lack of it, of people *about* to marry. He was preparing to direct his one-act play based on the latter theme, "The Angel Intrudes," for the Provincetown Players' second New York season. The play deals with the situation confronting a serious writer who is engaged to an arrestingly beautiful but empty-headed young girl, Annabelle. There was no one in the troupe who was exactly right for the role, so he issued a casting call. It was at this point in his life-story that Edna St. Vincent Millay entered the scene, almost as if she had come in on cue.

Dell wrote of his first encounter with the poet, "In response to that call a slender little girl with red-gold hair came to the green-room over the theatre, and read Annabelle's lines. She looked her frivolous part to perfection, and read the lines so winningly that she was at once engaged—at a salary of nothing at all, as was our custom. She left her name and address, and when she was gone we read the name and were puzzled, for it was 'Edna Millay.' We wondered if it could possibly be Edna St. Vincent Millay, the author of that beautiful and astonishing poem, 'Renascence' . . . ." Dell, tall and lanky, his pale, ascetic face alight with joy over his good fortune in finding such a perfect example of type-casting, could hardly wait till the next day to discover if the actress was also the poet whose work he admired.

As for Vincent, she must have been of two minds about the part of Annabelle, which hardly seems the role for a serious, sensitive poet. But she hoped the connection with the Provincetown Players would lead to Broadway roles, or possibly to the production of her own plays, so she showed up promptly for rehearsal the next day. Dell immediately pounced upon her about her identity. She confirmed that she had indeed written "Renascence" and was amused as well as pleased by his rapturous praise of its "astonishing beauty." He was still rather incredulous and was enchanted by the fact that the author of the most remarkable poem of the century should so resemble the fragile, frivolous Annabelle of his play.

After a few rehearsals, it was apparent that Edna Millay would give a "delicious" performance on opening night, December 28, 1917, an indication that she had considerable acting ability, since the success of the airy plot depended on a lightness of touch by the actress playing the part of the lovely but vacuous girl who is entranced by the intruding Angel, and who leaves her fiancé to go away with him. When it became known that the poet also had plays to offer, she was voted a full-fledged member of the company. On the strength of her prospects in the theater, the sales of her book due to appear in December, and an occassional acceptance of new poems, she asked Floyd Dell to help her find an apartment in the Village, and sent twenty-five dollars to Norma, telling her sister to join her right after Thanksgiving. The money may have come from Miss Haight, who now and then offered assistance with a check, which Vincent agreed to accept as a loan. The sisters would manage somehow, if they had to sleep on a park bench! Norma needed no second invitation, and with hilarious joy at being together again, the two Millay girls began "prying open their oysters" in a world feverish with the disease of war.

They lived from hand to mouth. Paying jobs in the theater, which both of them were seeking, were almost nonexistent. War work was plentiful, so Norma took a job "making airplanes" as Vincent put it in a letter to "Charlie" Babcock Sills, while the poet started sending her work to somewhat less than quality magazines in hopes of earning her way by means of her greatest love, writing. It was good to have Norma to "bum around with" in New York and comforting to have some member of her family to "cook breakfasts with" again. Floyd Dell had found an icy one-and-a-half rooms for them at 139 Waverly Place. It was "just a few doors from where Poe wrote 'Ligeia,'" he told Edna encouragingly, for there was little else to recommend the place.

He would gladly have shared his ramshackle apartment with her, for he had fallen in love with her almost at once: first with her voice, which could be "heart-breakingly poignant," he thought when he heard her recite "Renascence" one day after rehearsal. The Provincetowners frequently had coffee at Christine's "family" restaurant in back of the green-room, and it was probably here, early in their acquaintance, that Dell and Edna Millay began to discuss her long poem. Then it came out that part of "Renascence" had been written when the poet was only eighteen. "I don't suppose that anyone could tell where the two parts are joined together," she said.

Dell took a chance. "I'll bet I could," he boasted; and she scornfully bet he couldn't, flipping back a lock of unruly red hair that fell over her forehead when she was excited. The next evening he pointed out the two lines marking the end of the early and the beginning of the later part. He felt he had scored a real triumph when she admitted he was right, her green eyes opening wide in surprise.

Flushing with pleasure, he took another chance. "These first two lines of the second part were written later than all the rest of the poem," he said rashly, "and replace some lines by which the two parts were originally joined together." Again he felt triumphant as she registered complete amazement, and said she was astonished at his critical perception. He was rather astonished himself, but he tried not to let her know it. He felt that she was far above him, somehow unattainable, though he tried hard enough to capture her. When he saw how tenaciously she clung to her poetry writing, sitting huddled by the fireplace (the only warm spot in the tiny flat) with her hardcover notebook and pencil, perfecting her lines, and often forgetting to eat, or "existing on bread and tea," Floyd Dell fell in love with her spirit.

"But there was in her something of which one stood in awe," he wrote in *Homecoming*. "She seemed, as a poet, no mere mortal, but a goddess; and though one could not but love her, he loved her hopelessly, as a goddess must be loved. Perhaps because she was one's Lost Youth one felt sorry for her and worshipped her at the same time." She was twenty-five, and he, thirty. "The lonely, unreachable, tragically beautiful, inhumanly remote and divine quality in one who was, at moments, a scared little girl from Maine, and at other moments, an austere immortal," he went on, "drove everyone who knew her to writing poetry in recognition of her lovely strangeness." Dell's words were an unconscious commentary on the reactions the poet aroused in men from the time she arrived in the Village. His feeling that she represented "one's Lost Youth," that she was an innocent, starry-eyed nymph in need of protection, is especially revealing, since he was only five years older than she, and in some ways much more naïve.

He was also in a financial dilemma just then. *The Masses* had been forced to cease publication in October on government orders because of the magazine's continued pacifist policy and antiwar cartoons, prominently featured six months after the United States had formally declared war on Germany on April 6, 1917. Dell himself had been severely rapped for a piece he had written defending the rights of conscientious objectors. His regular source of income gone, he had to depend on selling articles or short stories to various publications, which was hardly a dependable living, and certainly did not include squiring about a "half-goddess" of a poet. He could scarcely afford to buy her dinner at Christine's or Polly's, let alone the Brevoort, the favorite spot of the Provincetowners who would save for weeks to be able to have one good meal at the Brevoort; in the meantime they contented themselves with a beer at the bar there if they wanted to drink in style.

However, he saw her as often as he could outside the theater, and when the Kit-Kat Ball (later the Beaux-Arts Ball), given by creative artists every year, came along, Dell, as one of the organizers, saw to it that Edna Millay had one of the complimentary tickets. The poet, who, from the beginning, had accepted Floyd Dell's attentions with mixed feelings, was delighted at the prospect of dancing at an artists' ball. But she was so busy rehearsing, acting, and writing that she had no time to think up a costume until the last minute. She had only a few scarves to work with but with sudden inspiration she decided to fashion a "seven-veils" creation. Taking the scarves she had, she called on a college classmate, Margaret Lovell, who lived on West 11th Street, not far from Waverly Place.

Her friend was glad to help; she ran downstairs to see whether "the Fullers" had any scarves. Winifred Fuller, who had been with Vincent on the famous motor trip before Commencement, was visiting her sister Maud, also a Vassar graduate living in the Village. Margaret burst in with the news that "Vincent Millay was upstairs getting ready to go to the Kit-Kat Ball and needed some scarves." They rustled around and found something that might pass, and all three went back up to Margaret's apartment. There, stark naked, kneeling on the floor in front of a mirror was the poet; a small, shapely figure, she was winding the scarves this way and that, over her shoulders and breasts and around her long red hair. She hailed them with gratitude for their contribution and went on fashioning her costume, and asking for suggestions. They all sat around talking until she had swathed and pinned her garment together, and, with a stitch here and there, was about ready to go.

The girls assured her that she was a vision of loveliness, but she wasn't satisfied. "I need something to give it a touch of distinction," she said. "Some kind of a bauble or bracelet."

She glanced speculatively around the room. Suddenly she pounced on a miniature artificial geranium in a pot; she fastened the whole thing to a piece of red ribbon and tied it around her wrist, letting it dangle. "*Now* I'm ready!" she proclaimed, and off she went to the ball, where she no doubt danced until dawn.

After her success as Annabelle, Edna Millay seemed to Floyd Dell the perfect ingénue, so when he completed another one-act play, "Sweet and Twenty," again based on the theme of compatibility between a man and woman who wish to marry, he offered her the lead. Before accepting, she asked if he would read the play to her, which gave him the opening he had been looking for. He invited her to dinner and afterward read the script aloud. It is largely a dialogue on marriage between two unmarried people looking at a house; each of them has a guardian the other mistakes for a spouse. Though the plot is thin and contrived, the lines are crisp and fresh, slightly Shavian in flavor, and not without poetic touches. One of these, which probably influenced Edna's decision to accept the role, was a pleasing ballad, "April-May." She was so charmed by its tone that she offered to set it to music.

Then Dell learned that she sometimes composed songs. She had just completed a musical setting for a recent poem of hers, "Mariposa," a lyric beginning "Butterflies are white and blue"; the poem compares man's love and life to the brief life-span of butterflies. Dell was eager to hear the music, which he found "singularly lovely," capturing the half-mournful mood of the poem exactly. He thought she should try to find a music publisher for it. But though Vincent enjoyed writing an occasional score, she was a poet above all else, not a composer. She wanted to try her skill with "April-May"; and "the music she composed was in perfect imitation of the old English ballad it was supposed to represent." Dell, who was directing his play himself, was so delighted

that he included it in the "business"; and Edna made her entrance
on one scene singing the ballad. A rare combination of talents
all around!

The unmistakable influence of Shavian dialectics on Dell's
comedies led to a discourse on his part for Edna's benefit, dealing
with his socialist aims and ideas. Carried away by his subject,
Floyd paced up and down the room, gesturing with both hands,
and Edna, like his other friends, often had to suppress a smile
when he started to declaim in stentorian tones. The painter Andrew Dasberg, who shared a studio apartment with Robert Edmond Jones in the former stables of the mansion that housed
Mabel Dodge's famous salon, knew most of the Provincetowners
quite well. He once remarked that "Floyd Dell was like a bell:
he could be heard in every quarter." For all that, everyone, including Edna, seemed to indulge the eloquent Mr. Dell in his
oratory.

In the early weeks of their friendship, still in awe of her strange,
fragile beauty, feeling he could not reach her through "sweet
nothings"—and "always the teacher when he had the slightest
excuse"—Floyd poured his own enthusiasms into her ear. Pacifism,
first and foremost; socialism, Soviet Russia, and revolution; and
finally, psychoanalysis. He was being psychoanalyzed at the time
as part of his quest for a perfect mate. An issue that later became
a bitter bone of contention between them was his unrelenting
effort to persuade Edna that analysis would clarify her emotional
impulses and help her to overcome her "sapphic tendencies,"
so that she would be able to discover the enduring love and con-
tentment for which she was searching as ardently as he.

Edna Millay was ready to lend a responsive ear to most of his
outpourings, since she was, in Dell's words, "very much of a
revolutionary in all her sympathies, and a whole-hearted feminist." She listened, fascinated, to his stories about her college
heroine, Inez Milholland, who in the early days of the suffragist
movement campaigned for the cause parading up and down Fifth
Avenue on horseback. Vincent had mourned Inez' untimely death
more intensely than the rest of her classmates; and she felt closer
than ever to "the Amazon beauty" when she learned that Inez,
like herself, had been "suspended in shocked disapproval" from

Vassar shortly before graduation. She since had become its "pride and boast," just as Vincent Millay was to become. Once Floyd casually handed Edna a bronze button that had been left in his rooms by one of the ardent believers who had suffered arrest and imprisonment during the militant suffragist campaign. As she gazed at the brown metal badge of courage, tears came into her eyes. "I would rather have the right to wear this than anything I can think of," she said softly.

The poet listened and, as a rule, wholeheartedly embraced all that she heard. She possessed a strong innate sense of justice and a certain amount of social consciousness. When sociophilosophic discussions and arguments rang out at Green Room parties after an opening night performance, Edna would sit quietly in a corner, absorbing the words of Jig Cook or Floyd Dell or Eugene O'Neill. She tried to catch the side issues at bay between Djuna Barnes and some other belligerently minded member, without being moved to contribute anything herself. She was undoubtedly influenced by some of the liberal thinking aired by the Province-towners, and her views were probably broadened; but the realm of sociology and politics seemed alien to poetry in her eyes, and she was to remain the pure artist for many years. If the subject of poetry came up at the parties, she might or might not join in; although her own ideas were definite, she said very little publicly about the technique of writing poetry. However, if someone asked her to recite, she would come out of her shell and read her poems from memory as no one else could deliver them in her strange, sweet, and somehow "lonely" voice. Then the discussions would cease, and the side arguments come to a halt, while they all listened.

She stubbornly resisted all of Floyd Dell's proddings about psychoanalysis. No matter how much he tried to convince her that treatment might help her clarify her emotional drives and so find happiness and the lasting love she claimed humankind could never know, she remained adamant. She held that it would be dangerous, even harmful to her creative process to strip off all the layers until she reached the "dour" depths of her being. If Dell had been more subtle he might have succeeded, but his constant promotion of psychoanalysis as the solution to the poet's complex problems, his prying and probing, and his attempts to prove that if they married and had children they could both find happiness only made her more stubborn. At this time she wrote in a poem called "Weeds," where she longs for a peaceful place to lie near the daisy and the sorrel, that "Life is a quest and love a quarrel." The year before she died she wrote "Journal," testifying that she still dreaded the "fearful thing" she might discover if she should find the "lost and ominous key to the sealed chamber of her mind." Perhaps she was afraid of losing what Dell has called "the heroic egotism of genius." In any case, the more he talked, the more irritated she grew. She finally told him pointblank that he asked too many questions and that there were doors in her mind that he must not try to open. She crystallized her sentiments in the sonnet "Bluebeard," a stern poetic indictment of Dell's meddling.

Nevertheless, he persisted for some time. By one means or another, he hoped to have the same success with Edna that Charles Ellis, Provincetown artist, set designer, and actor, was enjoying with the poet's sister, Norma. Ellis, on the production staff, and Norma, who called for Edna every day after rehearsal, for "The Angel Intrudes," had been immediately attracted to each other. Charles began to see the sisters home, and before long a romance developed between him and Norma that would result in an early engagement, and marriage a few years later.

Not so between Floyd and Edna. For all his ardor the poet remained tantalizingly out of reach. "She had a charm . . . . A sort of Celtic magic seemed to emanate from her like a perfume. She seemed a little aloof from ordinary concerns . . . ." he wrote in *Homecoming*. When he did manage to embrace her, she reminded him "of the Snow Princess, whose kiss left splinters of ice in the hearts of mortal men who loved her." She was more accurately, perhaps, a combination of fire and ice; or, as she demanded defiantly in "The Singing Woman from the Woods' Edge," written at this time, "What should I be but a harlot and a nun?" This bewitching, humorous, mischievous, but rather weird and bitter ballad was taken literally by many readers, and did much to engender the legend of Edna St. Vincent Millay as libertine poet. The chameleon-like nature which had baffled the schoolboys drove Dell quite daft. Edna soon tired of his mooning and his efforts to make her disclose her secret emotions. She tried to discourage him gently at first, but when Dell would not desist, she led him a merry chase, literally and figuratively.

From this time on, her physical beauty seemed to blossom: Where before she had been appealing in a poetically mournful and melancholy-looking way, she was now ravishing in the eyes of many men. Several in the Provincetown group were among her favorites, including Allan Ross Macdougall (future editor of the Millay *Collected Letters*), with whom she enjoyed a tender, fun-loving friendship; they were both devoted followers of J. Herriman's satiric comic strip, *Krazy Kat*, and enjoyed mimicking his dialogue lingo. Harrison Dowd, the musician and composer who joined the Provincetown company, had been an admirer of hers for several years; Scudder Middleton, to whom she wrote the poem, "If He Should Lie A-Dying," was another; Rollo Peters, of the newly formed Theatre Guild, was still another; and there were more during the six months or so that Edna Millay lived at 139 Waverly Place. Floyd Dell would flare up fiercely if she gave her favors to anyone but him, which made matters worse because it led to bickering over his rights as her most persistent suitor. At times she would tease and taunt him. He described her at a picnic, sitting between Solomón de la Selva and Dell himself, as "looking very demure and enjoying every moment of the encounter of an old beau with a new beau." One day she dared him to catch her and ran out of the theater and dashed around the corner of MacDougal Street, laughing, her red hair flying in the wind, with Floyd, laughing in spite of his anger, in hot pursuit. Out of this telling incident and others came such clever poems as "Daphne," in which the poet warns that she may turn into a laurel bough, but if he wishes to follow her, then, she orders "To heel, Apollo!" Dell called this side of her "the gamine of Greenwich Village"; when she was irascible, he called her "Vixen." Several sonnets mirror the madcap but inconsequential relationship between Edna Millay and the first of her serious "suitors."

It was through Floyd Dell, however, that two men came into the poet's rapidly revolving course of erotic adventures, who were to be fixed stars in her love constellation, lasting forces in the

future of both her everyday and creative life. One of these was
Eugen Boissevain, this second-appearance time for a longer interval, but again almost unnoticed by Edna Millay. On an impluse
one night, Floyd took Edna and Norma to visit Max Eastman's
communal household in Washington Place. Boissevain was a mainstay of the menage; he had been sharing living arrangements with
Eastman since the death of Inez Milholland the year before. His
wife, who suffered from pernicious anemia, was seized with a fatal
attack while on the speaker's platform during one of her speaking
tours. Eugen anxiously watched over her at the hospital, hoping
in vain for some sign of survival. Finally he asked, "Shall I come
with you?" Inez murmured, "No, you go ahead and lead another
life." But Eugen, who adored his dashing, indominatable wife
with the love that a bon vivant like himself would naturally feel
toward a live-wire, reckless, and charming revoluntionary, could
not think of another life for some time. His friend, Max Eastman,
who had been a onetime admirer of Inez (and whom Eugen had
met through her), suggested that they share an apartment. Eastman, who had just separated from Ida Rauh, a member of the
Provincetown Players, to whom he had been married for several
years, needed companionship as much as Eugen. Their friendship
had thrived, and by the time they moved to the Washington Place
literary boarding house, among whose members Max eventually
formed the staff of a new publication, *The Liberator*, Boissevain
had regained his equilibrium and a good deal of his former jovial-
ity.

The evening that Floyd Dell brought the Millay sisters there,
however, was by his own account dull. Edna was tired and more
than usually reserved; the conversation was rather strained. Max
had earlier turned down fragments of Millay poems that Floyd
had suggested for *The Liberator*; Eastman had refused them
mostly, he confessed years later in *Great Companions*, because his
own first volume, published by Kennerly at the same time as
Renascence, had been overshadowed by the glowing reviews the
latter had received. He hoped Eugen would provide some diversion. However, Edna seemed to take no interest in Boissevain
beyond a passing curiosity in the man who had been Inez Milholland's husband; and she radiated so little charm that both men

must have wondered what Floyd Dell had been raving about. At such moments even Edna's hair lost its glow, and seemed a luster-less brown rather than red. She appeared smaller than ever, and rather mousey. Nevertheless, a second meeting between the poet and the genial Dutchman had taken place, and it left a slightly stronger impression on her than the first. Eugen apparently stopped in at the Waverly Place apartment a few days afterward, when he met Mrs. Millay, who was visiting the girls for the week-end.

The other man who was to be a lasting influence on Edna Millay was the poet Arthur Ficke. She had long recognized his spiritual value, but now he entered her life with the blinding impact of physical beauty. She had corresponded with Ficke on and off for nearly six years, but she had been too occupied to keep up the letters to him during the last year, and she somehow never expected to meet him, certainly not in Greenwich Village, in the midst of a war-conscious world. She was surprised to learn from Floyd Dell that Ficke, an old friend of his from Davenport, "showed up wearing a Sam Browne belt and puttees,—*Major* Arthur Ficke, carrying dispatches from Washington to General Pershing." He asked Floyd if he would introduce him to the author of "Renascence."

Edna was delighted, but she was not prepared for the tall, broad-shouldered, superlatively handsome man in uniform who walked into the apartment of 139 Waverly Place with Floyd one evening in the early spring of 1918. He was much more than a good-looking Army officer. Arthur Ficke possessed that rare combination of sensitivity and strength that occurs when an athletic body is endowed with an artistic, creative spirit. He had a classical head, with dark wavy hair and a broad brow above his finely chiseled features. His large, luminous light-blue eyes dwelt on her with an arresting gaze that was almost hypnotic. His straight nose was in exact proportion to the rest of his face, and his full mouth was sensuous, with softly curving lips, but it was not weak. His chin and jawline were strong, clearly defined. His smile was brilliant; his laughter quick, contagious. Even his hands were "flawless," with slender tapering fingers, and oval nails marked by long half-moons. For once in her life, Edna was dazzled by male physical perfection, combined, as she already knew, with a high order of intelligence and a gift for poetry.

The callers had brought a delicatessen supper of sandwiches, embellished by a huge dill pickle, which was handed round "like a loving cup," Norma said laughingly, as they all sat on the floor enjoying an indoor picnic. The remark was Arthur Ficke's cue to seize a pencil and extemporaneously dash off a sparkling, satiric love ditty, scribbling the lines on the top of the cardboard lunchbox. It was a gay little party; and probably to Floyd Dell and Norma Millay seemed nothing more than a merry, informal supper. To Edna St. Vincent Millay, however, the lighthearted evening was a soul-shaking event: for the first time in her life she found herself falling in love. It was a miraculous yet terrifying sensation, fearful because she was irresistibly drawn to a man who had been her spiritual advisor for so long, and, though she knew he was not free, she was powerless to stem her emotions. And she could tell from the long look that occasionally supplanted the merriment in his eyes that the same thing was happening to Arthur Ficke.

Before the evening was over, both had acknowledged the unspoken, profound feeling between them. And both were shaken by it. The hour of their love was brief. A night, a day, and part of another night was all they had together before Arthur's ship sailed, carrying him on a mission that might well be dangerous. Beyond those ecstatic moments neither one seems to have considered a future, which was at best uncertain. Arthur Ficke may well have been sensitive to the fact that behind the pure white heat of Edna Millay's passion was the intense fervor of the poet. To her, love was an all-consuming emotion, a glorious artistry, of a mystic design far beyond the dull pattern of domesticity. Unlike most women, she was distressed by the ready proposals of marriage she received from men who fell in love with her; she did not care to compromise the beauty of love with the homely affection of married life. And, remembering her parents' quarreling and their casual parting, she was no doubt afraid of the loss of love through marriage or even through closeness to another human being. As she told him in a letter, Arthur Ficke was the first man she ever kissed without feeling she would be sorry for it afterward.

In *Homecoming*, Floyd Dell has said that Edna Millay "flashed into his life like a meteor." When poet touches poet in the glowing sky of passionate love, the impact is bound to engender artistic lighting and, to borrow a phrase from Emily Dickinson, "bolts of melody." Floyd Dell had been "driven" to writing more than one poem "in recognition of her lovely strangeness"; Edna had responded in the flippant poems of *A Few Figs from Thistles*, soon to bring her a fame and popularity she later found obnoxious.

Now, between Arthur Ficke and her, during the days and weeks following his departure, there was a rapturous outpouring and exchange of love sonnets such as probably never occurred before, and has never been duplicated. Ficke's sonnets have been overlooked in the annals of poetry, but they are among his finest work. And the love sonnets of Edna Millay inspired by Arthur Ficke are undoubtedly among her most lyrical and spontaneous. To her line, "After the feet of Beauty fly my own," he answered with the sonnet beginning, "For Beauty kissed your lips when they were young," and ending with an image of her forlorn quest, far out on the forsaken rim of the world, seeking on her wild feet a refuge that she could never know, a Beauty that could never be found.

And she wrote, knowing they could not be together,

> Into the golden vessel of great song,
> Let us pour all our passion;

They intellectualized their love, and immortalized it, but that did not make it any less real, as some writers have suggested. One has only to read Edna Millay's poignant, brooding lines in the same form, beginning, "And you as well must die, beloved dust," which, by her own testimony was written to Arthur, and became a bond between them, to realize that their meeting in person on that evening in 1918 was a momentous occurrence for both of them, although Edna was undoubtedly more affected by it than Arthur. In any case, the deep feeling on both sides was not a mere figment of her imagination. For a long time after he was gone she remained "dazzled" by the remembrance of his face and the brilliance of the light his presence had brought, as she expressed it in one of the sonnets. Only gradually could she become accustomed to the darkness in "the narrow room of her daily life" once more. (It was very early in the year, either February or March. According to a letter at "Steepletop," Arthur Ficke's ship sailed on February 19th, 1918; but in later notes he refers to this time as "March, 1918." However, the first period of ardent sonnet exchange went on through April.)

That room was literally dark and dreary even in spring; the poet would often seek refuge and warmth in a basement restaurant on Thompson Street, Grand Ticino. Here she would sit for hours, drinking tea at a back corner table, writing in deep concentration, resting her chin on one hand while she scribbled with the other, a lock of red hair falling over her forehead. The British sculptress Lu Duble tells of seeing Edna Millay there many times during off-hours when there were few patrons, but the poet rarely looked up. "All I want to do is write," she told Elizabeth Haight, who came down from Vassar to visit her one weekend at Waverly Place. The Latin teacher had warned her former pupil against "living dangerously" by working too hard and staying out too late; she cited in Latin the phrase, "healthy mind in a healthy body"; but Vincent would not listen.

"I know exactly what I'm doing, Elizabeth; I take no risks," she said earnestly. "Don't worry about me."

She hoped desperately to sell some of the poems she was writing, for, as she complained in a letter to Harriet Monroe, who had just accepted a group of the "Figs," she needed to be paid right away instead of on publication, because she was "awfully broke," more than she cared to admit in her mock-pathetic note signed "Wistfully yours." Although Renascence had finally come out in December, and had received universal praise, Edna Millay had received no compensation, nor, apparently, was there any word from Mitchell Kennerly regarding royalties, though he was urging her to complete a second volume, which he would be glad to publish. Originally she intended to call this volume "Poems," but changed the title to "A Stalk of Fennel," and finally to the more descriptive "Second April."

She still had to deal with Floyd Dell. Just before Arthur Ficke appeared, the editors of *The Masses*, including Floyd, had been arrested under the Sedition Act of 1918 owing to the pacifist and Socialist policies of the magazine. The fact that it had dissolved, and that the rights Dell had defended had been granted to conscientious objectors, made no difference: all of them had to stand trial. It was war hysteria at its worst, unreasoning and obdurate. Edna Millay's strong sense of justice and loyalty was aroused. She made slight distinction between friendship and love. As Floyd pointed out, "friendship had for her all the candor and fearlessness of love, as love had for her the gaiety and generosity of friendship." No matter how irritated she may have been with him as an overinsistent suitor, she was outraged at the unfairness of his arrest; and, along with some other members of the Provincetown group, she went down to the courtroom to lend moral support to the victims. The trial was a travesty of justice. Art Young, the famous cartoonist, who refused to make any defense of his cartoons, grew bored with the proceedings, and sketched all the principal characters in the farce, including the jury, after which, still bored with the long-winded testimony for the prosecution, he fell fast asleep. Several writers, Dell among them, spoke in their own defense. The jury, flustered and flabbergasted by such learned culprits, debated for two and a half days. The defendants could do nothing but wander through the corridors, waiting, supported by their friends. Edna, in true pacifist spirit, recited poetry, instead of hurling invectives at the court, to whittle away the tedious hours. Her quietly expressed but burning indignation helped to sustain the defendants through the long wait. When the jury finally did come out, it was to announce that they were unable to reach agreement! Having no verdict, the court dismissed the defendants pending arrangements for a new trial. They were free for the time being.

Floyd Dell, more than delighted by Edna's staunch loyalty, was quick to assume she had had a change of heart about marrying him. His ardor distressed her more than ever now, and she put him off, parrying for time, perhaps, until Arthur returned from the war. American losses were mounting every day. A diplomatic mission could be as dangerous as combat duty in a war that had brought new weapons of destruction to a so-called civilized world. She agreed with Floyd's antiwar sentiments, which she was soon to express in her finest verse play, and later in her greatest sonnet sequence. And she respected him as a writer, but she could no longer consider him as anything more than a friend. The sonnet beginning, "I think I should have loved you presently," was no doubt inspired by and directed to Dell. Yet she did not want to hurt him or to lose his friendship; so she temporized, and pleaded for more time to think, more time to write. And she made a point of seeing some of her other admirers.

Paradoxically, although she let herself be caught up in the gay whirl of the artists' life in the bohemian section of the metropolis, she was already beginning to long for the sight and sound of the sea once more, the countryside along the coast of Maine, where she had grown up. The trees around Washington Square and on a few Village streets seemed pathetically mute to her, for she knew the thin sweet sound of leaves in the wind could not be heard in the constant din of traffic. One of the early poems in *Second April* is "City Trees," in which the poet sympathizes with the plight of the "little leaves" whose music is lost in the noise of the city. "Eel Grass," an eight-line lyric, "Inland" and "Exiled," in four and eight stanzas respectively, all written around this time, express the poet's longing for her native scenery.

Some of her nostalgia for Maine was probably mixed with a yearning for family life; even though Norma was with her, and in spite of the fact that their mother had never been a home body, of necessity, the poet seems to have had so deep an attachment to her, and for the laissez faire, but lively, affectionate, and literary way of life in Camden that she could not be happy for long without it. And in June of 1918, which was moving time in New York, for it was customary until the late thirties to move to a different apartment every six months, she found a place at 25 Charlton Street that was large enough to accommodate all four of the family. She seems to have been proud of the new apartment. She wrote to Elizabeth Haight inviting the Latin teacher to visit her in surroundings she described as being much pleasanter than at Waverly Place. Cora Millay joined her daughters soon after the move, and Kathleen came down from Vassar, delighted to spend the summer vacation in the Village.

The residence at 25 Charlton Street was the most celebrated Millay menage in Greenwich Village. At least three accounts have been written describing the scene, probably the best known of which is Lawrence Langner's rather prettified view of the popular household. Franklin P. Adams (F. P. A.), whom the poet had met some time before, and who was to be a lifelong friend, compared the three sisters, each in different coloring, to the famous Botticelli figures, full of grace and charm. Mrs. Millay, with her usual vitality, ever alert to the latest trends, entered right into the spirit of Village life. Like Jig Cook's mother (familiarly known as "Ma-mie" Cook), Cora Millay helped with costumes and props at the Provincetown, willing to lend a hand backstage wherever it might be needed. She bobbed her hair and joined the fight for women's rights, which was finally granted by constitutional amendment in the fall.

Her three vivacious daughters, particularly the iridescent Vincent, whose piquant quality and changing moods only made her more appealing, attracted a variety of interesting beaux, so that there was never a lack of entertainment for an alert little woman like Cora Millay. In his picture of the household, Langner described the "swarms of young painters, writers, actors, and musicians that descended on the top-floor apartment every night. Those evenings at 25 Charlton Street were a perpetual soirée with Edna holding court in one room, Norma in another, and Kathleen in the third, while Mother Millay fluttered on guard over her fledglings, hopping from one room to another." From the evidence of her past history and the accounts of others, it is likely that if Mrs. Millay did indeed go "hopping from one room to another," it was hardly to stand guard over her "fledglings," but because she didn't want to miss out on any of the fun, the stimulating conversations and arguments that might take place. Sometimes the girls would put on an impromptu performance of "Oh, men, alluring!" and other three-part songs, or song-and-dance skits they had brought down from Maine.

With the family reunited, the poet set herself a schedule that would have worn down a much less fragile physique than hers.

She wrote prodigously, though she often forgot that she had to send her poems off in order to get paid for them. And though she commented airily, "Anyhow, wealth is vulgar," she realized that she must broaden the market for her work if she wanted to keep on writing not only for love but for her livelihood and for the partial support of her family as well. One of her earliest admirers was W. Adolphe Roberts, a writer then editing *Ainslee's Magazine*, and it must have been about this time that Edna Millay began to submit poetry to a popular publication, or, as Edmund Wilson labeled it, a "trashy" magazine. Whether it was or not, *Ainslee's* proved to be a steady source of income from mid-1918 to 1921. Roberts also asked if Edna had written any short stories or novelettes, of which he was always in need. She had written no fiction since "Barbara on the Beach," which appeared in 1914, but at Roberts' request she sat down and turned out a sparkling short story. It followed hard upon a sonnet by Edna St. Vincent Millay in *Ainslee's*, and she decided to use the pseudonym of Nancy Boyd for the story and for all subsequent light fiction or prose pieces. She wanted the name of Edna St. Vincent Millay to signify a poet and nothing else in the minds of her readers—"a whole poet," in Witter Bynner's often repeated phrase—and she never compromised her position on the question of her pen name.

For the next two or three years her output of work in addition to acting in the Provincetown and early offerings of the Theatre Guild, direction of her own plays and her gay night life, was staggering. In the fall of 1918, she directed and had the lead in her play, *The Princess Marries the Page;* she later directed her morality play, *Two Slatterns and a King* for a rebel faction of the Provincetown who felt that more poetic drama should be produced. It is no wonder that she had "a small nervous breakdown" from time to time. She "burned her candle at both ends," and she was evidently under an emotional strain after her unforgettable encounter with Arthur Ficke. Although she edified her actions with the "stunning" defiant candle quatrain in one of the "Figs," the four-line poem which was to make her reputation as wit and spokesman of the twenties, she must have undermined her health during this period. Armed with several packs of cigarettes, she would lock herself in her room, where she wrote "with the same inspired precision that a sculptor chips marble," spending hours trying to achieve a perfect poem. Or, if she was writing a story for *Ainslee's,* she would pound the typewriter for hours. When the deadline drew perilously close, Norma helped with the copy of the manuscript, getting "the carbon sheets all ready to stick into the machine the minute Vincent took the other out." Later Norma collaborated with "Nancy Boyd" on the novelette, *The Seventh Stair,* published in *Ainslee's* in 1919.

By September of 1918, the poet was a regular contributor to *Ainslee's* and enlarged the field of publication of her poems to other literary magazines besides *Poetry,* including *The Dial* and Reedy's *Mirror.* Kathleen, to whom Vincent wrote a tender, two-stanza tribute that summer, returned to Vassar reluctantly: she had been attempting to write a novel, probably influenced by the ardor of her older sister. The second *Masses* trial came up soon afterward, and Edna again went with Floyd and the others to court, parading the halls reciting poetry while awaiting the verdict. The jury again took a long time to deliberate, but this time those in favor of acquittal were able to win over the others, and the Gilbert-and-Sullivan-like trial ended in victory for the distinguished defendants.

One of these was John Reed, brilliant member of the editorial board and one of the founders of the magazine; at the time of the first trial he was in Russia as war correspondent covering the 1917 Revolution, recorded in his famous book, *Ten Days that Shook the World.* He was also a charter member of the Provincetown Players, staunch Socialist, and ardent libertine, and Edna Millay had often heard of his exploits from Floyd Dell, Jig Cook, Susan Glaspell, and others. When she met "Jack" Reed, she was not disappointed. Soon after the trial, Reed got wind of the forthcoming Armistice from one of his many contacts abroad; Edna, Floyd, and Jack celebrated the happy event in advance by riding back and forth on the Staten Island ferry most of the night, sharing a jug of wine. They pranced joyously in the moonlight on the Staten Island shore and took turns reciting poetry. Toward morning, Reed, a courageous fighter for human rights, began to recount some of his adventures in Mexico. He had been a reporter on the

Mexican border and had won the admiration of General Villa, who gave him several scoops in the early days of the Mexican revolution. Edna was fascinated by his remarkable tales, which he told with color and humor and without bravura or self-conceit. He was going back to Russia shortly; and, though none of them could know he would be fatally stricken with typhoid fever and be buried in the land he chose to champion, the poet was moved to kiss him good-bye as the threesome broke up at dawn. Quoting Desdemona's words to Othello, she said with deep feeling, "I love you for the dangers you have passed."

It was one of those moments that are suspended in time like works of art, one that Floyd Dell always remembered in connection with the "tremendous enrichment" of his life through knowing Edna Millay. A little later he again asked her to marry him, and she half-heartedly agreed; but before long they were quarreling once more, and the engagement was broken for good. Eventually Dell found the kind of girl he was seeking, one who shared his interests, but did not begrudge the time taken away from her own talents for domesticity and child-rearing. Edna could not bring herself to "forget Pieria," as she phrased it in a sonnet, in order to satisfy the needs of a husband who wanted a conventional marriage and children. She was a celebrant of love for its own sake, but she was not willing to forsake the Singing Mountain of her Muse for the sere plateau of daily domestic cares. She reveled in the warmth of human love, and had much to give in return for being loved, but she was afraid that marriage would mean she would have to relinquish the inner core of her being. She believed that love was too precious, too rare and perishable a flower to stand the strain of daily married life. Stressing the intrinsic value of love, she asks at the end of the poem, "Passer Mortuus Est," written around this time, "Need we say it was not love just because it perished?" And in a superb sonnet she sings with mournful artistry, "Love is no more than the wide blossom which the wind assails."

She longed to see Arthur Ficke again because she felt that he alone could understand her complex emotional structure. The Armistice was signed on November 11, bringing the war to an end, and the doughboys marched down Fifth Avenue in dubious victory, but her "cherished friend" did not stop in New York; or if he did, he did not call her. She was at the zenith of her personal popularity: Floyd Dell was followed by one suitor after another, but these affairs apparently followed the same pattern she had woven in her relationship with him, deliberately or otherwise. And none of them had the same meaning for her that, from her letters to Arthur and the sonnets inspired by him, she must have experienced with the man who had been first of all her "spiritual adviser."

CHAPTER VIII

"A Leprechaun Among Poets"

WITH THE SIX MONTHS' shift among New York's renting popu-
lation, the Millay residence at 25 Charlton Street came to an
end and, funds being low, was changed to a rambling tenement
apartment at 449 West 19th Street, near the Hudson River docks,
on the extreme fringe of the Village. By early January, 1919, the
poet was sending off a sonnet to Roberts of *Ainslee's* from the
rather dark and drab but roomy "railroad" flat, "large enough to
hold Norma's sewing machine," which was to be "home" for the
next year and a half. In 1919 there was a poem, either lyric or
sonnet, by Edna Millay in every monthly issue of the magazine,
and the May, July, September, October, and December issues also
carried Nancy Boyd pieces of varying kinds and lengths. Of these
latter she wrote to Arthur Ficke that, though some were good
and some bad, they were "almost invariably . . . beautifully
written, after a flippant fashion." She was rehearsing the leading
role of Tama, the Japanese girl, in Rita Wellman's *The String of
the Samisen*, due to open on January 17, in which she looked as
lovely as an Outomaro woodblock. Henry, one of the little boys
who were paid twenty-five cents to hold the door closed during
performances, thought the play was "very nice because the heroine was so pretty." By way of contrast, later in the season, in the
Jig Cook-Susan Glaspell satire, "Tickless Time," with Norma playing the wife, Edna assumed an almost unbelievable plainness as

Annie, the protesting slavey, maid-of-all work. This year marked the height of her career as poet-playwright and actress.

Like many other creative artists, the Provincetown playwrights reflected the wave of disillusion that washed over the country in the wake of the grossly unfair Treaty of Versailles and the let-down of the League of Nations by the United States' refusal to join the newly formed world body, both of which made a mockery of the premise that the recent struggle had been "a war to end war." The Provincetowners in fact, with their pacifist ideals, ante-dated the revulsion against the horrors of war, the debunking of its glamor in such plays as *What Price Glory?* (1924) by Maxwell Anderson and Laurence Stallings or Robert Sherwood's satiric comedy, *The Road to Rome*, which stripped the magic mantle from the famous war heroes of history. Even before the Armistice was signed, Jig Cook wrote the only three-act production the Provincetown group every attempted, *The Athenian Women*, a play that was against all war, urging the kind of peace that would produce art as the Greeks knew it. O'Neill's *The Sniper*, produced in the group's second New York season, was an antiwar play. His *In the Zone*, also a war-protest drama which became a classic, was considered too "conventional" for the Provincetown stage; it was presented by the Washington Square Players, with great success.

It was apparent, moreover, that the war which was to have made the "world safe for democracy" had done nothing of the sort. There was more suspicion of foreigners, more persecution of "radicals," and more brutal suppression of striking steel, coal-mine, and railroad workers in this country. The harsh terms of the Versailles Treaty only led to dictatorships abroad. Sacco and Vanzetti, arrested in April, 1920, were originally picked up in one of the routine raids on anarchists or "suspicious radicals" that the postwar politicos saw fit to promulgate.

The general discontent and disillusion which evoked the real-istic antiwar dramas swept through the soul of Edna St. Vincent Millay with equal force but subtler issue. During the months of 1919, when she was writing lyric poetry for her second volume, lighter verse for a separate one, and turning out Nancy Boyd "pot-boilers," the poet wrote her most distinguished verse play, *Aria da Capo*, an arresting allegory denouncing war as a means of settling disputes among men. Using the double framework of a play within a play and the device of a stage director, Cothurnus, the spirit of tragedy, who interrupts the frivolous scene of a harlequinade to present a pastoral tragedy of two shepherds, she wove an intricate and bitter pattern of irony: the irony and unwitting cruelty of everyday life as well as the tragedy of war. The scene between the two sheperd-friends, Corydon and Thyrsis, which starts as a "game" (actually a predestined game of power), including the construction of a crepe-paper "wall," and ends in a senseless struggle and the death of both shepherds, is as timely today as it was then. An added note of horror comes as Cothurnus shuts his prompter's book, summons Columbine and Pierrot back onstage, tells them they can go on with their feast. And when they object to the shepherds' corpses he has shoved under the table, there is a chilling moment as they follow his advice in pulling down the tablecloth so the audience will forget the tragedy as soon as they resume the farce. As the musical title indicates, the play ends with the light love twitterings between Columbine and Pierrot which open their scene at the beginning of the piece.

Aria da Capo was unanimously voted for production by the Provincetowners, with Edna directing, according to their custom. Everyone was warmly enthusiastic about the play, but made no attempt, as they sometimes did, to give gratuitous advice on casting or anything else. Norma, delighted with the role, played the part of Columbine, and Charles Ellis, who designed the settings and costumes, played one of the shepherds, so it was practically a family production. Edna's old friend Harrison Dowd was the Pierrot; James Light played the other shepherd, and the artist Hugh Ferris was cast in the role of Cothurnus. From all accounts there were few offerings at the Provincetown that shaped up in the allotted three weeks' time as smoothly as Aria da Capo did. And the opening night performance on December 5, 1919, was evidence of the overall harmony and success of the undertaking. "The play's beauty, its subtle mingling of satire and lyricism, and the excellence of the production marked it immediately as the best presentation of the year," wrote two of the members, Helen Deutsch and Stella Hanau, in their book, The Provincetown, published in 1931, long after the group had broken up. This was high praise, as there were sixteen productions that year, including O'Neill's *The Dreamy Kid*. Mrs. Millay, who had been visiting her sister in Newburyport, came home for the occasion, Edna furnishing the train fare. Evidently their mother had given up practical nursing when she joined the girls on Charlton Street, and from then on allowed her daughters to support her. She continued to write sporadically and to help out in the theater, but neither of these activities provided a living. From the poet's letters, all three Millay girls took it for granted that it was their turn to assume the responsibility of looking out for their mother; and although Vincent was often apologetic for being late or "broke" for one reason or another, she seemed particularly glad to be able to support her mother.

The play was an immediate success; the author herself was surprised at "how well it played," though she had written it for the theater and by now had acquired a fair knowledge of playwriting. Partly because the time was ripe for such an offering, *Aria* achieved widespread recognition: it was produced by little theater and college groups all over the country, and a French version was staged in Paris; later it was published in Reedy's *Mirror*. Edna received many letters and invitations to lecture before literary groups, one of which resulted in her first appearance as an after-dinner speaker at a meeting of the Society of Arts and Letters. Her reputation was growing, but she had made very little money from her poetry.

It is interesting to note that she wrote to Harriet Monroe in March of 1919, almost a year to the day after the shy missive asking to be paid "a lot" immediately instead of on publication. In her 1919 letter, sent concerning two more "Figs," which Miss Monroe had been considering for *Poetry* for some time, "Recuerdo" and "She Is Overheard Singing," the poet again needed the small check, but this time she showed more confidence. She reminded the editor in no uncertain terms either to find a place for the poems or "return 'em." It is true that she was asking a favor, for her poem had not yet been accepted, but even though her tone was again half-serious, the note revealed a no-nonsense attitude. Using much the same line that Robert Frost had taken

toward Ellery Sedgewick of the *Atlantic Monthly* a few years
before, Edna Millay threatened to "tell the world all about it"
if Harriet Monroe did not make up her mind about her "stunning"
poems she had been keeping so long. Evidently, if she wasn't
actually bitter, she was far less in awe of editors than she had
been a year before.

She was probably feeling bitter toward the world in general
during the spring of 1919. Aside from being disturbed and disheartened by postwar events, she must have been disillusioned
about her personal life. Arthur Ficke had not appeared in January, as he apparently had promised; and it was a year—the
second April—since they had met face to face after so many years,
and known a moment of mutual, almost terrifying wonder and
delight. The poem called "Spring," published in italics at the
front of the original edition of *Second April,* a keynote to the
mood of melancholy that pervades many of the songs in the lyrical
volume, sounds one of the few cries of complete negation in regard to the renewal of life that the poet ever issued. Containing
some of her most startling imagery, the lines reveal an intensity
of despair never repeated. Even her beloved Beauty was "not
enough" to solace her in this dark hour; even the return of April
seemed purposeless in its blossoming rebirth: "but what does that
signify?" she demands. Life, that "flight of uncarpeted stairs,"
amounts to nothing. It is "not enough that yearly . . . April /
Comes like an idiot, babbling and strewing flowers." This shocking figure is somewhat mitigated by the lyric which gives the
volume its title, "Song of a Second April," and might well be
called Lament for a Lost Love. In these stanzas the poet sings
of April's return with her customary eloquent simplicity in appreciation of nature's lowly gems, of hepaticas, mullein stalks,
and the sound of woodpeckers' bills on the trunks of trees, but
the scene is shadowed by a pervading melancholy because the
one whom alone she "cared to keep" is not there.

It may have been that some time between the writing of these
two poems Arthur Ficke sent her another packet containing a
sonnet sequence, which dispelled her rancor toward life. She had
read the poems eagerly, many times; she loved much of the sequence. She kept the sonnets throughout the spring and summer,

thinking seriously about them, jotting down comments until she had "marked them all up" without realizing it. She herself was writing an ode that summer, the "Ode to Silence," later published in *Second April;* it is one of her least successful poems because it attempts to relate Silence to the nine muses and becomes weighted in the process. The subject was probably provoked by the constant noise of the city, particularly in the neighborhood and apartment house on 19th Street, where the Italian families replete with children were always shouting at one another, arguing, banging on the piano. She did have a two-weeks respite in July when Walter Roberts loaned her his apartment while he was on vacation. While there she worked hard on the ode and other poems, and only allowed herself a little diversion if someone like her friend Rollo Peters called and invited her out to "feed her up once in a while."

She and her editor at *Ainslee's* were on the friendliest of terms, and she left an amusing confession on his desk telling him that she "had made good her escape" with two treasures; a little picture of a Shakespearean theater that he had once given her and a cigarette case that Salomón had given her a long time before. The Nicaraguan poet evidently went to London about this time and then possibly returned to Central America to live, as there is no further reference to him in the Millay correspondence or poetry. Roberts eventually wrote a memoir of her entitled *Tiger Lily.*

In early fall she received an inquiry from Arthur about his poems, with a broad hint that he wondered why she hadn't returned them with her opinions and reactions long before then. She hurried to reassure him that the sonnets had not "weighed her down." It was only that she got nervous prostration at the thought of trying to "parcel post parcels" and she was loath to part with the poems she so loved. Her letter was full of ill-concealed longing to see him again. There was a wistful tone to her words, a semisatiric pleading often repeated in her letters to Arthur: she was afraid he had changed his mind about coming to New York; she hoped he would not come to town without at least calling her up; she was "in the telephone directory." She enclosed a clipping about the production of *Aria da Capo* and promised to send him a copy of the play if she could find one.

Reedy's *Mirror* published the one-act play in the March 18 issue in 1920, and in April they brought out a group of twenty sonnets by Edna St. Vincent Millay, which greatly increased her reputation as a literary figure. The group included some of the sonnets that had been inspired by Arthur, as well as the defiant ones provoked by Floyd Dell and other suitors, to reveal a mastery of the form and a fresh handling of it at a time when the modernists were trying to erase the word "sonnet" from the world of poetry. The remarkable aspect of the sonnets published in the *Mirror* is that they are modern in language and feeling as well as strict and flawless in form. Gone was the classic "thee" and "thou"; in its place was the present-day pronoun "you." The diction, like Robert Frost's, was the language common to all; the figures were twentieth century. "Only until this cigarette is ended," she begins one of this group, which goes on to speak of the "jazzing music blended." And while it is true that Millay's sonnets are replete with classical references, they are brought in naturally, without pretension: "We talk of taxes," another opens; and ends with glimpses of Isolde, Guinevere, and Francesca, without seeming incongruous or anachronistic. Emotionally, the fourteen-line poems presented a modern woman who was at times almost masculine in her attitude toward love. It is the woman who often takes the initiative in ending a love affair: "I shall forget you presently, my dear / So make the most of this, your little day"; and, "faithless am I except to love's self alone," she vows. Here was the "new" woman, free in her attitude toward love, yet "stern in her soul's chastity," her loyalty to her first love, poetry, written as she saw fit to create it by singing out unconventional ideas in traditional forms, those stringent vessels she had revered since childhood. As Floyd Dell said, "She learned the molds first, into which she later poured her emotions while hot." Even the most *avant-garde* literary critics were outspoken in their admiration of these sonnets.

That spring Allan Ross Macdougall, who was going abroad, took along some of these sonnets, including the "Columbine" which she had written for Norma after the production of *Aria;*

a group of poems called "Personalities"; and a copy of *Aria*. He was to be her "li'l Agint" abroad, and did succeed in securing publication of poems in the British literary weekly, *The Nation*, and of the play in an issue of Harold Monro's Poetry Bookshop "Chapbooks," both enviable outlets for any poet; and there was a possibility of a production-contract for the play. Moreover, in May, she received the annual one-hundred-dollar cash award from *Poetry* magazine for her highly original poem, "The Bean-stalk," a delightful, if rather curious piece of whimsy, a complete departure from the kind of poetry she had been writing.

She should have been more than content, but most of the time she was inwardly "sodden with melancholy," as she wrote to Arthur, the object of her suppressed, and oppressed, feelings. Early in the spring he had written asking if he should send her another sonnet sequence inspired by her, which he had just com-pleted. She had answered eagerly that he must by all means send the poems. She cannot have helped hoping that, since she was so evidently on his mind, he might still come to New York to see her. But she learned that he was planning to accompany Witter Bynner on a long journey to the Orient. She wrote to the latter that her heart was breaking of envy, and though she made a joke of it, saying that if Arthur went along with him she would "asphyxiate herself in Pell Street punk-smoke" in Chinatown, she was no doubt terribly let down by the news.

Again she kept Ficke's sonnets a long time. She had to live closely with them, she told him finally, to make it seem as if she herself had written them before she could understand them "sufficiently to criticize them." For some reason, these sonnets oppressed her as his others had not, perhaps because of the "harsh and sombre restraint" she found in them. She was always honest in her letters to him as she was to all her friends and col-leagues whose work she was asked to judge; especially in the case of Arthur, she shows an amazing objectivity. She was deeply in love with him, and in some ways it saddened her to look into his mind through those sonnets, but she made herself forget him personally when she read for the purpose of criticizing; and she was not afraid to say that at first reading they struck her as want-ing the beauty of color and sound, which was important to her,

since it is one of the salient features of her own poetry. And
though in the end she found the sequence "a very fine and beautiful piece of work," she was forthright in her comments, and fear-
less in telling him that she felt he occasionally did something for
"an easy, and so unworthy, reason." No matter what the risk, she
maintained her own intellectual integrity. When her colleagues
in turn criticized her work, she was willing to accept their suggestions if she was unsure of some phrasing; but if she had definitely
decided it was *right* for the poem, she would not change it. Once
Arthur told her he did not like the line, "A bucket of blood in my
path," from a work she had shown him; she countered, "I had
rather give up a bucket of your blood, Arthur, than this bucket
of blood." She made no secret of the fact that she wished he were
not so far away; she yearned to see him again, to talk to him.
There were so few people in the world, she felt, "to whom one
had a word to say."

She did not lack admirers. They would hardly let her alone.
And she was soon to add two more writers to her list of suitors,
to one of whom she had many words to say, strained though they
sometimes became. This was Edmund Wilson, then an assistant
editor on *Vanity Fair,* who, with his friend John Peale Bishop,
also on the magazine's staff, had been eager to meet Edna St.
Vincent Millay for some time. Both of them were at a party at
Hardwicke Nevin's,[1] which Edna went to rather wearily after
her performance at the Provincetown one night in April, 1920.
She was exhausted, but was finally persuaded to recite some of
her poems; as always, her face was transfigured by the inner glow
that seemed to radiate from her entire being when she was stirred
by the spirit of poetry. She had something of the incandescent
quality of a Bernhardt at such moments, so that as she spoke the
lines in her cool, grave, yet melodic and strangely thrilling voice,
her face with its slightly irregular features took on an ethereal
beauty.

Wilson, who had never heard her read her poetry, was enthralled. He noted her "lovely and very long throat that gave her
the look of a muse"; her clear diction that made every syllable
distinct; and the vibrant haunting quality in her voice that seemed

---

[1] Nephew of the composer, Ethelburt Nevin.

to come from another sphere, the lonely dwelling place no one could invade, but whose solitariness she had the power to impose on her listeners, holding them hushed until the last note of her spoken music died away. Part of this quality of course came from the poetry itself, which when read aloud permits listeners to experience the full effect of the cadences and the tonal shading in the choice of words. The up-and-coming literary critic, with his eye for detail, noticed also that the poet was "dressed in some bright batik," which complemented the bronze of her hair highlighted by her burning flush of spirit.

Before long he and John Bishop were among her most devoted escorts and took her out together or separately as often as she consented to see them. She had so many admirers, most of whom fell madly in love with her, that hopefuls could rarely be sure of seeing her alone. Wilson wooed her by way of *Vanity Fair*, whose editor, Frank Crowninshield, had the same kind of ability that Jig Cook had in recognizing talent in others. He had been quick to foresee the future giant of literary prose and criticism that Wilson would become, as well as the potential of an eminent poet in John Peale Bishop; and now he was equally responsive to the fact, which Wilson no doubt pointed out, that the poetry of Edna St. Vincent Millay was far above the level of a magazine like *Ainslee's*, which, outside of an occasional poem in the *Dial* or *Poetry*, was publishing almost all of her work at that time. Soon she was a regular contributor to *Vanity Fair*, which gave the two younger editors much more opportunity to be with her. For a time the three of them traveled along the rugged but starstrewn paths of the Singing Mountain together. They discussed poetry and exchanged and quoted their respective efforts at all hours and places; Edna once read them a sonnet she had just completed on a Fifth Avenue bus while on the way to the Claremont for dinner. They went to a party at the Village home of actor Richard Bennett, then playing the role of Robert Mayo in O'Neill's *Beyond the Horizon*—where Wilson, sitting on the floor beside the poet, felt "very bohemian," more than he would have with any ordinary girl. Even the most casual experience was heightened by her intensity and sense of excitement. Like many others, Wilson, called "Bunny" by his intimate friends, including

Edna, felt the "intoxicating effect" of her company, of her mere presence. He observed that she "cast a spell on people of the most varied professions and temperaments, of all ages and sexes." One night very late, after they had consumed a bottle of bootleg gin while talking about poetry, all three wrote self-portraits. Edna's was a clever, self-perceptive piece, and perhaps a sly poke at free verse, ending with a delightful description of her body, based on a single word image (the adjective "unexclamatory"). Bishop's poetic sketch of himself was published in *Vanity Fair*, and the magazine wanted to print Edna Millay's as well; the poet herself had no objection, but Norma, though "amused," was disgusted by the portrait, which she considered "lewd." She convinced Edna that it should not be published.[2]

Occasionally Wilson took Edna to the theater, and she sometimes attended a Poetry Society meeting with Bishop; but more often in the early weeks of that spring of 1920, the three were together. Because of the poet's "disarming impartiality" toward all her friends, the idyll of these three continued longer than it might have otherwise. But after a while, when "Bunny" began to monopolize her and John felt neglected, a state she hastened to assuage, the relationship between the two young editors became rather strained; and Frank Crowninshield objected to having both his assistants distracted by love for the magazine's shining new contributor. Many of the Nancy Boyd "distressing dialogues" appeared in *Vanity Fair*, as well as the poetry of Edna Millay. For the fall of 1920 Crowninshield was planning a full-page feature on the poet with four of her lyrics, four sonnets, and a photograph.

Edna herself was distressed at the turn the three-way friendship had taken. She was fond of both Wilson and Bishop, but not in love with either. She kept hoping that Arthur Ficke and Hal Bynner would soon come home from the Orient; she missed them sorely. Even though she might not see Arthur, it would comfort her if he were not so far away. She was worn out with writing, and worried about the publication of her second volume. Before he left for China, Bynner had advised her to seek a new publisher, preferably Alfred A. Knopf, but she had done nothing about it

[2] It was finally published posthumously, in the Millay *Letters*, 1952.

because she had a certain loyalty toward Kennerly as her first publisher. She had read proof on the book early in April, and it was to have come out two or three weeks later, before the end of the month. Now it was nearly June, and she still had received no "author's copy" and no word from Kennerly. Moreover, she felt cramped in the apartment on 19th Street, where all four Millays were now living. Kathleen, bent on pursuing her own career as a writer, had left Vassar in the middle of her junior year. Vincent, chagrined at the thought that she had tried to manage her "baby sister's" life without giving Kathleen a chance to speak for herself, was nevertheless glad to have the family around her again. During the winter she had been too busy to notice the surroundings much, but now the place seemed grimier and noisier than it had the summer before. She was wondering how she was going to stand the next few months in the city; she was also troubled by the awkward situation with Wilson. Jig Cook and Susan Glaspell came to the rescue by offering the Millays the use of a cottage they owned in Truro, just over the hill from the Cooks' house and nine miles from Provincetown. It was a godsend to the poet; and though she had criticized Jig and had been a member of the faction in the Players that rebelled against his "paternalism," she was most grateful to him and Susan for their generosity.

The Millay girls and their mother happily stored their "worldly goods," packed their clothes, and went up to Cape Cod, taking along an old asthmatic Victrola that Allan Ross Macdougall had left with Edna, accompanied by his one recording, Beethoven's Fifth Symphony. The cottage, they discovered, was sparsely furnished and devoid of electricity and plumbing; the only running water came from a creaking windmill that pumped a small supply into a well. The place could have been called a shack; but to the poet it was "a dear little house," and the wind that blew through the pine woods behind it was sweet to breathe. Or when a gale came from the other direction it was good to smell the "outside surfy sea" again. Only a mile and a half away was a lonely strip of beach where the sandpipers were the only company.

The night they arrived it was raining, and, without knowing whether there were neighbors who could see them, all four took a shower under the spout from the eave. Edna was mortally tired, but she was exhilarated at being back on the seaboard. If the hills were hardly more than sand dunes with patches of green on top, if the whippoorwills' sweet scolding often kept them awake at night, or the mosquitoes sometimes swarmed around them, nature's bounty seemed more than rich. And what need was there of excess furniture indoors, as long as they had the Victrola? The poet did most of her "work to the tune of the Fifth symphony," she wrote Allan. Its noble music was "green pastures and still waters" to her soul. Before the summer was over she could whistle all four movements from memory.

The whole atmosphere must have refreshed her soul, for she began to write new poems almost immediately. Occasionally she saw Susan and Jig and some of the other Provincetowners, and she was able to get some advice in regard to the contract Allan sent her for a British production of *Aria da Capo*. Susan, who had received a similar offer from the same producer for one of her plays, advised Edna not to sign, as she was not going to. Neither was Gene O'Neill, who now was married to Agnes Boulton and living with their six-month old son in their coastguard house on the edge of Provincetown. In passing, one cannot help commenting on the fact that Edna Millay's "intoxicating effect" on people apparently did not extend to O'Neill, even during her first year in the Village, when he was still single and searching for a woman to take the place of playwright Louise Bryant, whom he had adored but with whom Jack Reed had won out. Nor did O'Neill's fatal attraction for women touch Edna Millay; it is likely that both were too predominantly possessed by their individual genius to succumb to or even notice the other's personal magnetism.

By August Edna had revived enough to answer a querulous note from "Bunny," and since she did not know exactly what to say, she suggested that he come up to see her. And here on a sweltering night as they sat on the battered porch swing swatting mosquitoes between words, Wilson managed to ask the poet to marry him. Parrying for time, as she had done with Floyd Dell, Edna told him she would consider his proposal. He thought he heard her murmer that " it might be the solution," or words to that effect. He could not be sure, and at that point the mosquitoes

Collection, The Museum of Modern Art, New York

The famous portrait of Vincent taken by Arnold Genthe under one of the huge magnolia trees on the campus at Vassar, spring 1916.

Mrs. (Cora Buzzelle) Millay in her practical nurse's uniform.

Vassar College Library

Henry Tolman Millay, c. 1892, when the Millays were living in the house on Broadway, Rockland, Maine, where Edna St. Vincent Millay was born.

Vassar College Library

Edna St. Vincent Millay

Vincent's first photo, taken at about three months. (The puppy was only a month old at Vincent's birth, according to her "Auntie Kem," Mrs. Clementine M. Parsons.)

Vassar College Library

A school-girl picture, c. 1905.

Vassar College Library

Vincent wearing the traditional hair-bows in her high-school graduation picture.

Vassar College Library

Vincent at the wheel of a boat on Penobscot Bay, near Camden, Maine, at about the time "Renascence" was written.

The Bettmann Archive

Vassar College Library

This photo bears the significant date of August 29, 1912, the day on which Millay read "Renascence" in the music room at Whitehall Inn, Camden. This reading inspired one of the guests, Miss Caroline B. Dow, to become her patroness. It is probable that the picture was taken in the garden at Whitehall.

Arthur Davison Ficke. A portrait made a few years after Arthur Ficke and Witter Bynner wrote to "E. Vincent Millay" about her poem "Renascence."

Yale University Library

Witter Bynner. From a photograph taken about the same time as that of Arthur Ficke shortly before he and Bynner wrote a book of verse, *Spectra,* under assumed names, satirizing the various cults of free versifiers of the period.

Vassar College Library

Vincent under the porte-cochère of the main building at Vassar, taken by one of her classmates, class of 1917.

Vassar College Library

Millay as Marie de France in the "Pageant of Athena."

Vassar College Library

Vassar College Library

The "Pageant of Athena," marking Vassar's 50th Anniversary, 1915. The setting is the outdoor theatre at Vassar with Millay as Marie de France reciting the lay of Tristan before the court of Henry II of England.

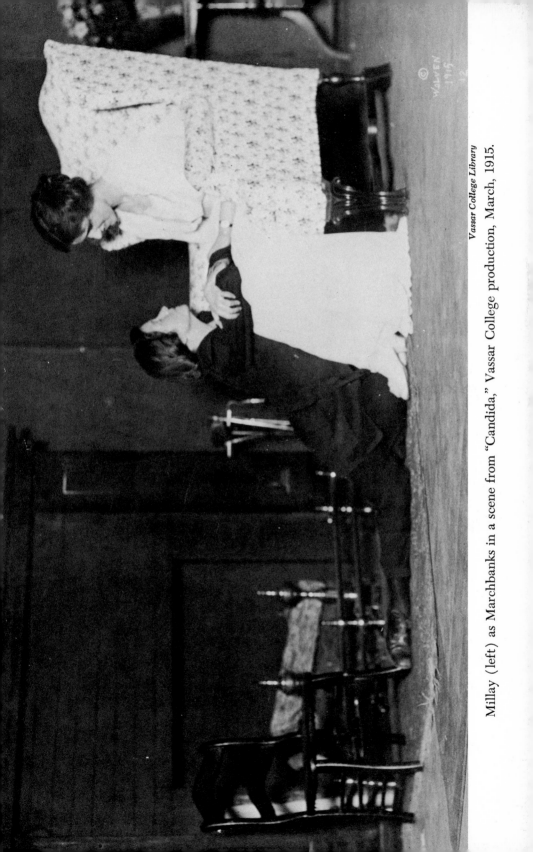

Vassar College Library

Millay (left) as Marchbanks in a scene from "Candida," Vassar College production, March, 1915.

Inez Milholland, Eugen Boissevain's first wife, a Vassar graduate and staunch suffragist, one of Edna Millay's college heroines, who died in 1916. Miss Millay and Boissevain were married in 1923.

Vassar College Library

Max Eastman, founder and first editor of the *Masses* in 1916, who was once in love with the dashing Inez.

Vassar College Library

Edna Millay during the period
of her years with the Provincetown Players, 1917-1920.

Vassar College Library

Portrait by Marcia Stein taken
at about the same time as the
picture by Arnold Genthe.

Vassar College Library

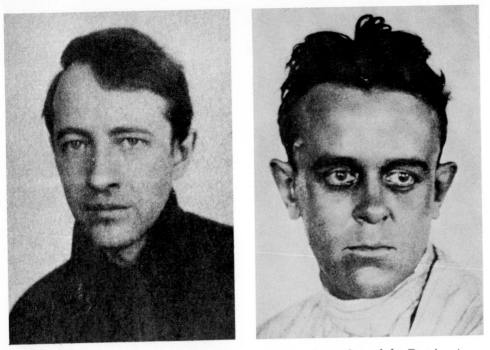

Left: Floyd Dell, who was an editor of the *Masses* and member of the Provincetown Players when Edna Millay joined the group. *Right:* John Reed, playwright, foreign correspondent in Russia, adventurer, author of *Ten Days That Shook the World*, shown in a photo shortly before his death of typhoid fever.

An early picture of Elinor Wylie as a young beauty in Washington, D. C.

Eugen Boissevain, Edna Millay's devoted husband, shortly before their marriage.

One of the Mishkin portraits in tailored suits, c. 1927-1928.

Vassar College Library

Vassar College Library

"Steepletop," the house in the Berkshires on the large berry farm bought by Edna Millay and her husband, Eugen Boissevain, in 1925.

Vincent during one of her appearances at Vassar as an alumna, reading her poetry. Photograph by Berenice Abbott.

Vassar College Library

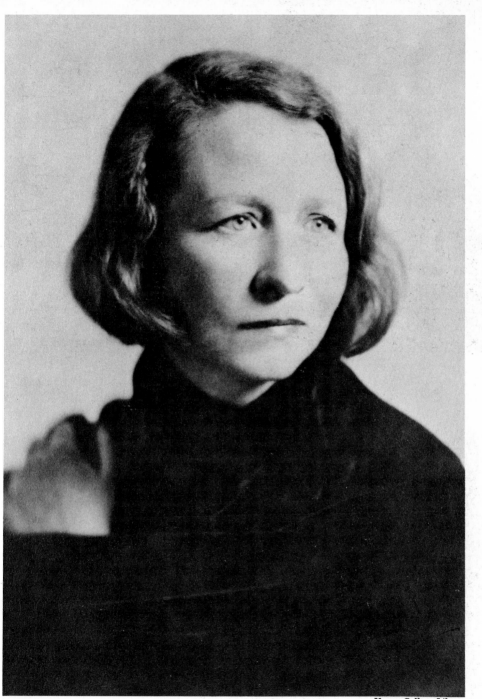

Vassar College Library

"Portrait in black velvet." In later years, possibly c. 1939. The picture is inscribed, "To Auntie Kem, with love from Vincent."

Vassar College Library

In the library at "Steepletop," correcting proofs for "The Murder of Lidice" before its broadcast over NBC on October 19, 1942.

drove them indoors. He had no further chance to probe that night nor the next day. In the morning she sat on the floor and recited her new poems for him. Her mother and sisters, listening with him, commented exactly as they felt—particularly her mother, who struck Wilson as "extraordinary . . . a little old woman with spectacles . . . very brisk and bright," though she could not have been more than fifty-some years old in 1920. He had not met Edna's family before, and was fascinated by the bohemian household. The Millays were still vague about meals, except dinner, and that was casually served on a "plain board table by the light of an oil lamp." He realized more fully than he had in New York that her life on "Pieria" meant more to Edna Millay than any mundane concerns.

He saw it in countless ways during that unforgettable weekend. The rapt attention she gave to the Beethoven recording, which she played for him, was so contagious that in spite of the blur of the rasping machine, he felt the heroic, mystic quality of the music as he never had before. Eventually her pleasure was transposed into the sonnet, "On Hearing a Symphony of Beethoven," in which she begs the music not "to cease, pleading with the sweet sounds" to "reject her not into the world again." When Jig Cook and Hutchins Hapgood stopped by and sat on the edge of the porch talking with Edna, the conversation was Olympian in flavor. The "light but learned" Jig, a "liberated Greek professor," quoted a poem in Sanskrit. And there were small things that Wilson remembered with startling clarity because Edna pointed them out, like the gull's egg they came upon, a neutral-colored oval nesting in the sand, which caused the poet to stop, and, with a meditative stare, pronounce it "beautiful." Somehow, he knew it would be pointless to ask her about her reasons for putting off his proposal. Nevertheless, after he returned to New York he was haunted by those half-spoken words that marriage to him "might be the solution."

He probably had heard correctly, for Edna was apparently in a quandry on the question of marriage. Years before, when she began corresponding with Ficke and Bynner, she told them she was going to wait for them; and she must have sensed when Arthur left his family in Davenport to travel for six months in

China with Hal, that his marriage was weakening. Yet she could not tell if Arthur, aside from the sonnets he kept writing to, or about, her, still cherished their brief encounter as she did. If only she could be certain that those sonnets expressed the same feeling for her personally that she had for him. She kept looking for a letter from China while she was in Truro, but when one came, it turned out to be from Hal, and she wondered if Bynner might not be a better, more stable choice. Norma was with her while she read it and she remarked casually, holding up the letter, that she "might marry this man some day"; but she was only talking, not speaking her heart. Not yet. It was as if she was standing in the wings, waiting for Arthur to give her the cue.

In the meantime, she responded to others who loved her with the warmth and joy she found in the act of love itself. As Ficke wrote in one of his many "Girl" stanzas inspired by her, "Her heart, born eager, generous and just, / Failed to perceive the sordidness of lust; / She thought it lovely, and she made it so." She drove herself with an inner fury to experience all that life had to offer. Before the tranquil summer in Truro was over, she squeezed in a three-week visit at Lawrence Langner's place in Woodstock, then in its heyday as an art colony and center for literary and performing arts as well. There she had a whirlwind affair with an Italian opera singer. His principal attributes were his divine voice and the fact that he could teach her Italian, of which she said she learned "a lot" in the three weeks. Beyond this, she dismissed any serious notions about him, as she ultimately dismissed all her suitors. If Edna Millay was "Daphne" to Floyd Dell's Apollo, she became a kind of Cassandra in regard to all her other relationships, consigning her love affairs to doom even as they began. The one exception was Arthur Ficke, and she was a most perverse Penelope to his Ulysses.

Back in New York in September she located a "lovely big room" for herself at 77 West 12th Street, less than a block from Fifth Avenue. Much as she doted on her family, she now wished to live by herself so there would be little distraction from her work, but she was shortly followed by Kathleen, who took the "one-and-a-half" right next to hers in the same building. The closeness of the sisters may have been tainted by rivalry after Kathleen's decision to become a writer, but the younger girl apparently always looked up to her poet sister and wanted to emulate her in every way. Kathleen probably had another reason for returning to New York early, for in December she married, in Vincent's apartment, Howard Irving Young, one of the hopefuls among the playwrights connected with the Provincetown group.

In his novel of Village life in the early twenties, *I Thought of Daisy*, Edmund Wilson has pictured the poet, an admirably drawn portrait in the character of "Rita," as she directed a crew of admirers helping her dismantle, pack, and move out of her old apartment. The one piece she was anxious about was her "little Buddha," which she would not allow to be packed, and was afraid of letting anyone carry. It was an authentic detail, since Edna had always been fascinated by Oriental art, and now furnished her apartment so that it looked "as Chinese as China," she wrote to Hal Bynner late in October. It was her only means of following Arthur and him to the Far East. She was frank about missing them both, and she poured out her publishing troubles with Kennerly, who now would not even answer the phone when she called. Though her letter was "silly" in some of its ramblings, she thought chattering was better than writing a sad one, and she was "sad so much of the time," she said.

Then, as if she could not bear to suppress her true feeling toward Arthur a minute longer, as if she suddenly decided she had received the sign she sought from some words of his, she sent him a note on the same day, October 29, 1920, releasing her love from the cage of convention. Headed dramatically by his name alone, and followed by an outright admission that she loved him "too," and always would, just as she did the first moment she saw him, this was the beginning of a series of tender and touching love letters from Edna Millay to Arthur Ficke. In a few eloquent, deeply poetic paragraphs, she set down her emotions for all time, just as both had done in their sonnets. It did not matter, she went on, that they never saw each other or that they wrote so seldom. In one prophetic sentence she stated simply that they would *"never escape from each other."* [3] After a burst of beautiful imagery equal to some of the sonnet lines, she ended with the

[3] Italics mine.

quiet vow that he would never be lost to her in any way; and without any salutation, signed it "Vincent." One has the impression that she mailed the letter with trembling fingers and that she awaited his reply with equal parts of fear and eagerness.

For all of that, she did not seclude herself, nor did she have much privacy in her own apartment. She was, according to Wilson, who continued to court her personally as well as professionally through his editorship, almost "besieged by suitors," who flocked to her door. In his novelized description of the poet's particular allure, Wilson mentions "the Irish fickle-mindedness" in her, who "exalted every impulse, and made dramatic every relationship" to a point where "neither happiness nor drama could endure." Among her physical charms, he included her feet, which, "like everything else about her, seemed to mange to be attractive in a curious personal way." Then he observes that she had, "for all her small head, her small hands and feet, the bosom of some divine being," and that "Flushed by the excitement of conversation, she burned like a little furnace." This last in a lesser way calls up her own stirring sonnet line in regard to the deeper excitement of romantic passion, in which she, along with the treacherous queens of antiquity, experiences "Love like a burning city in the breast."

One of her callers, and a lasting admirer, at the 12th Street apartment, was Llewelyn Powys, the scholarly and perceptive English essayist and critic. Shortly after his arrival in New York during the previous spring, he had read *Renascence*, and had been struck by the unique quality of her lyrics, which "amazed and enchanted" him. "They seemed to express a spirit at once daring and sensitive," he wrote later, "and to possess a beauty, which . . . was separate and authentic as only true poetry can be." Having heard of her beauty and charm, he arranged a meeting through a mutual friend, and called late one chilly fall afternoon. He was not disappointed, but she was not the sort of person he had expected. She received him with disarming friendliness and warmth, as if they had been longtime friends and colleagues. They were soon talking and laughing like intimates, and he found her moods that varied from moment to moment, her gaiety and staccato laughter, like explosive little balloons bursting in the room, irresistible; but the element that surprised him was the delicate, almost ephemeral fragility of her physical beauty, combined with an underlying earthiness or sturdiness of spirit, difficult to define.

"She was dainty with a daintiness that can be compared only with the daintiness of Queen Anne's lace, . . ." he wrote finally. "It is true that I did detect in her look an April shadow of vanity, but below this self-conscious protection was a living representation of the divine spirit of poetry, uncontaminated as the spirit of Catullus, gay as the spirit of John Suckling. I never became disillusioned; the more I saw of this young and beautiful girl, the more I came to appreciate the rash quality of her nature, heedless and lovely as a fieldfare rising from the wintry ground. She might disguise herself in all the pretty frippery she could buy at Wanamaker's, she might be photographed for *Vanity Fair* every day of the week, and yet below . . . there will always remain a barefoot poet, doomed yet redeemed, under the shadow of Eternity."

Powys, whose ascetic Welsh face, framed by his golden hair and beard, was belied by his subtle wit and sly humor, appealed to the poet as much as her "daintiness" did to him; she responded as always with her whole being. Her Irish impudence, not at all put off by his serenely handsome patrician countenance, prompted her that very afternoon to dub him "Lulu," which seemed to tickle his own sense of the incongruous. And "Lulu" he remained to the end of their long friendship. It is not surprising that in 1925 when he published his book, *The Verdict of Bridlegoose*, dealing with his initial visit to the United States, Powys dedicated the work, "To Edna St. Vincent Millay, A Leprechaun Among Poets."

His presence during that fall of 1920 must have been a blessing to the poet, who was suffering from physical as well as emotional problems. Her apartment, though "lovely," proved to be as poorly heated as the one on Waverly Place had been; she caught a severe cold that developed into bronchitis, which she could not shake off. She was tired much of the time, working mostly at her Nancy Boyd pieces for *Vanity Fair,* which now took the form of scintillating and often hilarious "dialogues" on numerous current topics. As usual, she neglected to take care of her health, keeping late hours, running out bareheaded into the rain if some errand had to be done at that moment. She had bobbed her beautiful long red hair while she was in Woodstock; and in a letter to Allan Macdougall commented that she now looked about twelve years old, when in good health. Most of the time, ill and depressed, she felt her actual age. "I'll be thirty in a minute," she said to Wilson one day, tossing it off lightly; but the thought made her shiver.

She was worried, too, about a curious circumstance in connection with her poetry. She had dedicated *Second April*, on the publication of which Kennerly continued silent and in hiding, to Miss Dow; but that lady was registering strong disapproval of Edna's recent poems which had been appearing in magazines, as she had objected to the stage career two years before. The poems in question were those the poet considered light verse, and, wishing to keep them separate from her serious work, had agreed, to let Kennerly bring them out in a volume to be called "Figs from Thistles," right after the publication of *Second April*. But since he was so delinquent and might default altogether on the latter, the poet could see another volume gone a-glimmer in "Figs."

Therefore, when Frank Shay, owner of a Village bookshop, suggested publishing the poems as a paper chapbook, *Salvo*, presumably patterned after the chapbooks of Harold Monro's Poetry Bookshop in London, the entire first issue to be "Figs from Thistles," Edna Millay was more than ready to accept the idea. She did not want to distress her beloved patron, who had frowned upon the light verses in the beginning, when *Poetry* printed the trial group in 1918. On the other hand, the poems were not carelessly constructed, and they expressed a certain side of her complex nature, the side that echoed the poetic wits of the past, not only Suckling but Andrew Marvell, Robert Herrick, and even the more recent Oscar Wilde, and she did not wish to withdraw them. The chapbook publication might be the solution: it would be a "light" publication for light verse.

She reckoned, however, without the tremendous response of the public to the poems in the little paper volume with the bright green cover, finally entitled *A Few Figs from Thistles*, that ap-

peared in November, 1920. The postwar generation that had been
disillusioned in its ideals of changing the social order and now
thought only of the freedom of individuals to behave as they
chose, identified immediately with the defiant spirit of the "First
Fig," the soon-to-be-famous and much-quoted, or misquoted
"candle quatrain." Those four lines, beginning with the calm
statement that her "candle burns at both ends," and "will not last
the night," but gleefully assuring foes and friends that it "gives
a lovely light," catapaulted Edna St. Vincent Millay into an enormous popularity as "the poet laureate of the twenties," a dubious
honor, and one she never completely lived down. She was also
hailed as "the spokesman for the new woman" and "the voice of
rebellious, 'flaming' youth."

Word of the double-burning candle spread like wildfire and
was taken up by the newly emancipated all over the country.
Floyd Dell, traveling out to the west coast shortly after its publication, was amazed to hear the quatrain quoted in California and
earlier in the Middle West. Before the month was out, the edition
was exhausted; and, although no further issues of the chapbook
Salvo were ever published, there were as many as five or six
subsequent editions of the one devoted to the "Figs" within the
next two years. People were utterly delighted by the pert, au-
dacious, flippant attitude toward life and love. The "Second Fig,"
taunting tradition in a neatly worded couplet—"Safe upon the
solid rock, the ugly houses stand: / Come and see my shining
palace built upon the sand!"—was almost as widely quoted as the
"First Fig" by a generation that was kicking its heels in revolt
against Victorianism. And the flaunting independence of women
in love exhibited in such poems as "Thursday," in which the poet
asserts, "And if I loved you Wednesday . . . I do not love you
Thursday"; "Daphne"; "The Penitent"; and "To the Not Impossible Him" brought Edna Millay the undying admiration and
loyalty of the "new woman."

Of the five sonnets in this small volume, including two of her
best, "Love, though you riddle me with darts" and "Oh, think
not I am faithful to a vow! / Faithless am I save to love's self
alone"—a dominant Millay theme—the latter became a kind of
credo among young neophytes of feminism. This, a finely wrought

sonnet of Shakespearean excellence, contained in the inverted
epithets of the closing couplet a powerful potion for defiance
in the face of the probable infidelity of the lover. "So wanton, light
and false, my love, are you, / I am most faithless when I am most
true." These impudent love sonnets, of a much higher caliber than
the other poems in the volume, possess the classical seriousness of
Mozartian gaiety in *Don Giovanni*, tuned to the undertones of
tragedy in the brevity and impermanence of love, even while
celebrating its intrinsic value. Whatever the shadings of merit
in the poetry, however, *A Few Figs from Thistles* was read,
quoted, and often parodied, from cover to cover.

Its publication seemed an effrontery to Miss Dow, and the poet
herself was rather dismayed by its popularity, not to mention
the notoriety the volume caused her over the next ten years. On
the surface, her decision to publish light verse separately had
seemed wise; but she probably would have done better to scatter
these flippant poems through her work like light color notes in a
symphony, or scenes of comic relief in a tragedy. As it turned out,
the volume created an image of Edna St. Vincent Millay that was
not easily dispelled, and yet was only a fragmentary view of her
essentially serious art.

Moreover, she apparently received little financial return from
the wide circulation the volume enjoyed in the fall of 1920. Besides her publication worries, the disapproval of her patron, and
her precarious state of health—she was never again to be "strong
as a pony," as she once had bragged to Floyd Dell—the poet had
to force herself into strenuous work on extra Nancy Boyd pieces
in order to pay her higher rent, buy clothes, and make ends
meet. She could have borne it all if there had been some sign
from Arthur that he had received her extraordinary love letter and
shared her feeling of destiny in regard to their love. But there
was nothing. And in spite of her popularity, the attentions of her
Village suitors, and her work, she was lonely and melancholy, with
an increasing tension and sense of doom.

As always, she crowded her waking hours, and was often wakeful when she wanted to sleep. In December she made her first
postgraduate appearance at Vassar, reading her poems at Assembly Hall. Most of the girls knew her by reputation, and many

in the class of 1921 knew her by sight from her visits to Kathleen. No doubt one reason the latter had dropped out was that she had found it difficult to follow in Vincent's enviable footsteps. *Renascence* was, of course, well-known at Vassar, and many of the undergraduates already knew the candle quatrain and other poems from *A Few Figs* by heart. They were eager to hear the poet herself recite them. The audience that gathered at Assembly Hall was so large "it was necessary to adjourn to the Students Building," the Poughkeepsie paper reported, so that all could get into the auditorium. The poet was terrified, as she always was before readings; but as soon as she got onstage she felt at home and said so. She read her poems "with an informality that captivated her audience at once," as if she were back at school, and they were all classmates together.

She started by announcing that she would recite some poems she "had liked well enough to learn by heart," among them, after a few of the "Figs," the series of six elegies she had written in memory of Dorothy Coleman. Some in the audience remembered the girl with the golden voice who had been so tragically struck down after graduation. Whether they did or not, all were hushed and moved by the poignant dedication and the unique, starkly realistic chorus, "Give away her gowns, / Give away her shoes." They were moved as well by the strangely beautiful closing "Elegy," in which she described the glorious voice that is gone in terms of her refusal to be consoled by other enchanting sounds, or by the fact that her friend's body will "bud and bloom" again through the earth's secret chemistry. Nothing can restore that voice: "Once the ivory box is broken / Beats the golden bird no more." It was this poem, and the drama of the moment when she ceased speaking, the spell over the audience before the burst of applause, that the paper chose to highlight in its review of her reading. Her friend Elizabeth Haight, sitting with the faculty, was especially touched by the fact that the poet had listed "the woodcock's watery call" among the lovely sounds that could not comfort her.

The recital was so successful that before she went back to New York, Vincent was commissioned to write a verse play for the fiftieth anniversary of the Vassar Alumnae Association, which

was to be celebrated the following June. She and Kathleen immediately blocked out the idea and plot for an Elizabethan drama,
but before the poet could begin the writing, she was seized with
a cold that sent her to bed. Her apartment was so chilly she could
not stay up long enough to type her current Nancy Boyd piece,
which she was now doing regularly for *Vanity Fair*. "Bunny" Wilson brought her his electric heater and found her looking so forlorn and miserable, bundled up in a bathrobe under shabby
covers, that he suggested she should have a complete change,
perhaps join the general exodus of American literary lights who
were all leaving for Europe.

The notion appealed to Edna Millay. She was ill, tired, and
sick of the Village, which had become a tourist attraction after
the war, and as a result had become both "cheap" and expensive.
Restaurants and teashops were "Village-y" to the point of absurd-
ity. In a delicious piece, "Art and How to Fake It," the poet as
Nancy Boyd advises a man how to be "artistic in the Greenwich
Village manner" in decorating a studio or a restaurant, with side-
splitting results. Rents were going up with the boom of the
twenties already evident. With Prohibition, the evils of gangster-
dom, hijacking, bootleg gin, and the speak-easy invaded the peace
of the Village. Edna Millay was not one of those who found the
speak-easy exciting. She was outraged when the Volstead Act
was passed, and wrote for a Nancy Boyd "dialogue" entitled
"Our All American Almanac and Prophetic Messenger," a bitter
and mocking satire which predicted the dates when all the private
habits of citizens including "venery," would be prohibited, one
by one, as a consequence of the forbiddance of alcohol. Many of
the writers who were migrating to Paris objected to government
interference in their private lives. The more Edna considered the
idea of going to Europe the more attractive it became. She was
tired of all the suitors that knocked on her door, and she was
weary of waiting for Arthur to return. Most important of all, and
this probably caused her depression, her poetry writing had come
to a temporary halt, perhaps because her life in the Village had
become arid. Her Pegasus needed "fresh grass to feed on," as
she wrote her mother.

And so "it was decided she should go abroad," according to

Wilson. Frank Crowninshield arranged for her to go technically as a foreign correspondent for *Vanity Fair;* she was to send in two articles a month, which made it possible for her to be paid on an allowance basis. He offered her a higher fee if she would sign her own name to her prose, but she refused. The Nancy Boyd dialogues and sketches, closely related to one-act plays, show the influence of her Provincetown training, the impromptu script-writing that often had to be done for the next bill. Unlike the short stories and novelettes she wrote for *Ainslee's,* the *Vanity Fair* pieces exhibit quality. Some of the incisive dialogue might have been written by Shaw or Wilde, except that it is distinctly feministic; certainly it leaves no doubt that she was a wit as well as poet, and she should have had no qualms about signing her own name. But she wanted to be known professionally only as a poet. When Wilson tried to persuade her to accept Crownin-shield's offer, she reprimanded him sharply from her "school-marmish side," as if he were an ill-mannered boy in a classroom. He saw that she would never compromise, and gave up. Despite their mutual admiration and respect, there always seemed to be a sparring edge between Edna Millay and Edmund Wilson. Edna, though frail in health and fragile in body, was indeed at that moment "the solid sprite who stands alone."

Eventually they formed an unspoken truce. Edna was able to get back some of her music, playing Bach on the piano in his apartment. Wilson read poetry aloud in his voice, "harsh and light as the scratching of dry leaves over the hard ground . . . . immortal page after page conceived in a mortal mind," allowing her to approach "the wild bright bird" of Beauty; but if she tried to tell him of her "rapture" and "sweet rest" when she rose to leave, he would "cry her down with a salty flail." So she wrote in her perceptive "Portrait" of him some years later. They had several evenings of "wonderful conversations" before she left, some of them in French so she would be refreshed in the language when she reached Paris. During one of these practice sessions he remarked that her ex-admirers ought to organize an alumni association, to which she flashed back at him in French: "They always talk about it, but they never do it!"

They laughed together and made their peace. And before she

went away, John Bishop, who was once more on friendly terms with "Bunny," joined them for an evening spent on the early "high and festive basis" they had all relished during the previous spring.

And then, after hectic preparations for her journey, in the midst of which Kathleen's marriage took place, and a hasty trip to see her mother, who was again living in New England, the poet sailed for Europe on the French ship, *Rochambeau,* on January 4, 1921. She had no idea what the future might bring. In breaking the news of her travel plans to her mother, she had written that it "had nothing to do with any love affair, past or present." She hoped for "something more satisfactory than she had had so far. She was going as a free woman, a business woman, and because she wanted to travel." These were bold words, meant to reassure her mother, written from a brave, but sorely aching heart.

CHAPTER IX

Peripatetic Poet

THE CROSSING took nine days, and on some of them the *Rocham-beau* ran into very rough seas; Edna St. Vincent Millay was one of the few aboard who did not suffer *mal-de-mer*. The sea-coast child proved a natural sailor. And when she came to Paris, among the rest of the literati who made the American exodus in the early twenties she enjoyed the sights along the Seine and the cafés that lined the boulevards along the banks. She visited the Louvre and the Tuileries; and she wandered through the crooked streets and frequented wicked cafés of Montmarte. During the first week she walked miles and miles because she found it all so "fascinating."

During her first week in Paris she also wrote two articles for *Vanity Fair* and had lunch with the French editor of the magazine. She soon met members of the famous circle who came to be known as "the lost generation." [1] F. Scott and Zelda Fitzgerald, foremost of the luminaries, made slight impression on the poet. In fact, as she later told Wilson, who arrived in Paris during the summer and stayed in a hotel around the corner from her, Fitzgerald was always self-consciously wise-cracking about his art. He made her think of a stupid old woman with whom someone has left a diamond: proud of the jewel, showing it off to everybody, to the surprise of all who see it, because she makes such

[1] A common but erroneous translation of Gertrude Stein's original phrase, which was, "la génération *du temps* perdu."

inept remarks about the diamond. It was a perceptive simile on Edna Millay's part; and though the image was literally far from the handsome, "exhilaratingly clever" Fitzgerald, Wilson admitted it was symbolically true.

At the Café des Deux Magots on the Boulevard St. Germain the poet bought small bouquets of flowers from "little bits" of girls; and at the Café Rotonde in rue Vavin, she sipped *un export sec* with fellow artists: poet-brothers Stephen Vincent and William Rose Benét, Edgar Lee Masters, and composer Deems Taylor. Allan Macdougall was on hand, editing a column similar to F. P. A.'s "Conning Tower" for the Paris edition of the Chicago *Tribune,* happy to see his "li'l Aingil," Edna, and ready to show her around the City of Lights. Other members of the Players, including Djuna Barnes, came over in the summer. The poet went dancing to "le jazz hot" with American boys and had no lack of partners. She bought a display sample of a Poiret evening gown. Even in the wintry weeks of January right after her arrival she was captivated by the beauty and charm of Paris, she wrote Wilson.

Yet the letters of Edna Millay, almost from the beginning of her stay abroad, betray the fact that she was lonely and home-sick for her family to the point of neurosis. It is true that all through this period, she gave lively accounts of her sometimes more than lively activities; but these accounts are overcast by a pall of loneliness and heartsick longing. The sought-after, sophis-ticated, "business woman and foreign correspondent" for *Vanity Fair;* the gamine of Greenwich Village, and the effervescent col-lege girl have all but vanished in the sometimes pleading, some-times wailing, sometimes wondering, and only occasionally happy or poetic letters to her family and her heart's friend, Arthur Ficke. Instead the poet reverted to childhood, the "scared little girl from Maine," the loving little girl in need of her mother. She wrote from Paris, scarcely six months out of New York, in one of these "love letters" to her mother that no matter how in-teresting it all was, and how beautiful, and how happy she was, and how much work she got done, she was nevertheless away from home—home being somewhere near where her beloved mother was. She was always looking for mail from home or from Arthur.

In writing to the Millays she frequently referred to childhood scenes or used the nicknames of childhood. Norma was "Hunk," or "Normie," or "Loved Sister"; Kathleen was "Wump," or "Wumpty-woons," or "Kay"; and Cora was addressed all the way from "Mother," to "Mo-thie," to "Mumbles," or simply some term of endearment, often "Dearly Beloved." The poet signed herself with various nicknames besides "Vincent"; usually it was "Sefe," short of Josephus, another boy's name, which she had dubbed herself in childhood. Often it was "Bincent," and occasionally "Eddyner." Some baby talk is sprinkled through the lines, and the effusive affection is almost embarrassing at times. Nostalgic recollections crop up unexpectedly. A quartet with a Negro jazz orchestra made the poet "homesick" for her sisters, the three girls harmonizing "My Baby Needs a New Pair of Shoes," a number they used to perform in Camden, with their mother putting in a rich bass note once in a while. And in England, where the poet went for several weeks in the fall, the taste of cambric tea brought back a childhood scene which Edna Millay recalled for her mother in a passage of a letter from Hertfordshire, September, 1921. It was reminiscent of Proust's opening in *Swann's Way*, with the homespun quality of a "barefoot poet" in a New England kitchen instead of the elegance of a French novelist's drawing room. Wherever she went, she confessed she was like the Ancient Mariner, buttonholing all who came near her with a tale of her delightful, dedicated, miraculous mother. In the first-mentioned letter, written after six months abroad, on June 15, 1921, one frequently quoted paragraph contains a clearcut tribute from Edna Millay to her mother as the *raison d'être* of the poet's whole career. In another vein, the first paragraph of the next letter, written in July in answer to one from Mrs. Millay, she showed tender appreciation of her mother's kindness to small animals, her feeling for birds and flowers, paralleling Colette's adoration for her beloved "Sido." The French novelist was perhaps more subtle and restrained than the American poet, but she was writing for publication, as part of her inimitable gift for creating fiction from the reality of her personal life. When Edna

Millay translated this flow of feeling in terms of her own particular genius, she was just as objective, raising her filial emotions to the realm of art. Rarely in literary biographical history are there two such examples of mother-daughter admiration and love.

In the July missive the poet made the first mention of bringing her mother to Europe; she predicted they would "have themselves a little honeymoon." Then in a double postscript she asked if her mother supposed, when they were dead that someone would publish the *Love Letters of Edna St. Vincent Millay & Her Mother;* in the second part, she mentioned sending a poem she had just written, telling her mother to "show it to the girls, too." This packet seems to have been delayed in the mail; but, as nearly as one can make out, the poem referred to was the work written in connection with her feeling for her mother, and the one which brought Edna St. Vincent Millay her most prominent award. For it was inevitable that her nostalgia, her subconscious memories of the past in the midst of a reckless, pulsating present; and above all, her homesickness, should evoke a poignant, deceptively simple, and unique poetic symbol of mother love and devotion.

It was a spontaneous creation, not planned, as the sonnet sequence would be, which she intended to write about the New England woman whose story her mother had told her, the latter eventually called "Sonnets From an Ungrafted Tree." Before she left New York she had said she needed to be by herself for a while; she was becoming sterile in the "congested" city; with so many people around, she did not get a chance to work. As things turned out, during the months in Paris she was hardly more alone than she had been in New York, and she plunged into the gay life of the boulevards with her usual intensity. But the scene was new and stimulating to her in spite of her homesickness, and she did get a lot of work done. Her power of concentration was strong once she set herself to writing, and she went her own way professionally. Though she spent time in the cafés, and even, on one occasion, blocked out a mystery story as she sat outdoors having lunch, she did not join the group of expatriates that gathered around Ezra Pound and T. S. Eliot. Nor did she try to nudge her way into Gertrude Stein's circle, then forming an enchanted ring of writers and painters. She did not seek to have her poems published in any of the "little magazines" which sprang up like mushrooms in Paris as in New York and often perished overnight.

Because she had always led a more or less nomadic life, Edna Millay did not need to make a cult of bohemianism, the way many of the "Left Bank" expatriates from America did, spending so much of their time in carousing and philosophizing that they forgot to create the works of art they claimed as their goal. She was always as highly individualistic as Robert Frost or Elinor Wylie, who was soon to come within her sphere. The most notable event of her stay in Paris was perhaps the dinner party for two in Brancusi's studio. The supremely gifted sculptor, in 1921 coming into prominence, had met the poet, and in one of his rare moments of relaxation from his rule of solitude, invited her to dinner in his studio with one other person. The other guest was delayed, so the red-haired Irish poet and the little black-eyed "Roumanian peasant and great sculptor" ate together off a wide round marble slab that, all dented and pounded, served as workbench by day and dining table by night. It was like "an enormous millstone," the poet thought. Brancusi lived like a monk in a huge, high, white-walled, white-beamed studio. He made his own furniture, consisting of a wooden bunk bed in one corner, a whitestone stove ("like a stove you build on the beach"), and roughly hewn, hand-turned chairs. And did his own cooking. To Edna Millay, who was used to the colorfully decorated and often cluttered studios of Village painters, the artistic purity of this sculptor's Paris atelier was a source of reverence and wonder. There were no "arty" trappings, no "kimonos flung over easels," no tapestries or batik wall hangings. In fact, there were no fabrics of any kind; there were only metal and stone figures on pedestals, many of them wrought into a frankly phallic beauty that gave a kind of unearthly majesty to the austere studio. But when "little Brancusi" began bustling around serving bowls of hot soup and broiled chicken, shuffling back and forth from the tiny kitchen to the bare marble table, his wooden sabots clattering on the stone floor, his black eyes crinkling with humor, the poet shed her sense of awe and settled down to enjoy herself. By the time they were eating the paper-thin slices of large, white turnip-like radishes and drinking sweet white wine with their chicken, they were chattering away in different French dialects (the poet probably in academic, the sculptor in colloquial French) as if they were two townsfolk from Transylvania, Brancusi's birthplace, meeting after a long separation. Brancusi was so retiring he would not let himself or his work be photographed and was suspicious if anyone brought a camera into his monastic studio. That such a rare creature should unbend toward the young American poet was a mark of distinction for Edna Millay.

During the first two months after her arrival in Paris, the poet, besides writing regularly for *Vanity Fair,* completed and sent off the first draft of her five-act verse play for Vassar. Eventually called *The Lamp and the Bell,* it was an outright ("frank, shameless") imitation of the Elizabethan dramas she had always loved, a form which lent itself to the pageantry of an outdoor theatrical presentation involving well over two hundred Vassar alumnae from as far back as 1883. Among the performers was to be Kathleen Millay Young, "ex–21." The drama dealt with the attachments of girlhood, the touching, tender friendship of adolescence which grows into a deeper, loyal friendship of womanhood, in this case so valiant it comes close to taxing the credulity of the reader. The setting is a medieval court; the two central characters, Beatrice and Bianca (in childhood, "Snow White and Rose Red," the original title of the play), are a princess-queen and her stepsister. Both fall in love with the same prince; Beatrice hides her love, relinquishing him to Bianca; some years after the marriage she inadvertently kills the prince-husband of her friend in battle; in the end, after Bianca dies from grief, she takes comfort in the final words of forgiveness from her friend and the fact that she is to bring up the two children of the marriage. All this nefarious business was not taken too seriously. In fact, Elizabeth Atkins, Millay's first biographer, states that the play is an allegory of academia, though her explanation of the parallels to college life and loyalty seems more farfetched than the play itself. The aspect of latent lesbianism implicit in the plot seems to have been overlooked entirely.

Moreover, there was ample room for a spectacular production, with colorful costumes and music, the melodies for which the poet composed, getting a composer-friend, Hiram Moderwell, to "harmonize" them. Three of the songs sung by the jester are equal in delicacy to any of the lyrics the poet ever wrote: "Oh, Little Rose Tree, Bloom!"; "Beat Me a Crown of Bluer Metal"; and "Rain Comes Down." They were included in her next volume and in all succeeding collections. *The Lamp and the Bell* was presented in June on the grassy stage of the outdoor theater at Vassar; and, in spite of its shortcomings, including a good many confessed anachronisms, it was the brilliant success the author expected it to be on campus. And in September, the production was featured in a long article with photographs in *Theatre Magazine*, which commented that it "struck the high water mark for college dramatics." The published version of the play was dedicated to "Vincent" Millay's class of 1917.

At around the same time that she was sending off the first draft of her Elizabethan verse play, in the early summer of 1921, *Second April* finally appeared on the stands in the United States. To Edna St. Vincent Millay, far away in France, preoccupied with emotional problems and involved in new work, its publication was an anticlimax; but it was hailed with shouts of praise by the critics at home. In Chicago, Harriet Monroe, writing in *Poetry* magazine, was eager to sound a fanfare and blow trumpets for the lyrical volume. It represented the serious side of the poet: some of the love poems were tinged with bittersweet irony; others, like "The Blue Flag in the Bog," strangely meditative and metaphysical; the "Memorial to D. C." which, with "Wild Swans," a brooding cry of eternal longing and loneliness, lyrically closes the volume.[2] *Second April* was especially welcome to many readers who had found the "Fig" poems too flippant for a poet of Edna Millay's stature. Her patron cannot have helped being deeply gratified by the universal acclaim accorded to the volume dedicated, "To my beloved friend, Caroline B. Dow."

However, the unfortunate timing in the publication of *A Few Figs from Thistles* formed the basis for an error committed by a number of Millay biographers, which was a tendency to regard the works that followed, particularly *Second April* and later,

[2] Exclusive of the sonnets, which always follow in a separate section.

The Buck in the Snow, as being "more mature," rather than a return to the serious mood of the poems in *Renascence.* Her most recent biographer speaks of Edna Millay as being "no longer" flippant or casual toward love, as if the poems in *Second April* were written after the "Figs," when in fact most of them were created during the same period or earlier. *Second April* was to have been published before *A Few Figs,* and, except for Kennerly's financial difficulties, would have been. The keen poetic quips of Millay's light verse are only indications of those intervals Proust has called "the intermittences of the heart," which enabled Edna Millay to be a gay companion, ready for a drink, a dance, a duel of wits, a momentary romance, and at the same time to create profound, passionate, and tender works of poetic art.

It was natural, as a result of the nostalgia that accompanied the recollections of her childhood that the work which broke the poet's fallow period was a fanciful Irish ballad, "The Ballad of the Harp-Weaver." Half-fairytale, half-fable, the rhthmic four- and five-line stanzas immortalized her mother's jaunty defiance of adversity; her dogged, yet debonair endurance of the practical nurse's demanding schedule; her consistent self-sacrifice; and above all, her mysterious ability to provide "most of the luxuries of life," including music lessons and pretty clothes. As the past came flooding back to her on waves of homesickness, the poet remembered the piano lessons her mother had given her when she was only four, and she no doubt recalled the yellow chiffon dress with the flowing sleeves banded at the wrist in gold metal cloth that her mother had magically furnished for her recital.

In the poem "Lament," composed some time earlier and included in *Second April,* a grief-stricken widow, in telling her small son and daughter of their father's death, says to the boy: "From his old coats / I'll make you little jackets; / I'll make you little trousers / From his old pants." And in the verse drama so recently completed, the jester sings, "Weave me a robe of richer fibre; / Pattern its web with a rare device." These two poems might be considered forerunners of the figure of speech that Edna Millay employed in "The Ballad of the Harp-Weaver." The concept must have come like a vision: the widowed mother and her son, in threadbare patchings and in want for food, "nothing in the house / To make a boy breeches," "nothing in the house / But a loaf-end of rye," glowing with the primary image, "And a harp with a woman's head / Nobody will buy."

In any other hands, a poem created from such a tableau could have become mere sentimentality. But Edna Millay's deft and delicate touch with words and meter and her Celtic sense of the magical and mystic made it possible for her to present the picture and its highly imaginative, poetically tragic outcome without cloying the reader's emotions. Just as Melville used the clumsy, handmade "grego" in *White-Jacket*, and the young sailor's old hunting jacket in *Redburn*, to signify his own penury and his forlorness of spirit, so Edna Millay created little jackets and breeches, woven by a dying widow on "the harp with the woman's head," fabricating "the clothes of a king's son" to denote the spiritual riches she had received from her mother. The symbolism is obvious, perhaps; indeed, so astute a critic as Wilson had thought, until he heard the poet's recording of it years later, that "The Ballad of the Harp-Weaver" should have been published in a woman's magazine. When he told her so, she objected, unhesitatingly and vehemently defending the tone of the work.

She evidently knew instinctively that this was an exceptional poem, different from any she had written, destined for exceptional notice. In sending Mrs. Millay a copy to replace the one she thought had been lost in the mail, she openly called the Ballad "a lovely poem," and she seemed to feel confident that her mother would understand and appreciate the tribute.

In September, 1921, just before she left Hertfordshire to return to the Continent, the mood of the harp-weaver ballad was still strong within her. She recalled the only romance she had had in Camden; the love affair that had been broken off abruptly came back to her, and her mother's kind understanding filled her with gratitude even now, a decade later. She expressed a whimsical notion, combining elements from *The Lamp and the Bell* with the "Ballad," that she would marry and have a son; that her husband would die; and that she and her mother and her little boy would all live together on a farm. She hastened to add that she was not being morbid, but merely wanted to share her intimate thoughts with her mother.

Morbid or not, she was obviously lonesome; and her melancholy must have been due in large measure to her longing to see Arthur Ficke. She knew he and Bynner had returned from China. He had sent her a large photograph of himself, which she carried with her on her travels through Albania and Montenegro, a costly and very rugged tour she decided to take, perhaps to gather material for an article. While traveling she thought about Arthur more than usual, though he was never far outside her psyche. She had always been completely open about her adoration of him. Whenever anybody asked if she knew Arthur Ficke, she would answer that she did; then, if the questioner wanted to know if she liked him, she would declare quite simply that she loved him. That was all. And the people who pried could think what they pleased. When writing to him, she tried to keep her comments objective and humorous, dwelling on the merits of his sonnets rather than on personal matters. But she could not submerge her feelings any more; and in October, almost a year after her first declaration, she wrote him another ardent love letter. She had sent any number of notes to him in between, but all she could ever think of to say was an anguished query—why wasn't he there with her?—a cry of longing to see him. Quoting one of the poems in *Second April*, she related it to her feeling for him, and poetically expanded the image to let him know all that she desired of him.

She invoked the "suns and moons rising in the purple edge outside most people's vision" and "the high music that only birds can hear" to intimate the deep poetic passion of her feeling for him.

He evidently had been in a state of conflict in regard to her, judging from his poems alone; and Edna, writing from her room in remote Albania, where she had just heard a muzzein crying his mournful prayer, as if calling them to worship, mentioned the expressions of love in some of his letters, which have hurt and healed her at the same time. She spoke of "the sweetness of being loved like that," and added that to be loved like that by him was "terrible and shaking besides." She named two of the sonnets in *Second April* that were written with him in mind. A third, concerning both of them, contained the line, "There is no shelter in you anywhere," but she assured him that it was no longer true; they had both changed.[3] She ended with another outcry against all the months and months she had had to spend apart from him, all the years with "only a glimpse of him in the face of everybody." It was a pleading missive; she was trying to convince him that they must somehow see each other again. Though there was a momentary flash of humor in her words, when she realized that all her reasoning "resolved itself into one pitiful female cry," there was no sign of the taunting Daphne, the self-assured, sought-after, popular poet, which was the public image of Edna St. Vincent Millay for many years to come. Without giving herself a chance to think it over, she mailed the letter from Albania, before going to Rome, where she stopped for two weeks.

She found a mound of mail awaiting her; there were at least ten letters from her beloved family, among them a happy note from Norma, announcing that she and Charles Ellis had suddenly decided to get married and were now living in a lovely apartment all their own. The poet was delighted to hear the news, but it made her ruefully aware that both her "little sisters" were now "young married women," while she was "just about three months from being an old maid." She joked about it at such length that she must have been perturbed.

She sought to calm herself with work, and, among other things, took on a reviewing assignment for the *New York Evening Post*. It was then that Elinor Wylie flashed into her horizon, for the paper sent her the latter's first volume, *Nets to Catch the Wind*. As she read the sometimes startling, skillfully wrought, clear-textured poems, among them "Silver Filigree," "Bronze Trumpets and Sea Water," "Velvet Shoes," and "The Fairy Goldsmith," she was more and more taken with the inimitable style of the gifted poet. After she had written the review, published in the *Post* on January 28, 1922,[4] Edna Millay sent an admiring note to the

[3] This sonnet, which he had asked her about, is number fourteen in the Ficke collection of Edna Millay's typescript sonnets at Yale University Library. The impassioned lines of protest against his "too poignant lovelinesses" reveal much of the same conflict he must have been going through. The poem was published in *Reedy's Mirror*, but never in a volume of Edna Millay.
[4] This was the only review Edna Millay wrote for publication.

author, expressing her keen delight in the other's poetry; and she characteristically complimented her by telling her to "keep well and strong; not to suffer her foot to be moved." Though they did not meet in person for nearly a year, this marked the beginning of a mutually rewarding friendship.

The trip through Albania had been costly, and living in Rome was expensive, so Edna Millay moved on to Vienna, where the rate of exchange was even higher than in other parts of Europe, for Austria was suffering from a prostrating, postwar inflation. But though it was the cheapest place in the world to live, it was also the gloomiest, she thought. It was early December, and there was not a shred of sunlight; if there had been, it could not have reached the inner-court room looking out on a gray slab of wall in the cheap hotel where she stayed. The whole city seemed gray; the people were pinched and gaunt-looking even though they were not thin. The food was heavy, starchy, and usually fried in grease, which was not only distasteful to her New England palate but harmful to her hypersensitive constitution. Even the famed Viennese pastries and coffee houses were a disappointment. Gone was the *Gemütlichkeit* of former days; in its place was a nervous, unsettled state of affairs, which seemed to reflect her own unsettled state of mind and heart.

She was still anxiously awaiting a reply to her letter to Arthur, but all she received from him was an inquiry concerning the safety of a rare Japanese print he had loaned her. She was piqued, even angry, though she could not believe he would have ignored the import of her letter if he had gotten it. The precious print was in her trunk in Paris and she had no money to go there and get it, nor could she have the trunk sent to Vienna. Arthur was a collector and something of an authority on Japanese prints, and she was genuinely sorry that she could not afford to send it back to him. She warned him not to "breathe it to a soul" that she was low on funds, and she did not want to worry anyone, or have anybody send her money to help her out, including *him*. She added with forced carelessness that she wondered if "he had got any of her letters.—Not that it mattered"; and she ended plaintively that it seemed a long time since she had seen anyone she cared about. This was one of the few letters to him in which she did not include love, and which she signed "Edna." [5]

She did not know exactly what she had expected from Arthur, but she certainly anticipated more than an inquiry about his Japanese print. In his sonnets, especially "To a Girl Singer," which he had recently sent her, he had revealed a reverent fear of the deep power dormant in the songs she had sung in solitude, of the "gigantic shadows" her spirit had flung against the sky, making him doubt her mortality. Such lines as these thrilled her and left her shaking with the terrible sweetness of their impact. She could not figure out, then, why he should suddenly write so impersonally, asking only about his art treasure. When she was not feeling actually ill from the food, from smoking too many cigarettes, or from the strain of a satiric novel she had begun—significantly called "Hardigut," concerning a land where people eat in secret, as if it were a scandalous, sinful habit—she was perplexed and disturbed by the difference in the mood of Arthur's letters.

And his next communication, a crazy little note scribbled on an index card with a postscript from Hal, only compounded her confusion; it was the first in a series of exchanges between the three poets, which might be called a melodrama of errors, enacted by mail. From all Edna could gather, Hal had sent a letter she never received, in which he asked her to marry him. Arthur had indicated that he felt they should wait until they had thought it over before taking such a serious step. But he had not mentioned his own feelings toward Edna. He was still not free, but his marriage was failing. She knew he had been in New York and had not written her from there, and she wondered vaguely if he might be having a love affair. After all, she had had many romances since that interlude in 1918: why shouldn't he? Of course she could not be sure, but she was again hurt by his impersonal attitude. She was lonely and miserable in Vienna, and the proposal

---

[5] She had begun signing herself "Vincent," the name she kept for intimates, early in their correspondence, in 1913; whereas she always signed letters to Witter Bynner, even after she began calling him "Hal," with the more formal "Edna."

from Bynner seemed at the moment a strong spar to cling to in
a sea of gloom.

On December 23, no doubt on the eve of the dreariest holiday
season she had ever known, she sent a halting, quizzical letter of
acceptance to Hal, fluctuating between fond reminiscence and
bewilderment. She would marry him if he really wanted her to,
she began, and admitted that she had thought for a long time
that she might marry him some day. She was twenty years old
when the correspondence with the two poets had begun while
she was still in Camden; but in her present state of mind it must
have seemed much earlier, for she wrote that he had known her
"since she was a little girl," and that he was "bound to her memories of childhood." Even allowing for the poetic license of figurative
speaking, including a reference to the age of innocence, her words
indicated that she was in a state of extreme nostalgia and emotional upheaval. She wished ardently that he were there, so they
could talk things over; if he only could know the "comical state"
of her mind!

The next two or three weeks were a time of impatient waiting,
during which she could do very little work; she was feeling more
and more wretched physically from the food as well as mentally
from the uncertainty. When she finally heard from the other two
protagonists in the three-way drama, she learned that it had been
further complicated by the fact that Hal had "opened her letter
to Arthur by mistake," and was having greater misgivings than
Edna. He was coming to Europe in the spring, he said, when
they would decide what to do. She also learned that Arthur had
fallen in love with a young artist by the name of Gladys Brown,
whom he had met in New York. Though she had suspected as
much, the news must have been a staggering blow; anyone less
generous in spirit would have fallen under it. But Edna Millay,
while she may have been momentarily shattered, rallied heroically.

Toward the end of January she was sufficiently in command
of her emotions to reply in detail to both letters. Still rather confused, trying to adjust to the situation, she wrote with warmth
and candor to each of the others in the odd mixup. To Bynner
she stated that she still wished to accept his proposal and that
she thought theirs could be a successful marriage. She insisted,

however, that she would understand if for any reason at all Hal felt his proposal had been a mistake. It was true that she loved Arthur and would always love him; but she felt it entirely possible to love several people at the same time. The world was so full of "gracious and noble spirits" that one must be either "undiscerning or frightened" to limit the heart to one individual. Her ideas on love and marriage as expressed in these letters are surely those of a poet and a free soul. She made it clear that it was not because he was single and Arthur was not that she wished to marry Hal. She claimed that she would not want to marry Arthur, even if it were possible.

To Arthur she sent a document that reached a high point in gallantry and generosity. She began by admitting that she "held a very nervous pen lately" and described her acute suffering in the gloomy suroundings, but went on with bravado, airily asserting that she had known "all about that girl in New York, long before he told her." She had sensed it from his letters. It did not matter, except that she was sorry if the girl was hurt; nor did it matter "with whom he fell in love, nor how often, nor how sweetly." It would in no way affect their relationship. Alternating between justification of her marriage to Hal and reaffirmation of her ardent vow to his closest friend, she again expressed with eloquent simplicity in poetic prose her profound feeling for Arthur Ficke. As they both had said in their sonnets, they would love each other for all time. She commented on some of those he had recently sent, especially the first of a duo, which were called "Go" and "Stay," in a two-part poem entitled "Girl Beside Pool." She hoped that when people read the lines beginning "Trouble not this dark pool! In shallower waters / Go dip the splendor of your naked feet," they would all know she was that Girl, and that he loved her in such a deep mysterious way. She offered critical advice on his choice of a verb in a poem that paid her a singularly lovely tribute and that foretold his future attitude toward her. She returned the compliment by sending him some new sonnets of hers, poems written in spite of, or perhaps out of, her despair. Several of the sonnets in her next volume contain lines which indicate that they must have been written at this time, especially the one ending, "But if I suffer, it is my own affair." And another,

which seems to point directly to Arthur and herself, in which
she bids him to

> forget not . . .
> How first you knew me in a book I wrote,
> How first you loved me for a written line:
> So are we bound till broken is the throat
> Of song, and Art no more leads out the Nine.

It is likely, too, that the group she sent him included, "I know
I am but summer to your heart" and the melodic, mournful, wise
sonnet beginning, "Pity me not because the light of day / At close
of day no longer walks the sky," and concluding with the sad,
perceptive, and philosophic lines "Pity me that the heart is slow
to learn / What the swift mind beholds at every turn." This sonnet attains a high degree of perfection in its flowing cadences,
subtle use of alliteration, and imagery drawn from nature, quite
apart from its reflective content. Whatever her suffering, and it
was undoubtedly genuine, there is ample evidence that she placed
poetry above all else. In writing to Bynner also, she had taken
time to remark, before delving into their dilemma, on the lovely
quality in his poems, "Web" and "Chinese Scholar." [6] If Edna
Millay had been any less wrapped up in her art, she could not
have weathered the emotional upheaval as well as she did.

Fortunately, her financial stress was relieved by a check Arthur
had sent her, drawn on his "reverend" father's account, which
she accepted gratefully in spite of her "man-sized talk" about not
wanting any help. She left murky Vienna and sped to Budapest,
where Dorothy Thompson and some other writers were spending
part of the winter. She took a "small but costly apartment overlooking the Danube" in the Ritz Hotel and plunged into a round
of parties to try to forget her recent turmoil, and to keep from
brooding about marriage to Hal. Whether she would have married
Arthur, in spite of her bold claims to the contrary, if he had asked
her remains an unanswerable question. They both may have con-

[6] Witter Bynner, whose interest in Chinese arts was as great as Arthur Ficke's
in Japanese prints, continued his study of Chinese literature for many years. He
was the first American poet to translate Chinese poetry into English.

ceded that there could be no union of two such intense personalities; that two poets of such complex and passionate sensitivity
could only destroy each other if they attempted to merge their
lives.

Certainly Arthur Ficke's sonnets and poems concerning Edna
Millay and himself present the picture of a torn soul, a deeply
disturbed love. His intense conflict is evident in a number of
poems, especially in "Sea Midnight," written on shipboard, right
after their 1918 tryst; "Questioning a Lady," in which the "lady"
speaks of her feelings about a former love, unmistakably Floyd
Dell ("His infinite curiosity too much pried / Into that darkness
which was mine alone. / *I am nobody's own* . . . ")[7] and from
the description in "To A Girl Singer" (I see you have a swift and
troubled smile / And odd secretive glimmerings in your eyes.
/ And I turn from you, terrified by the guile / Of this suave
simple exquisite disguise . . . "). And, while Edna Millay's sonnets
of the same period seem to be the joyous outpourings of a singing
heart and do not portray tortured feelings, they nevertheless point
to anxiety and ultimate grief for a lost love. The one beginning,
"Not with libations, but with shouts and laughter / We drenched
the altar of Love's sacred grove," goes on to fear that though
they might break their bodies in his flame, and pour their blood
on his altar, their grove will be forever nameless: "A pasture to
the shaggy goats of Pan, / Whence flee forever a woman and a
man." In another, she sees "the night pass, and the strange
morning break / Upon our anguish for each other's sake!" And
again, in "I know I am but summer to your heart," she feels she
has loved him "all too long and well / To carry still the high sweet
breast of Spring." During her early disillusionment, when Arthur
did not come to see her after the war, she wrote, "Here is a wound
that never will heal, I know," the opening of a sonnet she recited
to Edmund Wilson in the spring of 1920. Finally, it must have
been during the dark days in Vienna that she wrote the much
quoted sonnet, one that became famous for its free-flowing composition and ideas, a kind of gay-sad swan song to a love affair.
After opening, "What lips my lips have kissed, and where, and

---

[7] Italics mine.

why, / I have forgotten, . . ." and continuing with the unforgettable metaphor of the tree in winter that, quite simply, "knows its
boughs more silent than before," she concludes with the mournful refrain, "I only know that summer sang in me / A little while,
that in me sings no more."

All of the above sonnets were included in the volume Edna
Millay prepared for publication after her return from Europe;
Ficke's, too, were published in volumes in 1922 and 1924. Whatever the conflict of each was, they both must have feared that a
marriage between two highly gifted, inflammable spirits would
go up in smoke, and he probably thought that she would not
make a good wife.

Whether the marriage to Hal Bynner would work out, Edna
could not tell; she was still confused and upset by the whole
situation, as if "a bee was chasing her," and she did not know
which way to run. Then suddenly, a hysterically funny note
arrived from Hal, in which he let her know that he was more
frightened of the future than she. This was followed ten days
later by a long, intimate letter from Norma concerning their
mother, and the opposing desires that had been cluttering Edna's
mind were miraculously set straight. In a moment of panic at
the height of her distress, Edna had written her mother that
she would have to postpone bringing her to Europe; and, although
Cora had sent a "brave cable" on her daughter's birthday on
February 22, saying that she understood, Vincent sensed a tragic
undertone. Now Norma wrote that their mother had been ill,
and was so disappointed over the postponement of the promised
trip that she could not keep from crying. By the time the poet
finished reading the letter, for which she blessed her sister, she
realized that to her the most important thing in the world was
to get her mother over there beside her. She noted that of course
the famine in Russia was important, but in her life nothing, including marriage, could compare to the need to keep her promise
and bring her mother to Europe.

Luckily, she received a check just then from Otto Liveright,
who, with his brother Horace, was to publish Hardigut, with five
hundred dollars as an advance on the novel; she immediately sent
three hundred dollars to her mother for passage. With another

hundred from the *Vanity Fair* article, which Vincent would ask
Crowninshield to forward directly to Mrs. Millay, she should be
able to manage. The poet herself would get along somehow; she
was living on air as it was, at the mere thought of being with
her mother in Europe. And occasionally little extra income sources,
like the fifteen dollars she received from the *New York Evening
Post* for her review of Elinor Wylie's book, provided expenses
for a few days. All this time, in spite of her growing reputation
and popularity, she saw no royalty statements, nor did she realize
any returns from the volumes Kennerly had published. But that,
too, was less important than the fact that she was actually bringing her mother to Europe.

Early in April she left Budapest to meet the boat bringing her
beloved parent. They spent five or six weeks in Paris, most of the
time at a cheap, none-too-clean hotel in the Boulevard du Mont-
parnasse; but they did a great deal of sight-seeing, and had such
a "swell time" that they did not mind the rooms. Mrs. Millay,
looking like a little New England spinster with her dowdy clothes,
home-haircut (which she had given herself), and peculiar hats,
won everyone's heart. Vincent took her mother everywhere, even
on the "rough parties." Cora was completely in tune with the
gay bohemian life, and all that Paris had to offer. Her keen comments and Irish humor soon made people forget her odd appearance, which was in such contrast to that of her daughter, who
always made a point of being perfectly turned out. Unfortunately,
the poet was still ill from the food in Vienna and Albania, so that
she had to stay in bed a good deal; but she wanted to be sure her
mother made the most of this long dreamed-of trip to Paris, and
she often pushed herself into sight-seeing and other activities
when she should have been resting.

In the midst of it all she received the startling news that Arthur
and the young painter he had fallen in love with, Gladys Brown,
were in Paris! They had "eloped" on a sudden impulse, Gladys
said long afterward. Arthur wanted the two women who were so
important in his life to meet. He invited Vincent and her mother
to have lunch with Gladys and him at the fashionable Prunier's
restaurant shortly after they arrived.

Whatever she may have felt privately, Edna Millay rose to the occasion with her usual overt enthusiasm. When Arthur, who met the Millays at the door, escorted them to the table and introduced Gladys, Edna made a great fuss over the starry-eyed girl. Gladys had soft, light-brown hair, a slim figure, and a quiet, intelligent manner. "I just knew when I saw you across the room as we were coming in that you were Gladys Brown!" she exclaimed. "I said to myself, 'There's the girl who took my fellow away!' And then Arthur brought us over to you—and you look so pretty in your red hat and red dress, I just know why Arthur fell in love with you." With that she flung her arms around Gladys and gave her a warm hug. She was so disarming that Gladys was won over instantly.[8]

After weeks of constant sight-seeing by day and partying by night in the chilly rains of a Paris April, during which both Vincent and her mother suffered from colds, and the former's intestinal trouble grew steadily worse, the Millays decided to leave for England and the quiet of the Dorset downs. Llewelyn Powys probably suggested the locality near Chaldon Down, where the Powys clan made their home in Chydyok. Edna was exhausted, and her illness was alarmingly severe. She had a close call with peritonitis and was in dire need of rest. They found rooms with a retired army officer and his wife in the peaceful village of Shillingstone, where the poet could have a tiny work "hut" all to herself, with only the sheep and the song of the lark for company. The first time she heard the lark, which she was to call "a dark articulate atom in the mute enormous blue," she was so startled and overcome by the beauty of its song that she found herself face down on the ground in a field of daisies, crying—an experience she transformed into poetry. This was the free flowing lyric, "On First Having Heard the Skylark," published in *The Buck in the Snow* six years later. Here in the hut she spent most of the day, resting in a hammock, writing when she could. Her mother cooked and brought a warm midday meal to her in a covered basket.

On days when Vincent felt strong enough, the two took long

[8] Although Gladys Ficke much later became resentful of Edna Millay's high-handed ways, she could not help admiring her, and enjoying her scintillating, often unpredictable moods of gaiety during the early years of their relationship.

walks through country lanes to nearby villages, gathering flowers from fields and hedgerows. And as the poet grew stronger, they ventured further. They went up to Cambridge one day, not only to see the famed university, but because Edna Millay hoped to get a glimpse of one of her early idols, if not her model, A. E. Housman. And a glimpse was about all she had. She followed the Don of Trinity College, a post Housman held for many years at Cambridge, for half a mile, trying to catch up to him. Then, as his "thin grey figure and cotton umbrella" turned in at the college gates, she had a brief view of a very nice face before he vanished in the twilight gloom. Had he known she was trailing him, he might have made one of his rare displays of interest in a colleague. He knew the poetry of Edna St. Vincent Millay, and a few years later told an American reviewer that he got more enjoyment from her than from either Robinson or Frost. And in 1932 he was to write that some of her poems convinced him she was the best living American poet; but as he had heard she was "profuse and unequal," he had never "tackled" a whole volume of hers. He expressed a desire to read the book of sonnets she had just published; and after his correspondent (Director of the Fitzwilliam Museum at Cambridge) loaned him a copy of *Fatal Interview,* he pronounced it "mighty good." His phrase, in view of the fact that he was not a sonnet enthusiast, came as high praise from the diffident author of *A Shropshire Lad.*

The Millays lingered on in England. Esther Root, an accomplished pianist whom Edna had met recently in Paris, came to stay not far from them.

The poet and "Tess," as she was familiarly known, had taken to each other at once, and soon learned of their common interest, their love of music. It was enough of a basis for both of them to form a friendship which was to be lifelong. Their celebration of Tess' birthday together on June 4 became an annual event. Edna was glad to have her new friend nearby now to provide company for the Millays.

And word arrived that Gladys Brown would soon be there. Arthur had received a cable stating that his wife, from whom he was not yet divorced, had to have an emergency operation, and he was needed at home. Gladys, who was hoping to arrange a solo exhibit in London came to England right after he left, and found a room in a house in Dorset. She turned out to be an expert horsewoman as well as artist. Edna, who had not known the extent of her talent, that she painted "damwell," was more than ever charmed by her, and wrote Arthur Ficke as much. Lolling in the rope hammock of her little hut, she thought a great deal about Arthur, and the strange ways of Fate. She quipped lightly about its "star part" in the "Hicktown mellerdrammer" they all enacted; but her elaborate joking carried undertones of heart-break beneath the high-flown carefree phrases. Gladys taught her to ride a horse properly, even to getting back on when she was thrown one day, hurting her head on the asphalt road. She would have stayed right there; but Gladys helped her to her feet, went off calmly after the horse and brought him back, insisting firmly that she remount and start riding again, ignoring the blood on her scalp from the fall: that was the only way to recover from being thrown. And the poet obeyed her docilely, though it was difficult to climb into the saddle with one slightly damaged leg. But she was having a wonderful time in spite of it all and was full of admiration for Gladys as a veteran horsewoman who had survived a hundred falls. They accepted each other as friends, these two whom fate, in the person of Arthur Ficke, had brought together.

When Cora Millay saw that her daughter was well enough, she suggested that they do some more traveling. She wanted to make a pilgrimage to Ireland to find her family roots; and she would not go home without seeing the south of France. Vincent made the effort to grant her both wishes: after all, she had brought her mother to Europe as a treat, not to have her serve as a nurse. But first they went up to London to see the British representative of Brandt & Kirkpatrick (later Brandt & Brandt), who had just become her agents, to secure publication of her poetry in England; soon afterward, an offer came from Martin Secker, D. H. Lawrence's last publisher, who wished to bring out a volume of her selected poems. Needless to say, Edna Millay accepted at once. While in London, she took the time to write a warning letter to Wilson at *Vanity Fair*, cautioning him not to let Crowninshield or anyone else alter one word of *The Key*, the second prose piece under her own name, as someone had done in the manuscript of *The Barrel,* the first to be signed "Edna St. Vincent Millay." She had changed her mind about using her own name only because she needed the funds, and was furious at the idea of the magazine taking liberties with her work, even with the name of Nancy Boyd. This was always to be a vital point in Edna Millay's professional dealings, and later on she was rabid with rage if an editor attempted to tamper with her sonnets. It is significant that as much as she needed money at this time, she sent a small check, accompanied by a tactful note in *Krazy Kat* patois, to Allan Macdougall, who was without a job in Paris at the moment. Probably no writer took a more generous attitude, both materially and spiritually, toward her friends and colleagues than Edna Millay.

Esther Root and Gladys Brown left for home before the Millays, promising to look up Norma and Charlie in New York. Tess, who had taken many snapshots of Edna at Shillingstone, was eager to show them around; she would also be on the lookout for an apartment in the Village for the poet and herself. Edna would have preferred to go back right then. The wind in the ash tree had begun to sound like surf on the shore at Truro, if she hushed the "silly bleating" of the Shillingstone sheep, inspiring the lyric, "Memory of Cape Cod." However, she would not forsake her promise to her mother. They remained in England until November, while Vincent tried valiantly to get on with her novel; she sent Horace Liveright a description to use on the dust jacket, though she had only completed one chapter. The damp, disagreeable weather finally sent them to the south of France.

In Cassis-sur-Mer they reveled in a beauty and peace that became a poem, though its author was far from measuring up in strength to the pleasures of a plunge in the blue Mediterranean, followed by a walk through terraced vineyards. She was exhausted afterward, so then they moved slowly along the Riviera to Italy. When they sailed for home soon after the first of the year, Vincent was weak and wretchedly ill. Late in December she had written Arthur from Cassis that she could barely drag about. He had announced that he and Gladys were going to be married as soon as he got his divorce, and Edna responded that the news was "marvelous," telling him that she knew well what a "nice girl" Gladys was. Yet in the next paragraph she blithely, openly repeated her vow that she would love him till the day she died. And there was no danger of her marrying Hal: he had jilted her!

All her suitors seemed to be abandoning the idea of marriage to her. "Bunny" Wilson had informed her in June that John Peale Bishop had married; and perhaps by now Bunny, too, had found someone else. Floyd Dell had been settled with his "B. Marie" for some time. Edna Millay, the "old maid" of thirty, frail in health but burning with inner creative fire, could not have helped feeling that poetry was her fixed and guiding star.

CHAPTER X

The Poet Takes a Husband

THE CLOSE OF 1922, although a low point in the physical and emotional life of Edna St. Vincent Millay, marked a high point in her professional career. Late in the year, "The Ballad of the Harp-Weaver," printed by Frank Shay in much the same format he had used for *A Few Figs from Thistles*, appeared in a booklet by itself, dedicated to the poet's mother. It immediately won the hearts of American readers and reviewers throughout the country. For this unique volume, plus an expanded edition of *A Few Figs*, and for eight sonnets included in the *American Miscellany of Poetry*, 1922, Edna Millay was awarded the Pulitzer Prize, the first in the field of poetry to be won by a woman. Though the prize had not been established very long, it was a source of great satisfaction to Edna Millay that "lady poets" were being recognized at last, a principle that meant almost as much to her as the fact that *she* was the one whose poetry had broken down this particular barrier against her sex. The one thousand dollar award that went with the prize was a symbol of success in her eyes, and was not to be squandered on trivia or daily expenses. As extravagant as she usually was with money when she had it, she placed this award in a savings account. She would not "bust" her thousand dollars "for God or hero"; or even her beloved mother to whom she wrote the above in explaining why she hadn't sent the usual stipend. Mrs. Millay had gone back to Maine on their return from Europe.

Works were dedicated to Edna in 1922, among them the published version of Floyd Dell's *Sweet and Twenty*, which appeared in a collection of his one-act plays. Arthur Ficke's revised edition of his *Sonnets of a Portrait Painter*, 1922, contained four new sections of sonnets, all dedicated to different colleagues. After the revision, dedicated to Floyd Dell, there followed: *Don Quixote*, to Witter Bynner; *Rue des Vents*, to Maurice Browne; *The Middle Years*, to Edward Arlington Robinson; and last but certainly not least, a section entitled, "*Epitaph for the Poet* V (A Hymn to Intellectual Beauty), to Edna St. Vincent Millay." Composed of seventeen sonnets, it included most of those Arthur had sent to her at various times, though not the earliest ones that he had written after their 1918 encounter. The opening sonnet is based on the Politian philosophy that he who looks on a naked goddess leaves happiness behind, and is "doomed to all the splendor of her wrath, smitten blind . . ."; "blind to all save the wild memory / Of Beauty naked against a stormy sky." The second is the one often quoted in connection with her, beginning, "For Beauty kissed your lips when they were young." In sonnet XIV, Ficke made use of a phrase from her letter of October 29, 1920, to start off with, followed by an image similar to one of hers: "A swamp of violets stretches from my feet / To an horizon violet-hued with dawn";[1] Sonnet XV, beginning, "In times hereafter," is the one in which he had taken the advice she gave him in one of her letters from Vienna, changing the verb in the last couplet from "flee" to "turn." She, or anyone who knew the story of their extraordinary exchange of feeling and friendship, could easily discern in these sonnets a glowing portrait of Edna Millay, a high tribute to her individuality as well as her poetry.

Following the announcement of her award, she was invited to make public appearances, and the Liverights were clamoring for her to finish her novel, *Hardigut*, for which a jaunty dust jacket, with a surrealist design, had already been printed. But her illness prevented her from enjoying any of this acclaim as she should have, and she was too worn out to work. Tess had found rooms in a Waverly Place apartment, where the poet huddled

---

[1] The first phrase is a direct quote; the final one is the image idea he borrowed from her letter.

most of the time, trying to deal with her intestinal trouble as best she could. She saw few friends, and those only when she felt well enough to cover up her misery with a kind of feverish, brilliant chatter. Columnist F. P. A. was one who came to see her, his dark saturnine face deeply concerned as he noted her unnatural "high, bright gaiety"; it seemed to him that she was "full of eternal fragility" at this time, though she tried to conceal it. She introduced "Frank" to Tess, the beginning of a mutual attraction which culminated in their marriage a few years later.

Edna also occasionally went out with her erstwhile suitor, "Bunny" Wilson, and it was through him that the one gleaming event of those dreary winter months occurred—her meeting with Elinor Wylie. It must have been a proud feather in Wilson's literary cap to introduce these two arrestingly lovely and accomplished artists to each other as the trusted friend of both. Elinor, with her cameo-like, aristocratic face, framed by the marcelled hair she wore in the twenties; her tall, slim figure, always perfectly groomed, in keeping with the imagery of her poems; her incisive irony, and "harsh, unflurried, unembittered laughter," in Wilson's words, was an equal match for Edna Millay's warm, flashing wit and ravishing red-haired, incandescent charm, her impeccable appearance. An immediate and lasting kinship linked these two strong-minded poetic spirits, a feeling that was to become one of the rare remarkable friendships among poets of the same sex. Their lively sessions arguing over the relative suffering of Keats and Shelley, with Edna taking the side of "Mr. Keats" while Elinor championed "Mr. Shelley" became famous in poetry circles before long. They argued and harried and laughed and loved each other with literary and human fervor. They compared notes on techniques and preferences in poetry and people. Like Robert Frost and Edward Thomas, these two were "softly circled round in a relation of elected friends neither time nor foe could divide."

The winter wore away. Edna was able to do so little work that she finally decided to abandon her novel and concentrate on preparing a new volume of poetry, which was to be brought out by Harper's, her publisher from this time on. Through her agents, Harper's had also agreed to publish new editions of *Renascence* and *A Few Figs*, as Kennerly had gone bankrupt and was now out of business. However, it was an effort even to select and compile the poems she wanted to include, and she was feeling quite discouraged as spring approached. Tess, who had been visiting friends they had both met in Paris, Dudley Field Malone and Doris Stevens, persuaded Edna to accompany her one weekend in April.

Arthur and Gladys were there also, and in the evening various friends from the literary community that had sprung up around Croton dropped in, among them Floyd Dell and his wife, who lived nearby, and Eugen Boissevain, appearing like a benevolent giant or genie, for the third time in the poet's life. And this time his presence struck the dominant chord that would resolve her destiny and his. He was alone; he and Max Eastman had bought a small house on Mount Airy, in the neighborhood, but Max was in Russia, and by himself Eugen may have been more susceptible to Edna Millay's electric allure. In spite of her illness, she had never sparkled more brilliantly, perhaps because she was always inspired by Arthur's "divine absurdities," as she called them in a poem. Ficke's gift for devising games and literary diversions was well known, and his inventive mind was the *deus ex machina* that brought Edna and Eugen together.

They had all been discussing a Broadway hit, the plot of which involved the plight of an innocent young man from the country who falls into a lurid den of iniquity when he comes to the city, and is ruined. Arthur, his blue eyes blazing with wicked merriment, proposed that they put on an impromptu takeoff on the play. They would reverse the situation: in their drama, an innocent couple from the city is invited to spend a weekend in the country and unwittingly walk into an incredible clutch of depraved and evil country folk who avidly try to bring about their downfall. This was fine fodder to talents like Floyd Dell and Edna Millay, who had written many an impromptu scene for Provincetown productions, and before long they and Arthur had blocked out the action. When it came to the casting, Edna and Eugen were given the roles of the "innocent" pair who, in a prologue, meet on the train going out to the country. The rest all took parts depicting sinister characters: Gladys played a homosexual boy who immediately made eyes at Eugen; Arthur was a wily seducer of women who tried to win Edna's virtue by fair means or foul. Floyd was a sly con man with a dozen schemes for fleecing the unsuspecting guests. As the play progressed and the couple drew together in self-defense, refusing to fall from grace, the situations became more and more hilarious, and inevitably, the couple fell in love. Edna and Eugen, before the end of the third act, when they are trapped together in a locked bedroom and decide to take poison rather than ruin their reputations, took their roles literally, albeit unconsciously, and fell in love, to their own vast surprise, right before everyone's eyes!

It was a tale told many times in years to come, although recent erroneous accounts have disposed of the amazing experience by stating that Edna and Eugen were "paired off in a game of charades." At any rate, before she quite realized what had happened, Edna Millay found herself being loved and cared for by a man whose love she returned. Eugen Jan Boissevain had a kind of bonhomie about him, a combination of the successful man of the world and a sensitive, artistic spirit, though he was not creative himself. He was of Dutch-Irish descent; his mother's father had been Provost of Trinity College in Dublin, and his father was publisher of the *Algemeen Handelsbled,* Holland's principal newspaper. He could appreciate Edna's Celtic humor and mysticism, yet guide and protect her with his Dutch practicality. For generations his ancestors had been shipowners, dealing in East Indies trade, a tradition his family continued. He had come to America as a young man and had taken such a liking to the country he decided to adopt it as his own. He established a prosperous import firm in downtown Manhattan, dealing in coffee, sugar, and copra from Java. Yet he never lost his Dutch accent; and his genial manner, his hearty, booming laughter somehow suggested a provincial Dutch burgher. He was a well-known *bon vivant* who frankly and openly believed in free love. He had had some analytic treatment with Jung, and was able to view the world with an objective amiability that won him a great many friends. As Max Eastman said, Eugen had "the daring to enjoy life."

He now hoped to enjoy it with "Aidna," as he called her, or

"Vincie." He saw how ill she was beneath the exterior "high, bright gaiety," and he persuaded her to stay in the country and rest and to go into town only for diagnostic tests. It did not take much coaxing for Edna to surrender to his insistence on the intensive X-ray study of her insides. Eugen drove her into town in his big Mercer two or three times a week, and six doctors went to work on her. She had to rest fifteen hours a day, and was confined to a single hour of writing.

Before the month of May was quite gone, Edna wrote her mother that she and Eugen were going to be married. Big, jovial, generous, and kind Eugen had said the Mercer was now hers, and she promised to take her mother for a drive as soon as she was well.

To add to the complications of her physical condition, Vincent developed dental trouble, and during the period that the medical tests were being conducted, she had to have a tooth pulled. By a coincidence, Arthur had to have his tonsils out at the same time. It struck them and their friends as being a comical situation, and Gladys produced a cartoon-like drawing called, "The Twilight of the Poets," to commemorate their minor surgery. The pen-and-ink sketch depicted duplicate doctors in the foreground; Edna stretched with closed eyes and open mouth in a dentist's chair at the right; and Arthur, strapped to an operating table at the left. The duo of doctors is pictured holding up forceps, displaying Edna's tooth and Arthur's tonsils on their respective sides of the drawing. It created a diversion for both "patients," and helped momentarily to alleviate the apprehensiveness about the results of the X-ray series, which extended over several weeks. The doctors discovered serious intestinal trouble, requiring an operation.

On the morning of July 18, Edna Millay was married to Eugen Boissevain at Croton-on-Hudson. Arthur Ficke and Gladys Brown, who were to be married in December of the following year, were present at the ceremony; and in the afternoon they all drove into New York, where Edna entered the hospital for major surgery. Just before she went into the operating room, she said to Arthur, who had been as delighted as she over her Pulitzer award and had been helping her to prepare her new volume for the publishers, "Well, if I die now, I shall be immortal."

The operation for an intestinal complication was successful, but left the poet so weak that when she came out of the hospital, she could do nothing but rest at Mount Airy in Croton. When the proofs of her new book came from Harper's, Arthur had to correct them for her. There was probably no one else to whom she would rather have entrusted the task; he was a careful crafts- man, and she knew his eagle eye would pick up any errors. And while he was doing that, she may well have been memorizing some of his sonnets. When she was ill or convalescing it was her habit to pass the time in learning the poetry of those whose work she admired. She could recite Keats, Shelley, Gerard Manley Hopkins, some of the Latin poets, particularly Catullus, and the poems of her friends whose work she felt akin to, like Elinor Wylie and Arthur Ficke. Many years later, when he helped her prepare her own "Collected Sonnets," Arthur was amazed at how many of his she knew by heart, many more than he himself could recite!

One warm day (August 30, 1923), when he came to work on the proofs, she began to recite a poem of her own that had been tugging at her for some time in wretched moments during that summer of illness. This was the funeral-motif sonnet beginning, "I see so clearly now my similar years/ Repeat each other, shod in rusty black." She had not worked on the poem, and indeed, "had never put a word of it on paper before." Arthur wrote later in his notes on the preparation of *The Harp-Weaver*, "but had composed it entirely in her head, as she often does." She dictated it to him then and there, and he took down the lines word for word. He was amazed and excited by the unity of the imagery, the funeral-idea throughout. He felt that the work should be in- cluded in the new book as the thirteenth sonnet, along with two others dealing with somber subjects, disease, death and despair, one of which—Sonnet 16—had been written after the news of John Reed's death in Russia in 1920. Vincent agreed to the sug- gestion with little hesitation, for she trusted Arthur's judgment almost as much as her own in such matters.

She had intended to dedicate her novel to him, but her illness compelled her to abandon the project entirely; and when she realized that she could not complete the manuscript, she had taken a printer's dummy, covered by the modernistic blue and green jacket for *Hardigut*, and written on the flyleaf the tongue-in-cheek inscription: "To Arthur Davison Ficke, whose unfailing interest and earnest criticism made this book what it is." She signed it formally, "Edna St. Vincent Millay, July 3, 1923," and had presented the blank copy to him one night two weeks before her marriage, handing it to him with a dramatic flourish. Arthur, who always enjoyed a literary joke, accepted in the same spirit. He preserved the inscribed dummy, placing it among his papers for posterity; it is now one of the items in the Ficke collection at Yale University.

By the time the proofs were corrected, the weather was chilly, so Edna and Eugen moved into the Holley Hotel on Washington Square, where they were staying when the book, entitled, *The Harp-Weaver and Other Poems*, came out in November, 1923. The volume was widely reviewed and praised not only for its title poem but for its lyricism in general. Here were all the sonnets she had written in connection with Arthur and the strange tri-angular riddle over Hal Bynner's proposal that had now been re-solved into "two right angles" through Eugen and Gladys. There were thirty-nine sonnets, including the sequence of seventeen, "Sonnets from and Ungrafted Tree," the narrative of the New England woman estranged from her husband, who comes back to care for him on his deathbed during the least days of a fatal ill-ness. This was the only sequence of its kind, employing the third-person-singular, that Edna Millay ever wrote; and while it was an unusual genre piece composed with a stoical character in mind, the sequence did not have the appeal or the pure artistry of her intimate yet objective personal-experience sonnets. For those who voiced the opinion that Edna Millay was limited to love themes, *The Harp-Weaver* contained both lyrics and sonnets dealing with abstract ideas: the famous, "Euclid alone has looked on Beauty bare," an indication of that profound, "tough-minded" intellec-tuality which struck Wilson with such force, and was to become more sustained in the next ten or twelve years. The lesser known, "I will harvest beauty where it grows," and a number of poems concerned with death and the struggle or frustration of life, like "The Cairn," were intimations of purely philosophical themes to come from the poet who "sprang from the head of Jove" with the philosophic-religious "Renascence."

The Harp-Weaver, published by a well-established firm, was the first of Edna Millay's poetry to yield returns other than that of glory; and with her royalties, plus the enormous fee she had been offered for a lecture tour she planned to make after the first of the year, she began paying off all of her debts, as well as the family debts in Camden. Her only regret was that she could not have done so before she got married. Now she felt everyone must think it was her "rich husband" who paid her debts, and she took a fierce pride in the fact that every cent of the money had been made by her writing. Edna's spirit of independence, which Eugen well understood from the experience of his first marriage to the beautiful feminist, Inez Milholland, asserted itself in spite of the poet's willingness to have him take care of her. When she was invited to compose and deliver the dedicatory sonnet at the unveiling of a statue honoring three suffragette leaders [2] on November 18 in Washington, D. C., she made the trip, although she was still far from strong; and in the chill air, as she read the lines ending, "Take up the song; forget the epitaph," she must have felt deeply gratified at being able to contribute to the cause of women's rights. It mattered little that she suffered from a cold for weeks afterward. This was the sonnet she dedicated to Inez when she included it for publication in *The Buck in the Snow*. The fact that Inez had been one of her college heroines was a further bond between Eugen and herself.

The duality of her nature—the conflict between masculine and feminine impulses—seemed always present in Edna Millay's relationships, and might have caused her "neurotic illnesses," as Wilson termed them. It was probably the basis of the irritant in their friendship. It was that element, also, which probably contributed to Arthur Ficke's doubts and concern, and which had scared off Hal Bynner on the brink of their marriage. Any man less understanding, less affable and outgoing than Eugen Boissevain, would have been either lost and discouraged or annoyed.

Eugen was admirably suited to be the husband of a mercurial, complex, and highly gifted personality like Edna Millay. He was

[2] Lucretia Mott, Susan B. Anthony, and Elizabeth Cady Stanton.

twelve years older than she and, besides his love, offered her the kind of protection she had never received from her father: not only loving care but the adoration of a doting male parent. Her mother had given her encouragement and inspiration from the beginning, but not the adoration that Eugen now lavished upon Edna. In a few years, he was to give up his import business and devote his whole life to her career. This may or may not have been a wise move on his part, but it was a manifestation of his outlook on life as well as of his attachment to her. As he expressed his feeling, "Anybody can buy and sell coffee; but not anybody can write poetry." Moreover, his attitude was the more remarkable because there were no strings of possession or possessiveness attached to it. Perhaps his Jungian analysis had made him wise enough to know that if the cage door is left open, the bird may fly out but it will almost always return voluntarily. He and Inez had been married on a "free-love" basis, and there was probably a similar understanding between Edna and himself. He combined the virtues of a lover and companion with those of a devoted husband, almost to the point of ubiquity.

He watched over her like a nursemaid until she recovered from the operation, and so it would always be whenever she was ill. Ever solicitous for her comfort and welfare, he found a house for them in New York when she came back from Washington. Located at 75½ Bedford Street, right around the corner from the Cherry Lane Theater, it was one of the early three-story brick dwellings, only 9½ feet wide by 30 feet deep; and soon became famous as "Edna Millay's, the narrowest house in the Village." Shortly after January 1, the poet wrote a charming, playful note, although with an undertone of urgency, to "Dearest Bunny" Wilson, inviting him to call on them very soon if possible, before she had to "depart this life and leave for Pittsburgh and points west" on her reading tour. She was evidently apprehensive about the trials of the long tour in strange towns, standing before a sea of strange faces; yet she was determined to go through with it, to earn this money on her own.

Her fears, of course, were groundless. The tour, although exhausting, was a huge success. She missed Eugen's serene, solid, enjoyable presence; it made her laugh to think how different everything would be if he were beside her in the dusty parlor car en route to Cedar Rapids from Chicago. She wrote him a highly amusing account, in the form of a skit, of her frustration in trying to order breakfast in her room at the Windemere Hotel in Chicago that morning. Anyone unfamiliar with the mysterious workings of the East and West wings of that hotel would no doubt have been as distraught as she, but would not have been able to depict the scene with such riotous humor and accurate dialogue. She was glad that people everywhere enjoyed her poetry, that they were familiar with it to some extent, and that they showed their appreciation with tremendous applause. But between appearances she was lonely and bored. She did have one "lovely experience," which took place in Milwaukee, where she visited with the parents of Dorothy Coleman. Their deep gratitude for her "Memorial to D. C." was a distinct compensation for the discomforts of the tour.

She was eager to finish the tour, for Eugen had promised her that they would "go around the earth together" on a belated honeymoon as soon as she got back. Early in spring, they departed on a world cruise that lasted almost a year. They sailed on the S.S. *Taiyo Maru* and visited several of the Hawaiian Islands at the end of April; then left the first week in May and reached Japan at cherry-blossom time in Nikko. The "soft, clean pink" of the big double blossoms was a lovely sight; the only thing the poet thought prettier was a New England apple orchard in full bloom. It was a leisurely voyage, with ports of call at all the places she had often dreamed of seeing. Unfortunately, both Edna and Eugen came down with the flu as soon as they "hit the big cities"; most of the time in Peking and Shanghai was spent in bed, trying to recover. At Chefoo, a small village on the coast of the Yellow Sea, they stopped off to recuperate, and chartered a Chinese sailing junk, with a crew of two, a man and a boy. Every day they sailed to a different island among those dotting the seascape. They would build a fire and make coffee, swim and lie peacefully drowsing in the sun. That interlude was perhaps the most memorable of the entire cruise, and it was the only one a

poem was made of: a poem "For Pao-Chin," their boatman on
the Yellow Sea, who played his Chinese flute as they sailed back to
Chefoo in the evining.

They continued the voyage, heading for Batavia, Singapore,
and then India. They skirted the edges of a howling typhoon,
and when, with a flash of lightning, they saw a rainbow by night,
the poet felt a deep thrill coursing through her veins, as if life
had granted her one brief moment of perfect fulfillment. Touring
the teeming cities of Rangoon, Calcutta, Benares, Delhi, and
Bombay was a mixed experience. In spite of the exotic beauty,
Edna Millay could not help feeling oppressed by the tragic pov-
erty of so many millions of people, the helplessness of the poor
who were caught in the caste system. Combined with the impact
of Eastern mysticism, the strange spell of India haunted her for
years; and as late as 1948 she spoke of it with Vincent Sheean,
who visited the Boissevains shortly after his return from Jaipur.
From Bombay they went directly to Marseilles, and by mid-
October they were in Paris, just missing Norma and Charlie and
Gladys and Arthur, who had traveled to Europe together for
Norma's opera debut in Italy.

The Fickes, following their marriage in Edna and Eugen's Bedford Street house—a happy if hectic affair which the poet arranged
with her usual flair—moved into a studio apartment around the
corner, at 42 Commerce Street, above the Cherry Lane Theater,
overlooking the Boissevains' courtyard. The four were together a
great deal in an unusual rapport even among close friends. Arthur
dedicated his volume, *Out of Silence,* published in 1924, "For
Eugen Boissevain, And For Two Who Love Him," a fascinating
inscription, presumably including both Edna and Gladys, the two
women uppermost in his affections. This volume contained the
early poems Arthur had written to Edna: "To a Girl Singer" and
"Sea Midnight," composed on shipboard right after their momentous encounter in 1918. Here also were poems revealing Arthur's more objective attitude toward the poet from this time on:
that of an affectionate, close friend, whose feeling of admiration
still held a lingering flame of possessive love. The sonnet "Vista,"
often quoted in reference to Millay, pays her high tribute in the
lines:

I will confess that loveliness has stirred
Like a long music through me many a time
When all my courts and fountains with some word
Of yours were echoing in a silver rhyme;

and contains in the last six lines his vow to keep a memory of her safe from the outside world, safe within the high vault of his soul; a tall window, cherished beyond others, that gives upon her golden, unfenced ground.

His "Portrait of a Charming Friend," a triptych of sonnets in a lighter, more playful mood, begins with the lines of the "pickle" poem he had scribbled on the pastry box, but substituting the word "goblet" for pickle: "This goblet is a little loving cup." The last sonnet begins provocatively by referring to her as three little creatures, minx, marten, and mouse, and inviting her to enter his wide menagerie.

By Thanksgiving of 1924, as Edna had hoped, she and Eugen and the others were all home again to celebrate the holiday together. They were back in time, also, for the publication that year of the *Distressing Dialogues* by Nancy Boyd, which Harper's brought out "with a Preface by Edna St. Vincent Millay." Edna had written the latter at the publishers' request while she and Eugen were on their cruise. She had had little time or inclination for it and permitted Nancy Boyd no more than one brief paragraph of a Preface. With a literary straight face, she merely stated that "Miss Boyd had asked her to write a preface to these dialogues since she was already familiar with them, having followed them as they appeared in *Vanity Fair*"; and also since she was "one of the author's earliest admirers." She closed by recommending the "excellent small satires from the pen of one in whose work she took a never failing interest and delight."

The following February, her sense of fun prompted her to write to her friend, Deems Taylor, commenting on his remarks concerning one of his own compositions that the New York Chamber Music Society had performed the night before at a concert that she and Eugen had attended. Writing as if she were a perfect stranger, she took issue with the composer's claim that the audience must have been composed of "relatives of Mr.

Taylor" because they received his piece, "Portrait of a Lady" with such enthusiasm. She was warmly indignant in disagreeing with him, and suggested in closing that the audience was composed, not of relatives, but of "discerning and delighted strangers," and that he was probably the only relative of Mr. Taylor present. She signed the letter with her full name and sent it to the office of the New York *World,* where Taylor was then music critic. He no doubt enjoyed the joke and appreciated the implied praise of his work from one of America's leading lyric poets, as well as one of his most delightful café companions on the boulevards in Paris. It was shortly after this that the Metropolitan Opera Company commissioned Deems Taylor to write the first American opera ever to be produced by the foremost company in the world. The Board had recently voted in favor of such a production, long overdue in the repertory of the great company founded and developed in this country. Taylor immediately approached Edna as a possible librettist; the "book," he felt, should be in blank verse, and he preferred her to other American poets.

It was a signal honor, but one that the poet regarded with a good deal of trepidation, in spite of her unquestionable qualifications, her background in music and the theater. She felt it was one thing to write a verse play for the Vassar Alumnae Association, and quite another to write the libretto for a production of the Metropolitan Opera. Eugen, who was utterly delighted that "Aidna" had received an offer to share the commission with Deems Taylor, believed that all she needed was a proper place to work and that this meant the quiet and seclusion of the country. Indeed, they both felt after their return that the house at 75½ Bedford Street was too small. Free spirits such as theirs could not help feeling confined in the narrowest house in New York, no matter how quaint it was. Moreover, the quarters were too cramped for a big man like Eugen; and Edna had been longing for the sound of birdsong in the morning other than the "noisy chirping of the urchin sparrows" that had heralded the day from "crevice and shelf" under her hotel window on Washington Square. She had begun a mood-poem to them at dawn one day during her convalescence, but did not complete it till much later. The Mount Airy home was now occupied by Max Eastman, who had returned from the Soviet Union, bringing his Russian bride, Eliena. Since Eugen had always wanted to own a real country place, including some land, he and Edna began looking around early in the spring.

Before the end of March they located a sprawling fruit and berry farm in the Berkshires, seven hundred acres of rolling countryside near Austerlitz, New York, just over the Massachusetts line. The place had been unoccupied for some time and was run down; the ground was a tangle of overgrowth. But they both fell in love with it and decided to buy it. In April, Edna had scheduled a reading tour of several New England schools, including Bowdoin College, where she read with overwhelming success to a capacity audience. Eugen accompanied her on the tour, which they made by car, and they visited various members of the poet's family en route. On the way back, they were with Norma and Charlie, and decided to drive to Austerlitz so Edna could see what her sister and brother-in-law thought of the new place. Norma "was crazy about it" and Edna and Eugen were "even madder than before." They discovered a brook they had not known was there, and the orchards, in early leaf and blossom were more beguiling than ever. The old white frame farmhouse was in good condition, but needed much remodeling. They would have to knock out walls to enlarge the rooms, add an extra wing and a garage, and install a new heating system as well as plumbing. The outbuildings were all sturdy enough to stand, including a tiny "shanty" up in the fields, which the poet could use as a writing study; but there was so much to be done on the house that they decided they probably would not be able to move in before the first of July.

It was agonizing to have to stay in the little Village house in the city till then, but they often went to the country for weekends with Arthur and Gladys or other friends. Elinor Wylie and "Bill" Benét, who had eloped to Europe and were married after Elinor's divorce in 1924, had a house in New Canaan. And in May, Tess Root was married to Frank Adams in a lovely outdoor ceremony at the country home of friends near Greenwich, Connecticut. Afterward, Edna and Eugen drove to New Canaan with Arthur and Gladys and the Benéts.

The six notable personalities "spent Saturday night and all of Sunday together" in both intellectual and social harmony, punctuated no doubt by fierce verbal sword-play between the two female poets over the sufferings of "Mr. S." and "Mr. K." It was an argument they never settled, yet they never tired of sparring on the subject. The "lively malice" that would gleam in Elinor Wylie's hazel eyes as she dug up some quotation to make her point, and the bright pink flush that would flood Edna Millay's face when she got excited only added an edge to the active pleasure both took in each other's company. Arthur's presence was a continual joy. His brilliant nonsense in play and his dead earnestness in serious matters would always keep him in a secure place in Edna Millay's heart. All six were congenial. Sometimes they would all talk about poetry and contemporary poets. Again through Wilson, Edna became acquainted with Leonie Adams and Louise Bogan, both highly original poets whose work thrilled her, and she was to have a warm, enduring friendship with the latter.

None of the poets at the weekend party, except possibly Bill Benét, was physically fit. Arthur had a persistent cough which was perilously close to consumption; Elinor had been warned by the doctors against overtaxing herself in any way because of high blood pressure; and Edna was still not strong after her operation, and was beginning to suffer from the continual headache which was to plague her for months. Gladys, the painter of the group, though wiry, was thin as a birch wand and inclined toward bronchial trouble. Yet all of them burned with the high intellectual and emotional fervor of the artist. They reveled in the recklessness of the era and scorned prudent health care as they scorned Prohibition. They had all "consumed rafts of caviar and oceans of champagne" at Tess and F. P. A.'s wedding, and were not inclined to let down the mood of celebration. They acted and spoke as they felt, on impulse and inspiration. Eugen, who occasionally had his own bouts with an "amoeba" he had picked up in his world travels, was probably the healthiest of the lot. Although he entered into discussions and was an integral part of the intimate circle, he usually sat back and enjoyed the scene with the benevolent eye of its most interested spectator.

He seemed to marvel at his good fortune in being married to a gifted, fascinating, unpredictable creature like Edna St. Vincent Millay—his incomparable "Vincie."

May was beguilingly warm, so the Boissevains often drove up to the Berkshires to see how work was progressing on the farmhouse. It was typically slow; the workmen seemed to have difficulty getting started, and then there was trouble at every turn. Edna had had one long conference with Deems Taylor, who said he would leave the story line of the opera to her. He was resigning temporarily from his post on the *World* to compose the music, and hoped she could furnish him with the general idea of the book before long. She was eager to begin, but she wanted to wait until she and Eugen were in the country where she could work in peace and quiet. She received word that on June 15 she was to be awarded an honorary Doctor of Letters degree from Tufts College, another milestone for her, and the Boissevains decided they would move into their new home right after the presentation, no matter how little progress had been made on remodeling the house.

On June 22, 1925, Edna wrote her mother that they were there at last and, she was sure, "in one of the loveliest places in the world." The house overlooked wide stretches of Lebanon Valley; the place was surrounded by the forested rims of neighboring mountains; it was covered with wildflowers, particularly steeple bush, whose tall, pink spires predominated in the fields and meadows roundabout. This was the "weed" that prompted Robert Frost years later to call his seventh volume *Steeple Bush*. Edna, with Eugen's approval, combined the flower name and the site of the estate to form "Steepletop." And Arthur Ficke, following her lead when he and Gladys bought a home in nearby Hillsdale, called his place "Hardhack," another common name for the same wildflower. Though it took much longer than they expected to remodel the house and reclaim the farmland, "Steepletop" came to be a true haven, the home base for Edna Millay and her husband for the next twenty-five years—the rest of their lives.

CHAPTER XI

Lyricist, Opera Librettist, Champion of Justice, Gentleman-Farmer's Wife: *Lover of Life*

FOR SEVERAL MONTHS life at Steepletop was a hectic, if delightful furore of carpentering, hammering, and drilling, until the poet, who could not keep from participating, hardly knew whether she was "writing with a pen or a screw driver." She was diverted, too, by the digging, pruning, and spraying of the orchards and berry patches. Eugen's nephew, Freddie, who was a landscape gardener, left his Long Island business in charge of his partner to provide professional advice and service. Edna, with her "earth-ecstatic soul" and curiosity, was eager to learn the whys and wherefores of running a fruit farm. However, she spent the greater part of the day working on poetry in her little "shanty" in the fields. She had fixed it up as a study with only a table, a chair, and a small pot-bellied stove to "roast her back" when the winter winds should come.

She and Eugen were usually up by six in the morning to meet the workmen who came plunging through the house. Edna, after surveying the work being done on all sides every day, would proceed to her private retreat, often accompanied by a kitten or one of the dogs they had acquired. Along the way she might be thrilled by the sight and song of the birds, or she might be tempted to pick wildflowers, but would not stop for long, if at all. She had in mind a fairytale opera libretto based on *Snow*

White and the Seven Dwarfs. She worked most of the morning and part of the afternoon, usually stopping in time to enjoy the sunset if the weather was clear. Before the summer was over she had completed the first act. However, she suddenly decided the idea would not suffice for grand opera. She wanted a different sort of theme entirely. As usual, she consulted those whose advice she valued, but kept her own counsel in the end. Arthur and Hal Bynner suggested that she use an American Indian legend since the opera was to be an American one. Edna disagreed, believing that it would be better to trace the roots of Americans, an English-speaking people, to Anglo-Saxon times. She finally turned to an old, half-historical legend from the Anglo-Saxon chronicles of tenth-century England, to which she added an ancient tale of Allhallows Eve.

She carefully researched the language of the period so that no words of Norman derivation or later would appear in the text. Only "authentic"—simple, terse, virile—phraseology was used. The play relates the story of Aethelwold, the king's henchman, who went to seek a wife for his liege and married the maid himself, with tragic consequences. Although the requirements for an opera libretto placed certain limitations upon her, the poet succeeded in making her characters move by their emotions to the music of poetry, particularly in the love scene of the second act. In his criticism of the published version of the play, Wilson was to write, "Miss Millay, who is perhaps a little deficient in visual imagination, writes verse as a pupil of Shakespeare and Bach; and in the second act of *Henchman* as a pupil not unworthy of her masters. In the exquisite music of the love scene, at once so irregular and so smoothly running, at once so exact and so free, she has reached one of the high points of her poetry. It is the magic strain that strikes the ear, seeming wordlessly—by the very clear outline of its phrases, the definiteness of its images—to convey the exaltation of young first love, all its awkwardness turned to beauty."

Her achievement was the more remarkable since she wrote the libretto with very little knowledge of the composer's score. She and Deems Taylor had only four conferences in the year and a half they spent creating the opera. Most of their exchange was by mail. (In sending him scene 2 of the second act, for example, she commented that she was "out of her mind" to hear his music for scene 1.) Moreover, she was working under various handicaps. In addition to the hubbub of the household, she could not get rid of her constant headache, which was now accompanied by dancing spots in front of her eyes. If she and Eugen left the farm at all during the next year or so, it was to consult doctors in hopes of discovering the cause of her mysterious malady and, if possible, a cure for it. The various specialists seemed as baffled as the patient, for apparently there was nothing wrong with her eyes. At one point she narrowly escaped having an unnecessary operation on her nose, recommended by a doctor in Augusta, Maine.

She was worried, too, about the health of her closest and most cherished friends, Arthur Ficke and Elinor Wylie. Arthur's cough was growing progressively worse, and his condition was alarming. In the summer of 1925 he and Gladys took a cottage at Saranac Lake, a health resort in upstate New York. Edna and Eugen were to come for a weekend, but Edna had a commitment for a reading and could not go; so she wrote a poem, which she dedicated, "To Gladys and Eugen, entreating them to take good care of Arthur." Later published in *The Buck in the Snow* under the title, "To the Wife of a Sick Friend," it is a tender and touching lyric. The opening line, "Shelter this candle from the wind," indicates at once a serious treatment of the "candle" theme. The poem, describing the effect of the light cast by this candle on "the cave wherein all wander lost," the terror and darkness if the wind should snuff out the flame, is a tribute to Arthur's poetic and brilliant spirit. Toward the end of 1925, since he had not improved at Saranac, it was decided that he should go to Santa Fe, New Mexico, where the high altitude and general climate was supposed to be helpful in curing tuberculosis.

As soon as the house was livable, Mrs. Millay and the rest of the family were invited to visit. Edna was eager to have her mother see and enjoy the beauty of the countryside, to be in her new home, and to share, at least in some degree, the life that she and Eugen made in the Berkshires. In spite of frequent arguments between Norma and Edna, the Millay sisters, their husbands, and their mother remained close as long as they lived. It was at this time that the three daughters agreed on a plan to contribute regular amounts a month to their mother's expenses, a practice they kept up religiously until her death.

Considering the myriad changes and constant activity, it is remarkable that the poet was able to persist with her manuscript for the opera libretto. But once she took on a commitment, she usually delivered the work on schedule. The only exception was the manuscript for *Hardigut*, and she never attempted another novel. Fiction was not her métier. And though she was not a dramatist either, the theater, and especially the verse play, was closer to her heart than prose, fiction or otherwise.

During the winter, Steepletop was "an island in the snow." It was an "expedition" even to get to Austerlitz for the mail; Eugen often went on snowshoes. But whatever the weather, Edna worked in her study every day, the hot fire in her little stove toasting her back as she continued work on her libretto through the first three months of 1926. Her headache and spotty vision persisted, but, as she wrote to Frank Adams, it was so beautiful there that even looking at the snow-covered hills and fields "through a dotted veil" didn't bother her. She was sending F. P. A. a note of thanks for having awarded "Nancy Boyd" a gold watch for the best "poem" printed in his column during the previous year. This *Conning Tower* poem, "The Armistice Day Parade," a satiric jingle, was the last thing Edna Millay published under her pseudonym; and, although she promised Frank Crowninshield she would write some more articles for *Vanity Fair* as soon as the libretto was finished, she did not have enough interest in the field to follow through. Only one more piece was published in the magazine, a poem under her own name in 1928.

They were snowed in for more than six weeks. When Eugen came back up the hill from the post office, he usually had an armload of mail for "Edna St. Vincent Millay," forwarded from Harper's, all sorts of fan letters, most of which included a request for information about the author's working habits, hobbies or experiences. Once or twice she classified her mail in a humorous account for the benefit of her family and Arthur. But whatever the caliber, all of it was an indication of her immense, and ever increasing, popularity.

With the winter came starvation or death by the hunter's gun for the deer and for the game birds. One afternoon toward dusk Edna glanced out of the window in her shanty and saw a big, antlered buck, standing with his doe in the nearby apple orchard. They were poised, listening, almost as if aware of her gaze. Then suddenly, their tails up, they moved as one, in lovely long leaps over the stone wall into the hemlock woods beyond. She worked a little while longer, then gathered up her things, wrapped herself in the warm outfit Eugen insisted she wear, and started toward the house. At the edge of the orchard, she looked over the wall, and to her horror saw the handsome buck lying dead, his "wild blood scalding the snow." Only a few minutes before, he had been so full of life, leaping with grace and ease at the side of his doe.

After the shock at the tragic sight caused by the cruel sport of killing, the poet was struck by the strangeness of death, with its power to still in one instant a beautifully mobile creature like the buck; and the equal strangeness of life that allowed the doe, probably under some hemlock tree a mile away by then, to stand looking out at the white world with "attentive eyes." Inevitably, the musing led to poetry, a penetrating view of the mysterious process governing life and death, the hairline breadth between the two. Edna could no more help turning emotional or mental experience into poetry than she could refrain from breathing the cold mountain air, or from loving nature and all its creatures.

She set up several feeding stations outside the end window, one of three or four in the long living room, and often sprinkled birdseed on the sill of her bedroom window, so she could watch her winged friends from dawn until dark. Once she went so far as to spread a few grains on her bedroom floor, opening the window beforehand; when a warbler came to peck at the seed on the sill, he flew inside for the food on the floor. As Edna and Eugen watched, the bird, after finishing, emitted a trill in the middle of the room and flew back outside. And though Eugen teased her about "running a hotel for the birds," Edna filled the feeders in summer as well as winter, and kept a record of birds seen or heard at various times. One spring day—May 13, 1938—she listed thirty-eight different kinds for Llewellyn Powys. A small bird guide was always close at hand on a table near the bird-window in the living room or upstairs, so she could consult it quickly, jotting down her own notes and observations, which often disagreed with the comments in the guide.

Toward the end of March in that winter of 1926, the libretto was nearing completion, and a tentative title, "The Saxon," was chosen. Both composer and librettist were as eager to have the Metropolitan begin rehearsals as the opera company itself was. By midsummer the extra wing of the house was completed, and Eugen was marketing berries and fuit. Mrs. Millay made a long stay at "Steepletop," putting up jams and jellies, which stood in rows on the table, the color shining in the sunlight, so pretty to see, Edna thought, admiring her mother's skill. Whenever she herself put up anything, which was not often, she considered it a miracle if the canning kept, or the preserves didn't turn to sugar.

For some inexplicable reason, her health did not improve as one would expect in view of her happiness in her new life, the surroundings, and especially her success as a poet, including the libretto, which was completed before the end of summer. She changed the title to *The King's Henchman,* and Harper's wanted to publish the play soon after the opera *première.* Deems had sent her some of the score, which she played on the piano and found enchanting. Joseph Urban, the famous architect and set designer for the Metropolitan, was going to do the sets for *Henchman,* as Edna had hoped. All was running with comparative smoothness at the farm. Yet her headache, and the puzzling spots in front of her eyes continued with maddening monotony. In the midst of everything she was trying to do, including a prose piece for a book of poems by her old friend Abbie Huston Evans, which Harper's agreed to publish if Edna Millay wrote the preface, she would sometimes have to drop it all and go to another specialist for one more examination. Everyone who knew about the constant headache offered advice.

Among the many was a psychoanalyst who cornered Edna Millay at a cocktail party and tried to get at the cause of her trouble. This was probably Merrill Moore, who was a friend of poets, and who wrote over a thousand love sonnets himself, for relaxation. According to Max Eastman's account in his book of biographical memoirs, *Great Companions,* the analyst invited the poet to come into the library with him, and when they were alone, by a series of circuitous questions, came around to asking if it ever occurred to her that she might, perhaps subconsciously, have an "occasional erotic impulse" toward someone of her own sex. Edna's typical reaction was to exclaim, "Oh, you mean I'm homosexual! Of course I am, and heterosexual, too; but what's that got to do with my headache?" Her forthright retort no doubt put an end to the discussion, or to a possible cure of her headache by means of psychotherapy. But if she was not speaking tongue-in-cheek, if she was jesting in earnest, her remark indicates that she was as dead-set against analysis as she had been ten years earlier, in the days of Floyd Dell's courtship. She always scoffed at the idea that physical illness might be a manifestation of emotional problems, aside from such ordinary things as making oneself sick with worry, as she felt her mother did before Kathleen's book of poetry was published. But she would not countenance the theory that her peculiar spotted vision and almost constant headache, which lasted well over a year, was in any way due to her complex emotional makeup.

Arthur and Gladys had invited her and Eugen to visit them in Santa Fe at their expense as soon as the play was finished. Arthur seemed to be improving, although he did not adhere too closely to doctor's orders, and the Fickes both felt that Edna's condition might clear up in the high altitude of New Mexico. About the middle of October, after Edna had received a printed, paperbound copy of "the first act entire, words and music," which carried on the cover the exciting words, "Solely for use at the first performance of the Metropolitan Opera Company, New York," she and Eugen went out to Santa Fe for a few weeks' stay. It was a relief just to think about going somewhere for a good time with close friends "instead of to consult a doctor," as she wrote to an aunt and uncle in Maine.

The Fickes, especially Arthur, were overjoyed to see them. Witter Bynner was also in Santa Fe, and it was a merry household. Edna spent part of the time preparing the manuscript of "Aethelwold" (*The King's Henchman*) for the publishers, assisted by Arthur, who freely counselled her on changes she wanted to make. The sun was strong, the air clear, and the atmosphere in the house sparkling; and by December 6, the work was ready to be mailed to Harper's. Now the poet could relax completely and enjoy the southwest. They went to a Zuni Indian village to attend the ceremonial dances held at that season, a thrilling sight. The trip took them past the Petrified Forest, through the Painted Desert, and home by way of the Enchanted Mesa. It was during this visit that Edna wrote "Pueblo Pot," a rather strange lyric, involving the ancient shards of broken clay found in a courtyard where a pair of flickers were flaunting their colors and song.

The day they were to leave for Zuni, Eugen came down with an intestinal attack of the amoeba trouble that often plagued him, and could not accompany them. He told Vincent and Gladys to go on ahead, and that he would join them in two or three days. When they got to the little hotel on the desert, the two women took a room together. Then, when Eugen sent word that he was coming, Vincent said to the desk clerk, "Will you reserve a room for Mrs. Ficke? Mr. Eugen Boissevain is coming to stay with me."

The astonished clerk said the hotel policy prohibited such arrangements; she had registered as Miss Edna St. Vincent Millay, as she always did, whether on an official tour or otherwise. She was an ardent member of the Lucy Stone League, called after the early suffragist leader who retained her maiden name even though married; and Edna Millay, like Ruth Hale, Heywood Broun's wife, a suffragist writer and friend of hers, staunchly observed the rules of the Stone League by using her maiden name at all times. Now, instead of enlightening the clerk— whether out of some quirk, or because she thought he should have known who she was—she became angry, growing red in the face, all but stamping her foot. She refused to say she was married to Eugen until the clerk proved completely unmoved and refused to register Gladys.

Then Vincent finally told him that Eugen was her husband, and when the clerk asked why she didn't say so in the first place, she demanded, "My dear sir, don't you know famous women always use their own names?"

At first Gladys thought she must be joking, but she evidently was not, and the desk clerk in New Mexico obviously had never heard of her.

Arthur was writing in spite of his illness and restricted working hours. He was not strong enough to make the journey to Zuni, but he was considerably cheered by their stay in Santa Fe, and the poets had many an exchange aside from the preparation of Edna's manuscript. Altogether, the sojourn was just what both needed to bring them back to better health. Just before the end of the Boissevains' stay, one of the New Mexico papers carried a saccharine feature story about Vincent, headed dramatically, "Poet Wins Battle with Death," telling about her recent peculiar, puzzling illness in sensational terms, and mentioning briefly that the Fickes were living in Santa Fe for reasons of Arthur's health. Accompanying the article was a murky drawing of "Miss Millay" and Arthur Ficke, "deep in work on *The King's Henchman* at the Fickes' mountain retreat near Santa Fe." Arthur, with typical biting humor, crossed out the word "Death" in the caption, and wrote above it, "Misprint for 'Booze.'" It was his way of poking fun at false publicity stories, at the same time making light of the continual trials with sickness that he and Vincent seemed to suffer. Edna and Eugen left in time to be at "Steepletop" for Christmas; they had been gone exactly two months. Two weeks after their return, Vincent sent a copy of her poem concerning Arthur's precarious health and brilliant spirit, inscribed "with love, Jan 8, 1927." At the time the lyric was composed, when the Fickes were at Saranac Lake (as previously related), she had neglected to write a personal inscription on the original.

"Steepletop" was thickly covered with snow, which turned pink in the sunset every afternoon, the color deepened by the bright blue shadows of evening; and, whether she was writing a letter or a poem, Edna would stop to stare out of the window until the glow faded away, as she did on January 13, when she was writing to her mother about the details of the opera presentation. February 17 had been set as the *première* of *The King's Henchman*. The Metropolitan granted no extra passes to composer or librettist for the occasion, so Edna bought a ticket for her mother, who was to come with Norma and Charlie or Kathleen and Howard.

Opening night was a gala event indeed. A spectacular audience, including celebrities from all the arts as well as high-society patrons, filled the hall to capacity. From the moment the gold curtains of the Metropolitan Opera House parted on the first scene of *The King's Henchman,* the opera was a success. The audience applauded the set, the singers, and at the close of the first act, the opera itself. Edna, who had been waiting tensely for the reactions of the spectators, sat back relieved and enjoyed the rest of the performance. Cora Millay, from seat C108 in the third row of the orchestra must have felt that the rewards of her sacrifice and hard work were sweet indeed; but she was calm in her pleasure, and considered the dues no more than just. She had known from the start that Vincent would be a successful and famous poet. And when, at the close of the final act, there was tremendous applause for the cast, followed by cries for the composer and librettist, and Edna appeared onstage with Deems Taylor to acknowledge the ovation, little Mrs. Millay nodded approvingly at Edna's brief expression of gratitude: "I thank you —I love you all." Taylor, also bowing, seconded her words gallantly, with equal simplicity: "That's just what I was going to say," he told the audience.

This was probably the high point in the Millay family's history. All three sisters were well launched in their careers, although the younger two were not as successful as Edna. Norma was singing the leading role in Mozart's *La Finta Giardinera,* presented by the newly formed Intimate Opera Company at the Mayfair Theater; and Kathleen's first novel, *The Wayfarer,* had been published in the fall, while her first volume of poetry, *The Evergreen Tree,* was coming out in spring. All three daughters were happily married. Much as Mrs. Millay might profess impartiality, Vincent was naturally the star of her life.

The King's Henchman received excellent reviews from the music critics and was given four or five performances directly following the *première:* on February 21 and 28, and twice in March, playing to capacity audiences. The production was taken

on a highly successful road tour. The opera did much to sweep
away the barriers against American opera and opera sung in
English; yet there have been few written since then to match
Henchman in quality or popularity. The published version appeared less than a month afterward and within three months was
in its nineteenth printing. It was dedicated to "Eugen Jan Boissevain," without indicating his relationship to Edna St. Vincent
Millay in any way. Like most professional women in the arts, she
kept her own name in private life, and many people who read
the dedication did not know that this was her husband. In May,
Edna received a deluxe edition of the play, signed by all the
singers and staff members of the Metropolitan Opera Company.
She had never thought autographs very interesting, but when she
saw that "bunch of names" and read Deems Taylor's touching
inscription, "To whom so much of it belongs," it made her gasp,
and somehow "brought tears" to her eyes whenever she opened
the copy to show it to someone.

The year 1927, which began so auspiciously, ushered in a por-
tentous period in her life, one that involved an increasing social
consciousness, sense of justice, and a greater concern for human
welfare and world affairs as well as in the arts. Two days after her
own *première*, she wrote to Alexander Woollcott, then drama
editor of the New York *World*, on behalf of the Intimate Opera
Company's production of *La Finta*, not necessarily because Norma
was in it, or because she thought the young people who organized
the opera company "had worked hard and deserved encouragement," but because they had given the people of New York a
fine presentation of a work of art, and it would be to the benefit
of the city as a whole to foster and sustain the Intimate Opera
Company.

In April, she sent a scathing letter to the League of American
Penwomen which had condemned Elinor Wylie because of the
latter's personal life; she had eloped with Bill Benét and was sub-
sequently divorced from her husband in Washington. Edna had
been invited to be the guest of honor at a League function in
Washington later in the month. She had written that she was
unable to attend, but that she was honored by the invitation.
Now she wrote with indignation and anger that it was not possible

for an organization that had insulted one of the most distinguished writers of the day, Elinor Wylie, to honor *her*. She would consider it unbecoming for her to sit as guest of honor at a gathering of writers which placed the "circumspection of one's personal life" above literary accomplishment. She ended her denunciation by saying that she, too, was "eligible for their disesteem," and wished to be struck from their lists, to share with Elinor Wylie a "brilliant exile" from their "fusty province." She enclosed a note to her "darling" with the letter, sending it to Elinor with instructions to read it over, change the address if necessary "on the typewriter," and mail it at once.

She was full of concern for her friend's health during this year. Elinor had been straining herself far beyond her physical capacity to publish two novels, *Jennifer Lorn* and *The Venetian Glass Nephew*, in addition to two volumes of poetry, *Black Armour* and *Trivial Breath*, in the four years since Edna had met her. During their last visit, she had shown signs of breaking under that strain when she and Edna were alone. She had suddenly buried her face in her hands for an instant, after confiding that the doctors had predicted fatal consequences if she continued her long hours of arduous labor at her writing desk, her late parties, though these were now less frequent than formerly, and her refusal to "avoid all alcoholic beverages" or to stop smoking. Edna's heart had been torn between the desire to comfort her beloved friend and the will to keep from breaking down herself. In the end she did not even stroke the other's bowed head, but maintained a sympathetic silence till Elinor's mood passed and she brought her body upright with a crackling remark about her weakness. Some time later in 1927, Edna wrote a beautiful "Song for a Lute," expressing her deep anguish for the poet she revered, the friend whose life she feared for, "loving her utterly" as she did.

"Steepletop" was a bower of beauty in the spring of 1927, and late in May Edna sent a note to Tess Root Adams saying that she must be sure to come up to spend her birthday at the farm, bringing the baby, Anthony, recently born to F. P. A. and his wife. Edna, in furnishing the living room had included two pianos, on which the two friends celebrated Tess' birthday by performing duets. The room, which had been remodeled into a long drawing room by combining two small parlors, was sunny, comfortable, and had the charm of several bizarre touches. A startling head of Sappho, done in bronze, painted black, with fierce eyes whose black irises stared out from glowing whites, mounted on a marble pedestal, had been sent to Edna Millay by an Italian admirer of her work, and stood at one side of the white brick fireplace, an aggressive icon of the Muse. Sofas and chairs were ample enough for the relaxation of numerous guests in days to come. One winged chair in front of the end window soon came to be "Edna's chair," because she always sat there watching the birds busy at the feeding stations when the weather kept her indoors. On the walls were two exotic green hangings embroidered with golden birds, which Edna and Eugen had brought home from India.

In a small room off the landing of the stairway, Edna had set up a den or library, which eventually became her poetry room. Here were the complete works of the great poets in all languages, from Sappho in Greek to Catullus and Vergil in Latin, to Dante in Italian, to Baudelaire, Rimbaud, and other French poets, to Shakespeare, Chaucer, and John Donne in English. In short, as Vincent Sheean said, "All the good poets that have ever written" were represented in their native languages. In later years, a portrait of Robinson Jeffers, one of the few writers of free verse for whom Edna came to feel true admiration, hung on the wall, along with a pen sketch of Shelley and two sailing charts of Penobscot Bay. A sign commanding SILENCE in large red letters completed the decorations. When Edna was in the house, and was not writing, she could usually be found at her place beside the "bird window," or here, in her poetry room. On days when she did not work in her shanty preparing manuscripts on the typewriter, she was apt to write anywhere in the house and at all hours, using the hard-cover ten-cent store notebooks which she preferred, to jot down notes or block out the first draft of a poem. She kept notebooks and pencils handy all over the house, and always on her bed table, in case she was struck by an idea in the middle of the night when she could not sleep, a frequent occurrence. She seldom spoke of her own creative process, but once observed that the initial draft was set down in a fever of excitement, assuming form magically, as if conjured out of steam. Then came careful study, deliberation and rewrite, "chipping away at words in a painful kind of sculpture." Sometimes she and Eugen would discuss an idea for a poem early in the morning before they got dressed, and at ten o'clock they might still be talking, to Eugen's great delight. "Any day I may have an hour or more of extraordinary beauty," he told someone happily.

The farm was in good working order that spring; they picked about ten quarts of strawberries a day through June. Shortly after Tess' visit, Edna had to have another operation; it was just a "tiny" one, but it again left her weakened. She was never entirely free of health problems from the time of her serious intestinal trouble in 1922; and in spite of Eugen's solicitude, his determination that she consult the best diagnosticians and surgeons when anything went wrong, she never regained full health for the rest of her life. And although they had servants part of the time to do the heavy work and cooking, she became exhausted easily and was often forced to spend a morning if not a whole day in bed.

However, when driven by the power of poetry, or some burning issue of the times, Edna Millay seemed fired by an inexhaustible supply of energy. She had been involved to some extent ever since her return from Europe with the movement to save the two anarchists, Sacco and Vanzetti, from the electric chair, a fate to which the two men had been consigned by an unrelenting jury and judge, on insufficient evidence. In the seven years since their conviction on April 15, 1920, innumerable committees had been formed to aid in the attempts to petition a new trial; but all appeals had been denied by Judge Thayer of Massachusetts, who took advantage of a state law allowing the judge who tried a case initially to refuse appeals for retrial. A committee of literary figures had joined the movement midway in the struggle, and Edna Millay, her sister Kathleen, along with Robert Benchley, Dorothy Parker, John Dos Passos, Maxwell Anderson, John Howard Lawson, Arthur Ficke, and Witter Bynner, wrote on the subject in their respective fields and sent letters and signed petitions on behalf of the prisoners. As the months and years passed, the basic gentleness and honesty of the two Italians were revealed, and many who had originally believed them guilty reversed their opinions or began to doubt the decision of the court. It was a celebrated case, comparable to the famous Dreyfus case in France. World figures like Albert Einstein and George Bernard Shaw wrote strong articles criticizing the United States courts of justice, and appealing for flexibility and a fair trial for the condemned men. The United States embassies in Europe were picketed by protest marchers as controversy over the case spread.

The date of the execution had finally been set for August 23, 1927, and the judge remained obdurate. As the date grew near, there were strikes led by union members in New York, Chicago, and other big cities; a Ford plant in Argentina was bombed, and riots occurred in France and England. The fate of a fish peddler, Bartolomeo Vanzetti, and a shoemaker, Nicola Sacco, had aroused half the world. Edna, who had gone to Boston a number of times to attend meetings at the headquarters of the Defense Committee, now went again to join her fellow writers in protest and to plead with the Governor of Massachusetts, Alvan T. Fuller. She and Eugen drove down from "Steepletop," and early on the morning of August 22, she was standing in the line of paraders in front of headquarters, holding high her placard, ready to march at the given signal. They were to move in groups, marching from the Defense Committee's office in Boston proper to the outlying Charlestown area, where Sacco and Vanzetti had been held for some time in the state penitentiary.

The moment the first group of marchers reached the Boston Common, the police moved in and shouted, "You are warned that you are violating the law. If you do not disperse, you will be arrested!" But the paraders, continuing their march, acted as if they had not heard. Edna, her face set with intense determination, led the group of writers with John Dos Passos and "Jack" Lawson. Two patrol wagons rolled up to the first group, and they saw each marcher dragged down Beacon Street in the viselike grip of a policeman. But they kept moving steadfastly toward the Common. At the shouted warning, Edna only raised her card the higher, and instantly felt it hauled down and wrested from her hands by a burly policeman. She and Dorothy Parker, along with the others, were taken to the nearest precinct station, charged with violating an ordinance against "sauntering and loitering," and held on bail. Eugen, who did not participate in the protest, but wanted to be

on hand to protect his "Aidna," stood bail for her and several
other writers. They were released pending trial on October 16.
Eugen, hovering over Edna like a guardian angel, tried to make
her rest, but she was burning with outrage that was intensified
by the terrifying nearness of the hour of execution. She must
see the Governor immediately!

Fuller, who had previously seen Robert Benchley, granted her
an audience in the afternoon. She was in his office a full hour and
presented a plea for clemency with all the vigor she could sum-
mon. But after she had seen him, and watched his face as he
listened in stony silence, promising at the end to think it over,
Edna could not let the matter rest. She sat down and wrote him
an ardent, eloquent letter, exhorting him to think carefully about
the story she had told him in the afternoon—of a similar case in
Maine, when an innocent victim of injustice had died by capital
punishment because of a verdict based on insufficient evidence.
She called on Judge Fuller to "think a long, long way back to
Jesus" and to try to imagine which way He would have turned
in this hour; then the judge would know that he was moving in
the wrong direction, in a cruel decision that had already aroused
the anger and animosity of half the world. If Edna St. Vincent
Millay's symbolic middle name had not left its mark on her actions
before, the crusading spirit of the saint in her makeup now rose
with all the fire of the biblical martyrs and champions of the
downtrodden. St. Vincent, who established the Order of the
Sisters of Mercy, might have been guiding her hand as she wrote,
"I cry to you with a million voices. . . . Exert the clemency which
your high office affords." She sent the letter by special messenger
to the Governor's mansion. She also issued a statement to the
press containing her story about the miscarriage of justice in
Maine.

Then she joined the group of writers who were part of a gathering in Salem Street bordering the Boston Common, standing in a
deathwatch directly in the shadow of the Old North Church, one
of many such watches held throughout the country on that fateful
night. Police in turn watched them with a wary eye, armed for
trouble; but for the most part, the crowds were silent, bereaved
before the deed was done. Prayers were said; Edna read the first

of five poems she was to compose in commiseration for the condemned prisoners, "Justice Denied in Massachusetts." The title
was a variation of the sign she had carried, but the imagery of the
poem came from nature. In it she speaks of the cloud that covers
the earth and has soured the soil so that the larkspur cannot
blossom nor the corn grow into tall blades: evil has blighted
them. She counsels her fellow sufferers that the only thing to do
is to "abandon our gardens and go home / And sit in the sitting
room . . . until we die." She mentions "the quack and the weed"
that we have unknowingly nurtured, the "unfruited tree," the
blue hayrack, all earth symbols of suffering that will outlast her
generation.

Less than half an hour after midnight Sacco and Vanzetti had
both gone to their deaths in the electric chair. The people in the
Boston Common remained silent and grieved. Then they separated and went their ways. In New York's Union Square, ten
thousand people wept openly; the violence the police had expected was overcome by sorrow.

Edna and Eugen would have gone right back to "Steepletop,"
but she had to appear in court the next morning, where she and
the others who had been arrested were arraigned and fined ten
dollars each. They all pleaded not guilty; they had merely been
exercising their rights of freedom of expression and peaceful per-
suasion. When the police sergeant who made the arrests identified
Edna and started to describe the placard she was carrying before
he wrenched it from her, she objected indignantly, "I did not
carry that card!" He claimed that she certainly did, but her
retort in no uncertain terms was that the sign she carried bore
the words, "If These Men Are Executed, Justice is Dead in Massachusetts!" Her cohorts applauded, and they all announced they
would appeal the case to the State Supreme Court. Arthur Gar-
field Hays was their counsel and, they hoped, Clarence Darrow.
They would spend a fortnight in jail if necessary. She and five
others who were singled out to set an example to the public, were
determined to do "Anything to keep people from going to sleep
on the subject."

Edna was not only saddened, but infuriated by the gross injustice, and the tendency of the general public to avoid facing

the truth by carping on trivial details. Her statement to the press brought a letter, printed in the New York *World*, pointing out several errors in her account of the last hanging in the state of Maine; it was followed by a number of letters in Maine newspapers asserting that both Miss Millay and her assailant had been wrong; and offering still more variations of the story. Cora Millay, who had kept track of the Defense Committee's efforts through the years, occasionally giving her own active support, carefully clipped all the letters from the Maine papers and sent them to her daughter at "Steepletop." On the basis of these, Edna wrote a letter to the *World*, a "swell" letter, she thought, in which she sought to establish that the succession of mistakes, all committed by people who were convinced that they were right, only proved her point: that human beings, with the best intentions in the world, often make mistakes, and therefore Governor Fuller might have made a mistake. She hoped her reasoning would "shut up the raucous mouths of the whole darned bunch," but it had little effect.

Toward the end of October, she wrote her mother that she had just finished an article for the *Outlook*, taking precious time from her poetry writing which was at fever-pitch just then, because she felt it important to keep people aroused. And the article, entitled "Fear," had the passion of dramatic poetry. Largely a sweeping and stinging castigation of the indifference of the American people toward the injustice that reigned without protest for the most part, the piece was almost biblical in tone. It was as if an oracle was speaking, warning of the dangers that lay in the path of mankind if he continued to "quarter the troops of unkindness, hypocrisy and greed in his house." Without mentioning the names of either Sacco or Vanzetti, or any statistics of the trial, she wrote a heated jeremiad in moving and poetic prose in the hope of awakening in American people an awareness of the enormous miscarriage of justice that had taken place on August 23, and that could take place again if they did not change the laws and rid their lives of the real criminals—greed and blind prejudice.

Some years after the Sacco-Vanzetti executions the Massachusetts law was revised and improved in some respects: a judge who tried a case could no longer refuse appeals on it; instead, the State judicial court rules on new trials. But Edna Millay's article, published November 9, 1927, instead of bringing enlightenment and rue to the reader, brought invective and denunciation on its author. She was called a Communist, an advocate of anarchy, and a "parlor pink" for her efforts to insure a true measure of justice in the future; and many of the letters that poured into the editor of *Outlook* condemned the article as "vicious, false, wicked," or "a ludicrous piece of nonsense." The one piece of mail she received in regard to the article which brought her pleasure and comfort was a note from Witter Bynner, full of praise for the writing, and admiration for her courage. When she thanked "Dearest Hal," she told him that she read his words over and over, tears of happiness in her eyes, and she put the little note away, saving it to read again when she was sad.

Disillusioned temporarily, she nevertheless continued to write poems relating to the case, in company with all the other writers who felt as she did—novelists, playwrights and other poets—and it may very well be that the literature produced by the case aided in bringing about legal reform. A Sacco-Vanzetti Memorial was established to hold annual meetings on August 23 in the Old North Church, at which Edna read her poem, "Justice Denied in Massachusetts," and the further works, "Hangman's Oak," "The Anguish," "Wine from These Grapes," and "To Those without Pity." All were published in her next volume.

From 1927 on, Edna and Eugen spent part of each winter in a warm climate, and usually part of the spring or late fall on tour. Edna occasionally went alone, but as a rule Eugen accompanied her, making the hotel arrangements, seeing to it that she was not disturbed by phone calls, reporters, and other interruptions that might prevent her from resting or writing between appearances. Now and then his overzealous care was resented by professional people who had scheduled the poet to read. When Robert Frost's oldest daughter, Lesley, who ran a highly successful bookshop, *The Open Book*, in Pittsfield, Massachusetts, invited Edna Millay to appear in one of a series of poetry readings, she planned and she naturally expected the poet to greet people afterward. The bookshop patrons and friends of the Frost girls were eagerly looking forward to meeting the popular and much-heralded Edna

Millay. The shop was jammed with poetry lovers and appreciative listeners, many of whom had been promised an introduction by Lesley. But just as they came crowding up, after Edna had read the last poem and acknowledged the applause, Eugen rose up out of nowhere like a protective genie, a short sable cape over his arm. Placing it around her shoulders he said, "Come, darling, we must get you out of here!" and he whisked her off before a single person was able to shake her hand. Lesley, aside from being chagrined at having to face the disappointed audience, was rather a forthright feminist herself, and did not see how one like Edna Millay could allow herself to be pampered and led around like a child by her husband. And indeed, it was a riddle to everyone who had seen Edna Millay in action during the recent controversy, but did not know her well enough to realize that Eugen's protective attitude filled a long-neglected need in her life, or that this was another paradox in her complex makeup. She was feminist and feminine, militant and reticent, intellectual and emotional.

Moreover, apart from looking out for her interests, Eugen left her free, to write, to think, and to live and love as she pleased. During the months they were at "Steepletop," she concentrated on a new book as soon as the latest was off the press. Her life was in her poetry; her husband occupied himself in running the house and the farm. Edna once remarked that she and Eugen "lived like two bachelors," and both seemed content to have it so.

In the fall of 1927 and the winter of 1928, Edna was writing many of the poems which where to form her volume entitled, *The Buck in the Snow,* after the profound, philosophical lyric evoked by the sight of the dead buck she had discovered that winter day, not long after seeing the buck and his doe leap over the wall into the hemlock woods. The question of life and death, the imposing inevitability of death still engrossed or terrified or angered her. Eventually, out of her meditation grew a brooding ballad, "Moriturus," in which she conceded that she might "dicker with death" if she could have the light of the sun and the peace of the grave at the same time, if her senses could still be aware of life's beauty, its earthly joys like the "flight of the golden flicker" while her body was at rest, relieved of all its aches. She

knows only too well, however, that Death is "nothing at all," that
when the body becomes dust not even the thrust of the summer
gnat consoles it; so, no matter how ill or broken her body becomes
she will fight Death to the finish: he will have to drag her away
from life.

The unusual concept, different from her earlier invectives
against death in that it begins with a feeling of compromise, ends
with even greater defiance than before. The short, staccato four-
line stanzas in rhyming double iambics (abab, cdcd, etc.), provide a half-mournful, half-militant song that sets the keynote of
The Buck in the Snow as the opening poem. This was to be a
more somber volume, and, in a subdued tone, her most lyrical to
date. There were only a few sonnets to be included, one of them
the noted, "Sonnet to Gath," cited by her friend Edmund Wilson
as among her finest; and the one inspired seven years before in
Truro, "On Hearing a Symphony of Beethoven." Here also was
the rarely quoted but remarkable, "To Jesus on His Birthday,"
decrying the commercialism of Christmas, the fact that the message of Peace had been forgotten "for the thousand years since
the angel rolled away the stone."

In preparing and proofing this volume, she had the help of
Arthur Ficke, who with Gladys returned to the east to live in the
late spring of 1928. They spent several months at "Steepletop"
with Edna and Eugen and at first planned to build a house on
adjacent land. The four friends were frequently joined by Max
Eastman and Eliena, who also thought of moving to the Berkshires, largely because Edna and Eugen were there. Eliena, like
Gladys, was a painter, and preferred to live in the country. Croton
was getting "pretty thick," so they were planning to sell the
Mount Airy place and move into the neighborhood of Austerlitz.
In August, Arthur and Gladys heard of property they could buy
with a good house on it, just fourteen miles away from "Steepletop." They decided it would be quicker and less expensive to do
the small amount of remodeling necessary than to build a house,
so they closed the deal in summer and stayed on with Edna and
Eugen until their place, "Hardhack," was ready. It was a joyful
comfort to Edna to know that her beloved poet-friend and still
her "spiritual adviser" would always be close by. When, in 1920,

she had written that they "would never escape from each other," she must have sensed that their lives would always be in some measure intertwined. Max and Eliena eventually settled at Martha's Vineyard, where he established something of a nudist colony during the summer months, but they still came to "Steeple-top" often. The circle of intimate friends was completed by Elinor Wylie and Bill Benét, who drove over from New Canaan occasionally, when Elinor felt she could make the trip. Edna was increasingly concerned about her friend's condition, which grew more precarious with the added strain of each new book.

The Buck in the Snow was published in September, 1928. It was not received by either critics or readers in America with the enthusiasm that greeted her earlier volumes, probably because the gravity of the poems did not match Edna Millay's public image. To most readers she was a less serious and more amorous personality. Those who looked for more of the bittersweet love lyrics of *Second April* and *The Harp-Weaver* were disappointed; and those who still expected to find the gay flippancy of the *Figs* were disgruntled. Max Eastman, one of the few who had high praise for the volume, rating the title poem as "one of the most perfect lyrics in our language, a painting of life and death unexcelled . . . ," observed in his review in the *Nation* that it was "fashionable" here to be disappointed in the book.[1] Most readers did not expect Edna Millay to be so contemplative or objective. They wanted her to be passionate, forever flaming youth.

Such reviews of course were deeply disappointing to the poet; but, as she wrote in a note of appreciation to Max, in England, it was a different story: the British press had universally praised the volume, placing *The Buck in the Snow* above any she had published so far. She was astonished and thrilled at the wonderful response to her poetry in England. It was around this time that Thomas Hardy stated that in his opinion the two great contributions America had made to the twenties were its architectural innovations and Edna St. Vincent Millay. Whether the reviews were discouraging or gratifying, however, they did not cause the

[1] Much later Wilson lauded many of the poems in *Buck* for their lyrical quality and objectivity, including "Dawn," "The Bobolink," "The Cameo," and the telling "Portrait" of himself.

poet to change her ways. She wrote as she felt, and in the style which she considered best, or the best for her, no matter what the dictates of modernism, T. S. Eliot and others who arbitrarily laid down laws to the contrary.

In the fall of 1928, she went on a long and wearing tour, which ended in Brooklyn at the Academy of Music. She had been worried about Elinor Wylie all the time she was away; and thought to herself that as soon as this last "chore" was done, she would rush up to New Canaan to see her lovely friend. It was the evening of December 17 and she was backstage getting ready to go on, when one of the people on the staff of the organization that had booked her, without knowing of the close attachment between the two poets, casually mentioned that Elinor Wylie had just died (December 16, 1928). It had been very sudden: she was at home, spending a quiet Sunday for a change, since she and her husband had been going out a good deal. She had just finished preparing her last volume, significantly entitled *Angels and Earthly Creatures,* and was pausing to catch her breath before beginning to write again. Late that afternoon she had been reading in her novel, *Jennifer Lorn,* and near dusk she closed the book with a bang, saying in her definite way of speaking, "Yes, *Jennifer Lorn is* better than *The Venetian Glass Nephew!"* With that she decided to start getting supper. Only a few moments later, Bill heard her calling from the kitchen, and when he ran in to her, he found her fainting. She wanted a glass of water, and as he gave it to her, she murmured, "Is that all it is?" He carried her to the bedroom, where she lasted only a short while before she died.

All this Edna learned later; at the moment she was stunned. She felt as if a crushing blow had hit at the vitals of her own life. There was no time to collect herself before she had to make her appearance. She walked out on the stage, and, instead of her own poetry, began to recite the lines of Elinor Wylie that she had loved and learned by heart. It was a beautiful gesture, and one made spontaneously, unconsciously. She hardly knew what she was doing.

Like Robert Frost's bereavement for Edward Thomas, Edna Millay's for Elinor Wylie did not find its full expression until ten years later. Now she wrote only a few heartbroken lines, beginning, "When I think of you / I die too," included in the dedication of *Fatal Interview* to the departed poet, but never printed elsewhere. She also wrote "1928," which later became part of the elegiac series of six poems she was to compose as a memorial to her dear, witty, beautiful, and unique friend. At "Steepletop" ten days later, December 28, she sent a long, intimate, almost empathic letter to "Dearest Bill" Benét, much the same sort of communication that Frost had sent to Helen Thomas—a letter of consolation such as only a close friend could give. She told Bill that she and Eugen had been saving a tiny keg of choice wine, "Seven Shires," just for Elinor, and when he came there they would give it to him, and they "will all drink to their 'beautiful, brilliant, adorable one.'" She and Eugen spoke of her constantly; she was never "off their tongues" for very long. When they were with Arthur and Gladys, all four spoke of her, and Arthur read aloud a "marvelous" letter he had received from Elinor in answer to a letter from him about her poem, "Mortal Image." Edna counseled Bill not to torture himself by thinking that he might have been better to Elinor, or remembering tactless words he perhaps had said. As Edna was doing, he must think mostly of the happy times they had, of the things that gave her joy, not the ones that wounded her. He must remember how delightful Elinor was, and how funny: "so gay and splendid about tragic things, so comically serious about silly ones." Vincent felt "there was nobody like her at all." Those words must have reminded him of Elinor's strikingly similar words about Edna Millay: "She is like nothing at all but herself. . . ." These two remarkable poets recognized each other's qualities in every way. Prophetically Elinor had added of Edna: "when she and this generation are gone, the die which stamped her style will be broken."

To Stephen Vincent and Rosemary Benét, Edna wrote nearly two months later, after congratulating "Steve" on the success of his "splendid piece of work," *John Brown's Body* that, the loss of Elinor was still so great that she wondered how people could bear such things. Her brief paragraph was one of those rare expressions of grief that are in a language of their own, fully comprehended only by fellow artists. In *The Buck in the Snow,* written over a period of several years and published two months before Elinor died, she had been preoccupied with the theme of death as opposed to life; and in the prescient lyric, "Dirge without Music," she sang in subdued rage against death which took the lovely, intelligent, and tender people down into the dust. She could not be consoled by the fact that their deceased bodies blossomed again as roses. The flowers could in no measure replace the loss of loved ones; she was "not resigned," nor would she ever be to the law of life and death. Quite possibly she was brooding over Elinor's dangerous condition and incipient fatality at the time of writing the poem.

Ten years after it was published, one of her critics [2] deliberately misinterpreted the phrase "not resigned," which he took out of context and used as a subtitle for an article seeking to establish the proposition that Edna Millay, though a woman in her forties, was "not resigned" to loss of youth and desire for sexual love. He probably found his premise in the fact that Edna, staggering under the blow of Elinor's death, was more vehemently than ever "not resigned" and, by way of showing her defiance after the wave of grief had somewhat subsided, determined to pack every moment, while she herself was still above the ground, with the joy of living. And despite further blows, sorrows, and unexpected reverses during the next ten years, she carried out to the letter the hedonistic facet of her mystique.

Slowly, one by one, additions and improvements were made at "Steepletop." After Eugen gave up his import business, he had only a small income from some investments, so their household expanded according to the financial rewards of Edna's careers. *The King's Henchman* brought ten thousand dollars in gate receipts to the librettist, which, with the royalties from the widely circulated published version, plus the fees for a successful reading tour, probably went into building a garage with a studio apartment above it, reached by an outside stairway. Her shanty in the field was made into a small guest house. Finally a tennis court, a swimming pool, and a sunken garden were added; the last was

[2] James McBride Dabbs, in the *South Atlantic Quarterly*, 1938: "Edna St. Vincent Millay; NOT Resigned."

more or less a family project, with Mrs. Millay contributing three white lilac bushes and some yellow tulips from her garden in Maine, and other relatives sending bulbs or hardy annuals. Then there were many gay parties, house parties, and nude bathing parties on summer nights. They always went swimming in their or Gladys and Arthur's pool without bathing suits when "just our own crowd" was present.

Eugen was a gracious host, inventive in entertaining. One of Edna's favorite relaxations was tennis, at which she was a skillful if somewhat erratic player, and often there were tennis matches at "Steepletop." In organizing them, Eugen set up regular rules and presented the winning team with a loving cup. He and Edna sometimes arranged rehearsal-recitals by students at the Bloch Hillsdale Music College, which took place in the long living room. One summer two students from the school stayed in the guest house. More than once writer-friends stayed there to work.

When they were alone at "Steepletop," Eugen prevented any unnecessary interruptions of the poet's work. If they had a telephone at the time, he would run to answer it after the first ring so that she would not be disturbed by shrill repetitions. Sometimes they would have it disconnected for months to insure quiet and privacy. However, when Edna felt the need of company, or when she had just published a volume of poetry and wanted to have a change of pace, they would take a trip into New York to see Broadway shows and go shopping, if funds permitted. According to a reliable source, they were never as "rich" as people imagined, or as Edna let everyone believe. Their income like that of the Fitzgeralds and many other literary and theatrical figures, went up and down with the shifts of economic prosperity in the outside world. Eugen, who was from a well-to-do Dutch family, had lost some of his money as a result of World War I and was not as rich when they were married as he had been before; but it was probably a matter of pride to Edna, since the Millays had always been so poor, that she had married a man of wealthy background, and she fostered the image.

Frequently she turned to music, as she did in the late fall of 1929, when she indulged in an "orgy" of playing Bach, Beethoven, and Mozart on the piano for several hours a day. As always, she felt refreshed, and a resurgence of gratitude toward her mother, who had early taught her to play and had spent so much hard-earned money on her music lessons. She never failed to be thankful for the "beautiful gift" her mother made her years before; once again she wrote an expression of heartfelt appreciation to Cora Millay, who was now back in Camden.

It took until the summer of 1930 before the plans for "Steeple-top" had all been carried out, and the farm was running at what was probably the peak of its productivity. There was livestock in the barns, including a horse Edna could ride, and Eugen was marketing the fruit with some profit. Luckily, they had a very good caretaker, John Pinnie, a neighboring farmer, who stayed at his post with matter-of-fact efficiency and loyalty throughout the years. Arthur and Gladys had finished remodeling "Hardhack" by then, and the four friends decided to celebrate by throwing a "grand house party" around the time of Midsummer Eve, from July 21 to 24. Edna was seized with the idea when an old friend of hers from the Provincetown organized a traveling summer theater, The Jitney Players, and proposed a presentation in their "outdoor theater" on the hillside. Her enthusiasm was so infectious that two new neighbors "with new houses" wanted to join the festivities and offered their homes for guests. By the time Edna wrote to invite Deems Taylor and his wife Mary Kennedy (the singer), greeting them, "Dear Kids," she announced gleefully that some fifty or sixty "souls" were coming! As usual, her dynamic energy took over, and she ran the whole project, unknowingly stirring up resentment in Gladys, who not unnaturally felt she should have some say in the matter. Before the plans were fully laid, angry words had passed between them.

Though Gladys had often seen flashes of Vincent's temper, she herself had never clashed with the poet, and for the first time came up against the overpowering ego that had overwhelmed and forewarned Arthur against marrying her. Both women were "sore as hell" up to the day the house party began; but once the guests arrived they seemed to calm down. The play, the weather, and the ample supply of gin all contributed to the success of the festival. One night Edna suddenly decided to do the Samurai, a Japanese dance she had performed in *The String of the Samisen* at the

Provincetown; and in the spirit of the hour, the quarrel was forgotten. After the party was over, she was all charm and good nature toward "Gladdie" once more, and the latter could not help forgiving her. Edna Millay was temperamental and often unreasonably angry; but her anger usually disappeared as quickly as it came. She rarely bore a grudge or nursed a grievance in silence.

A month after the party, Edna and Eugen drove to Boston, where the poet attended the third Memorial Meeting of the Sacco-Vanzetti executions on August 23, and read the five poems, printed in Part II of *The Buck in the Snow*, that had been "inspired by the case." One of them, "The Anguish," an eight-line lyric that is a gem of power in poetry, never failed to stir the audience, and was later included in the recordings she made. While in Boston, she and Eugen were invited to have lunch in the historic Longfellow home at 105 Brattle Street, Cambridge, with a grandson of the venerable Victorian poet, Henry (W. Longfellow) Dana, and Mr. Dana's aunt, a Mrs. Thorpe, who told them she was the "laughing Allegra" of "The Children's Hour." It was a delightful event, and Edna sent a note to her mother on the stationery at the famous house, knowing Cora's great interest in historic places, especially those connected with poetry. Mrs. Millay had not written for some time, and they were rather worried about her.

In the late fall, Llewelyn Powys and his wife, American writer Alyse Gregory, came to stay in the guest cottage at "Steepletop." "Lulu," who was in process of completing the manuscript for *Impassioned Clay*, was suffering from lung trouble and was planning to go to the West Indies later in the winter. "Steepletop" was already deep in snow, and Powys enjoyed driving down for the mail with Eugen in the horse-drawn sleigh, the most recent acquisition at the farm. In the evenings he and Alyse would come over to the main house, and there would be much good talk in front of a blazing fireplace. Alyse was to write of their kind hosts in the preface to a volume of Powys' Letters published after his death: "The beautiful and famous poet had always entranced Llewelyn's imagination, and her husband was, in his own way, as rare a character as she." Between Llewelyn and such a free spirit there was naturally a strong mutual attraction, and it was especially appropriate that *Impassioned Clay,* his trumpet call to youth, should have been dedicated: "To Eugen Boissevain, under whose roof, and in the presence of whose daring spirit this book was finished." Certainly it is indicative of Eugen's "rare" qualities of geniality and warmth combined with a high order of intelligence, that three writers dedicated books to him within eight years.

Edna and Eugen were planning to go to Florida in December. The poet had been troubled again by her strange headache and a persistent cough following summer flu. In October she had sent Arthur, "Dearest Artie," a half-comic note, complaining that life was not so much "one damn thing after another" as "one damn thing over and over": sickness, in one degree or another, fluctuating among the variants of sick, sicker, not quite so sick, very sick, and so on and on. Illness seems to have been a constant plague, whether real or neurotic. Although she and Eugen had to leave, they had arranged for Alyse and "Lulu" to stay until it was time for them to go to the West Indies.

On February 5, just as Edna was beginning to feel a little better, she and Eugen received word in Florida that Mrs. Millay had died suddenly in Camden. It was a terrible shock. They knew she had not been feeling well, but there had been no sign of fatal illness. They left for Maine at once, where they were met by Norma and Kathleen and their husbands. They all stayed at the little hotel in Camden, and after the funeral, Edna arranged to have her mother brought to "Steepletop," where she was buried on February 12, 1931. On February 14, the poet wrote a broken-hearted "Valentine" for her beloved mother, an appropriate title, tinged with irony, of the lament that came from her innermost being, a cry for the lost parent she had called "sweetheart" in one of the "love letters" to her mother from abroad. The poem was the first in a series she was to write, expressing her grief, and published in her volume of several years later, *Wine from These Grapes.* It is notable that Edna Millay wrote three elegiac series, of six poems each; and all three to women important in her life. Just now, she was unable to work; she could hardly think for weeks, and read nothing but detective stories. She put aside the manuscript of *Impassioned Clay,* and it was April before she could bring herself to write a letter returning it, still unread, and thanking her friends for the sympathy they had sent. She knew they were sorry but there was little anyone could say. She revealed the depth of her grief in a few brief sentences telling of her "changed world," confiding that "the absence of that presence was everywhere."

She remembered, everywhere, the unusually happy relationship she had enjoyed with her mother, the close tie of affectionate love between them, which had been free of the knots of compulsion and utterly spontaneous. She recalled all the things they shared; the gay little jokes, the joy of earth's flowers, the intense love of poetry, literature, and music. And despite her despair over the loss of her mother, Vincent found one small consolation in her grief: they had had "a grand time."

CHAPTER XII

"Strange and Fatal Interview"

IN MAY, 1931, a few months after her mother died, Edna St. Vincent Millay was named among the "ten greatest living women" by John Haynes Holmes. At the same time, her volume of fifty-two sonnets in celebration, or commemoration, of a recent love affair, *Fatal Interview*, dedicated to Elinor Wylie, was published by Harper's. Hailed by the critics generally for the sustained quality of its passionate lines, its artistic maturity, and, two decades after it was published, called by Edmund Wilson one of the great poems of this century, the sonnet sequence traces the course of a troubled and fervid love relationship from its inception, through its heady Olympian consummation, to its deep, sorrowful, poignant close.

Intensely personal, though completely objective, the appearance of such an emotion-fraught work, which was the first to follow Millay's most contemplative volume of 1928, quite naturally caused an immediate furor. Those who had been disappointed by the philosophic character of *The Buck in the Snow* rushed to read *Fatal Interview*. They praised the poet whether or not they fully understood the poem, and inevitably, they speculated on the identity of the lover. Idle speculation, for, as open as Edna Millay was in her championship of equal rights for women, including the single standard in sexual behavior and marriage, she could also be extremely reticent. She might admit frankly that she "never settled down," but she was always very discreet, and would never divulge any details of the circumstances surrounding the birth of a sonnet sequence, or any poem portraying a love affair. The importance of *Fatal Interview* as far as its origins were concerned lay in its honesty of feeling and its universality. Anyone who has ever gone through the exquisite ordeal of a passionate love affair could not fail to recognize the secret procession of emotional events: the initial pangs of love as yet unannounced or unrequited; the hot, sweet anguish of desire and longing for the mere sight of the beloved; the glory of consummated passion; the false feeling that this love will never fade despite the foreknowledge that it cannot last; the unbearable pain of the first separation; the vow to rejoin the lover, no matter what the danger; the resurgence and high tide, followed by the ebb of passion in an "ailing love"; the vain struggle to prolong the life of the affair despite the realization that it cannot continue; followed by the gallant renunciation before it is necessary, or before the living flame dwindles to ash and dies; and finally, the tragic, mournful lament for the dead love.

The outstanding universality in *Fatal Interview* consists of its elevation of the human experience of the birth and death of love to the highest level by the music of its expression, by the touch of classical beauty in its allusions, and by the architecture of its imagery. This love epic, as it might be called, could very well have been a summation of all the loves in the poet's life, though it was inspired by a recent passionate interlude. It may always remain one of the mysteries in Edna St. Vincent Millay's colorful history, unless time and the passing of those closely connected with the affair permit names and dates to be revealed. Nevertheless, human nature being what it is, readers at the time of publication, and for several years after, continued to conjecture on the identity of the lover.

A few reviewers were critical of *Fatal Interview* because it ignored the Depression, the prime social problem of the day. Those who had followed the course of Edna Millay's social awareness from the early days of *Renascence* to her fervor in defending Sacco and Vanzetti, not only in the five poems published in *The Buck in the Snow,* but in the personal vigor of her protest during the deathwatch parade, could not understand how the same poet could give birth to a book concerned with a subject so personal and so far removed from the larger cares of the country. But the timelessness of love, and the sweet agonies of an extramarital love affair, portrayed in the framework of a sonnet sequence in the language of exaltation, was the touchstone of its wide appeal and tremendous success.

The quest of the curious, however, was not satisfied; and when one prying reporter discovered and stated the fact that Edna Millay was married, and was "living quietly with a husband of eight years standing," many readers expressed general indignation, feeling that the poem had been a hoax. It was a rather peculiar reaction, but it was understandable, since Edna Millay was known as the champion of free love, free living, restricted, perhaps, by the flexible bonds of intelligence and discretion, but not repressed by hypocritical mores and legalities. The poet must have found herself in the position of Melville who, to his astonishment, had to defend the veracity of *Typee* both before and after publication of his Polynesian adventure. Both writers set out to record human experience, and neither could have foreseen that readers would be concerned with the factual reality of a work that was intended as literary art, quite apart from its basis in reality. Edna Millay could scarcely prove her case as Melville did, by locating his shipmate and fellow runaway, Toby, calling upon him as witness to the amazing adventure. In *Fatal Interview* the second sonnet states clearly that the scar of the encounter will lie like a sword between the poet and her "troubled lord." Such an admission should have satisfied most readers, but the speculation went on until 1936, when Elizabeth Atkins, the first Millay biographer, came forward with testimony from Eugen himself. He first commented that the assumption that the poet was living quietly for eight years with her husband was false; he added that it was not the word "quietly" that was at fault. Some of Edna's contemporaries read into Atkins' discussion, especially in the 1963 printing of the biography, that the identity of the lover was disclosed; one poet vowed that Atkins had named George Dillon, with whom Millay translated Baudelaire's *Les Fleurs du mal*, which also appeared in 1936.

They had met during the reading tour in the fall of 1928, when

Dillon introduced Edna Millay at the University of Chicago, a "brilliantly successful" appearance, according to his account. Dillon, a distinguished scholar, Pulitzer prize winner and later editor of *Poetry* magazine, was known as one of the most charming men in literary circles. There was an immediate rapport between the two poets. But Atkins at no time named anyone. She merely stated unequivocally, if in rather quaint language, with Eugen's approval, that "a still-breathing married woman, name and dates given, has written a poem of extra-marital passion, not as an exercise of purple penmanship, but as an honest record of immediate experience."

Millay herself maintained a scornful silence. She had written a sonnet sequence depicting a love affair in the tradition of love poets from Sappho and Catullus to Shakespeare and John Donne and seventeenth-century sonneteers, on down to Emily Dickinson, George Meredith, and Gerard Manley Hopkins. Beyond that, as she had said in admitting her love for Arthur, people could not expect to learn any more. She would not deign to enlighten anyone. As far back as 1921 she had written her mother from Europe that she was considering a book composed entirely of sonnets, after which she might never write another sonnet again; or if she did, it would be "a big one, and inevitable." Whether or not she had conceived the idea for a work like *Fatal Interview*, it seems clear that she had had the concept of a long sonnet sequence for at least a decade.

In 1927 or 1928, when she was discussing "The Bobolink" and several other poems published in *The Buck in the Snow* with Edmund Wilson, she took offense at his criticism of the studied attitude of the poem. She angrily accused him of implying that she sounded like Mary Carolyn Davies, who was widely known for her pretty magazine verse, and she would not be placated by his explanation. All he meant was that there had been "an element of panic" about her earlier poems, especially those in *Second April*, so that people thought of them less as literature than as emotional experiences. Flushing bright pink in sudden rage she flashed at him, "Yes, and I still want to knock 'em cold!" She was wearing a high brown dress the color of the thrasher's wing, which brought out the copper lights of her hair, and Wilson could not help noting that "she looked quite beautiful." Eugen, who was sitting in on the conversation as usual, protectively interposed his opinion that this poetry was "more objective," and Wilson agreed, but Edna was not to be soothed. Later, when most American reviews tended to ignore the literary value of the volume, she was justifiably annoyed as well as depressed, and the cool reception of her work rankled sorely. If her aim in writing *Fatal Interview* was in part to prove that she could still create poetry that would "knock 'em cold," she was eminently successful.

This is in no way to suggest that the sonnet sequence is exhibitionist or was motivated by a desire to shock. Like Frost, Edna Millay wished above all else that her poetry might be "lodged" in the minds and hearts of readers not only in 1931, but long after she was gone. If some of the spontaneity of earlier sonnets is lacking, the passion is deeper, the technique is surer, and the artistry is more clearly defined. Taking her title from John Donne's sixteenth elegy in his celebrated series immortalizing a tragic love affair, which begins, "By our first strange and fatal interview," Edna Millay sought to answer, in terms of her own experience, and in her own inimitable style, all the poets who had sung the praises and trials of love. The Atkins biography gives a lengthy analysis of the influences and parallels from the first to the final sonnet in the sequence, which, although detracting from the exhilarating artistic effect of the poem as a whole, is interesting as a record of the background material the poet wove into her work. The closest source of inspiration, however, is virtually overlooked, or so briefly mentioned that it is easily discounted, and that was Arthur Ficke's *Sonnets of a Portrait Painter*. Published originally in 1914, it appeared at the height of a mad, undisciplined movement to destroy the sonnet as an art form which culminated in a solemn public "burning" of the sonnet accompanied by absurd incantations of the free versifiers in 1916. Consequently his work, although praised by some reviewers for its mastery of the form and its narrative value in recounting the story of a love affair, was largely neglected by American readers. Few people even realized that there was a consecutive story line to the volume, that it presented the emotional struggle between two lovers, analyzing the "modern" American woman from the man's point of view. Arthur had sent a copy of the work to Edna Millay early in their correspondence, and it undoubtedly made a deep impression on her. And while most of his friends and colleagues were discouraged from attempting a similar sequence by the poor reception of Ficke's volume, Vincent, with her affinity for the sonnet and her enthusiasm for Arthur's strong intellectual poetry, went on serenely writing sonnets. And probably, even at that time, when she was occupied with academic chores and distractions, she unconsciously planned to try her hand at such a work some day.

Whoever served as her inspiration, if indeed there was one specific person, she knew the proper moment had arrived. Like Arthur, she began the sequence by questioning the worth of her objective, seeking to discover the secret charm that her "tall oblivious gaoler eyed with stars" possessed more than any other man to capture and hold her spellbound, to rouse her sensual desire to the point of forsaking her spiritual wings "to journey barefoot with a mortal joy." It was also the old conflict between the New England puritan and the Celtic pagan in her, the same sort of struggle which plagues all the poets of Christendom; but in Edna Millay the broad streak of ancient Irish paganism won out easily. By the second or third sonnet she is rapturous over an irrational and as yet unreturned love. The phase culminates in an outburst of disarming generosity toward her lover, the desire to give all, openly and without guile. Neither Arthur Ficke's analytical appraisal of his love, nor John Donne's "The Token," which has been called the source of Edna Millay's sonnet, can rightfully be compared with her highly individualistic point of view. The lilting lyricism of the opening lines, "Not in a silver casket cool with pearls/ Or rich with red corundum or with blue," leads to a figure of speech as lovely and refreshing as a field of wildflowers in the morning, yet with an eloquence that seems to epitomize the poet's entire philosophy.

"Love in the open hand," the first phrase of the sestet, which she read with deliberate emphasis, almost too slowly some thought, in readings and recordings, represents the core of Millay's concept of sexual joy. It is the prelude of the supreme ex-

pression of the poet's desire to give herself to the beloved, a
revelation of the everpresent child in the artist. To picture the
gift of love as a brimming hatful of freshly gathered cowslips or a
skirtful of shining apples, is to relive the early morning of one's
life, to see love as the constant and timeless rejuvenator. Only a
creature who lived by herself in the duo-land of "Millayhood"
(in the phrase of Arthur E. Dubois, in *The Sewanee Review*,
1935), could have conceived such a metaphor, containing in its
resolution in the sonnet's often-quoted final couplet the presentation of all her poems to every reader for all time. Like Emily
Dickinson, who had presented her "letter to the world" two
generations before, Edna Millay now came with overflowing arms,
"calling out as children do, 'Look what I have! And these are
all for you.'"

     In the sequence, the sonnet just referred to, number eleven, is
followed by the ecstatic, exalted sonnet of joyful sexual consummation, called rather pontifically by Atkins a "pagan Magnificat,"
and certainly a powerful paeon of the pleasures of sexual joy,
endowing the lover with the gifts of the gods. But there a sinister
note is sounded beneath the joyous cries, the source of which lies
partly in the strange words that speak of bearing a son *"branded
with godhead,"* implying cruelty and ruthlessness on the part of
the lover no matter how divine. The images are overwhelming,
in direct contrast to those of the preceding sonnet; the woman in
the poet had superseded the child. There were those who thought
her reference to the gods was pretentious, here and in the sixteenth sonnet, the record of a dream in which she moves at ease
among Elysian fields, conversing as an equal with "mortal women"
of classical history who, like her, had had sexual intercourse with
gods. And in the twenty-sixth sonnet, in which Millay calls up
the ancient royal chronicles of love as witness to her own "un-
regenerate passion," comparing herself to the treacherous, wilful
queens who "took their knights to bed," annoyed some readers
who found it arrogant when it was first published in *Poetry* magazine, some months before *Fatal Interview* came out. By itself, and
taken out of context, the picture must have seemed presumptuous.
Yet most readers applauded such an attitude and thrilled to the

"love like a burning city in the breast," one of the most felicitous images in the entire sequence.

The fact that this sonnet appeared prior to the book, and the notation, in the fiftieth sonnet, that it had been "half a year since her heart broke in two," would seem to indicate that the experience out of which the full sequence was created must have occurred in late 1929 and early 1930. No poet of merit can write a work of fifty-two sonnets in a few weeks or even months and expect to create anything of literary value, let alone a volume of the extraordinary stature of *Fatal Interview*. Arthur Ficke wrote three revisions of his *Sonnets of a Portrait Painter*, and each was published in a separate edition. Edna Millay undoubtedly revised each sonnet individually. *Fatal Interview* was a tour de force, a calculated masterwork on the subject of love, yet the intensity of the passion is felt in varying degrees throughout.

In the course of the narrative, certain psychological aspects of the poet's complex nature inevitably come to light. For all her fine derision and flat dismissal of psychoanalysis, she frequently employs Freudian symbols, particularly in the sixteenth, twenty-first, and thirty-third sonnets, in all of which she makes use of the Dream, each time in a different way. In the already discussed sixteenth, it is an idyll of sexual bliss following gratification; in the twenty-first, the dream portrays a sexual longing for the departed lover in tender terms denoting the shadowy shimmer of a mirage in sleep; and the thirty-third reveals " a dark and secret dolour," a foreboding of the final, sorrowful phase of the love affair. Both of the last-mentioned are rife with sexual symbols consciously or unconsciously included. The subjective mood is sustained by the almost exclusive use of the first-person-singular (or occasionally the first-person-plural) throughout the sequence. Only a few times, in deliberate craftsmanship, does the poet depart from this device.

The midway sonnet, the twenty-seventh, is addressed to the Moon, bidding her to "hold off the Sun" as she did on the Carian hill in Keats' *Endymion*. The twenty-ninth commands the heart to "have no pity,—to shake the poet's house of bone with dancing, break it down with joy." The forty-second, again in the imperative, counsels an ailing Love to be "content to die"; and the fifty-second, the last, addressed to Endymion, once more invokes the Moon, described in the third-person-singular. The concentrated subjectivity is counterbalanced by the objective point of view Edna Millay was able to assume toward her various erotic adventures. At two points in the poem, the twentieth and thirtieth sonnets, both of which recall Gerard Manley Hopkins in their philosophic evaluation, she is serenely meditative. Her reading of the latter, which begins by observing that "Love is not all," and ends by asserting the opposite, was eloquent and quietly passionate, as if in these lines she sought to establish the full measure of her considered esteem for the treasured experience. In the closing sonnet of *Fatal Interview*, the poet stands apart, viewing the entire episode with the contemplative eyes of a religious mourner for the dead. If the consummation sonnet is a "pagan Magnificat," the finale could be called a hedonistic High Mass for a lost love, invoking the Moon gone mad, "being all unfit for mortal love, that might not die of it."

Although there were other sexual episodes in Edna Millay's life from time to time, as recorded obliquely in the five poems of "Not So Far as the Forest"; more realistically in "Theme and Variations," a group of eight lyrics; and in "Rendezvous," an account of a meeting in an Eighth Street apartment, it is clear that the fifty-two sonnets of *Fatal Interview* were offered as the poet's definitive statement on sexual love, impelled by an affair of tremendous impact. Presumably Eugen enjoyed the same privileges as she, whether or not he chose to exercise them. His complete personal devotion to his "Vincie," which included washing her hair when they were isolated at "Steepletop," and tending her like an affectionate nurse during her frequent illnesses and his delight in her public career, which he managed with the acumen carried over from his successful import business, seems to indicate that he had little erotic interest in other women. In any case, the volume in question represents the zenith of Edna Millay's ardor for the act of love no matter who served as its inspiration; indeed one has the impression at times that she was more in love with love than with any one person.

The immediate effect of *Fatal Interview* on her public career was to increase her popularity, doubling the demands and the fees for her readings. Everyone was eager for a look at the poet who had written such an amazing book of love sonnets at a time when the form was being actively denounced and repudiated, just as it is today, but with greater vituperation. T. S. Eliot was more arrogant and dictatorial than either Robert Bly or Karl Shapiro in laying down the law against the metrical line and any set form.[1] One cannot help remarking that the sonnet must have substantial literary value and appeal, since it has survived all attempts at annihilation during every decade from 1910 on, and is still standing firm under attack. Edna Millay found this particular form best suited for the expression of the evanescent beauty of love, and she paid no heed to her detractors; she had more than enough admirers. People everywhere jammed the halls to hear her. She received offers for a series of radio broadcasts, which soon materialized in a nationwide hookup of poetry readings by Edna St. Vincent Millay, an unheard-of venture in entertainment on the air. Magazines and newspapers clamored for interviews. And all the time controversy and rumor ran wild over the "names and dates" of the principals in *Fatal Interview*.

Edna let Eugen handle everything and took no part in things aside from the readings. When the book came out she was still deep in sorrow over the death of her mother, as well as that of Elinor Wylie, and was writing memorial poems that caught the spirit of both women who had meant so much to her. The fact that she dedicated *Fatal Interview* to Elinor, whose work she esteemed so highly, is indicative of the value she herself placed upon it. This volume and the sequence which followed it, "Epitaph for the Race of Man," represent Edna Millay's contribution to literature as a sonneteer of the first rank and a major American poet.

[1] Mr. Shapiro, indeed, not too long ago recommended a rereading of Millay's sonnets and lyrics to her detractors, citing her as "a poet of lyric genius."

CHAPTER XIII

Island Retreat From Worldly Strife

N O MATTER HOW imposing a figure she may have cut professionally and publicly in the thirties, Edna was forever
searching for peace of mind; she seemed possessed with an eternal
restlessness that kept her and Eugen constantly on the move.
They were rarely at "Steepletop" more than five or six months
of the year. As beautiful as the Berkshires appeared in almost
any season, the poet again felt confined by the tree-covered hills
surrounding the house. Before they had been there two years, she
found herself longing for the ocean, and she began to wonder
how she, a child of coastal towns, could live on a farm in upstate
New York, "tilling an upland ground." The feeling was expressed
in a nostalgic little poem, "Mist in the Valley," published in 1928
in *The Buck in the Snow*, a lyric likening the hills shrouded in
soft white fog on a moonlight night to the islands in the bay at
Camden, the illusion bringing back the sound of breakers rolling
in, and the plaintive cry of the "sand-peep."

She was stricken by a surging homesickness for the briny atmosphere of the seacoast; her longing was not satisfied by occasional trips to the shore, or by trips to the semitropical sands
of Florida or the Riviera. The hankering for some safe retreat on
the New England coast where she would relax completely and not
even write poetry gnawed at her. Although "Steepletop" was
physically isolated, particularly in winter, psychologically it was
her working ground. She loved to get up early in the morning

at "Steepletop," particularly in the summer, when she could go
out to watch birds busy at the feeders, noting the number of
indigo buntings that always came back, flapping their electric
blue wings boldly. She waited to see the pair of flickers flying
from their nest in search of food. She had predicted in *Fatal
Interview* that her love affair would be over "before the flickers
mate," so familiar was she with the habits of this particular favorite. The flicker, the blackbird, the bobolink, the meadowlark, and
the lowly sparrow came most often into her poetry; she saved the
song of the nightingale for the rarest of human creatures, like
Elinor Wylie and her recent lover; usually she chose for her bird
images the species less known to poetry and more common to
men. If there was time on those mornings, she would work in
the flower garden, cultivating the phlox, the iris, and the "spiny
poppy," perpetuating the love her mother had shown for garden
flowers, as well as her own for the mullein, burdock, hawkweed,
bindweed, blue vervain, and all the other wildflowers she still
loved, and which appeared in one of the poems to her mother,
"In the Grave No Flower."

Now she did the cultivation with the same enthusiasm she
gave to everything else, and was proud of her flourishing beds
of annuals, fond of making flower arrangements for the living-
room. Once, when Arthur and Gladys were staying at "Steepletop," she picked a handful of red poppies and put them in a
shapely, old-fashioned gray vase once belonging to her grand-
mother; and Gladys had painted a charming still-life of "Vincent's
poppies." If poetry had not been the stronger call, Edna might
have been content to be a fruit-farmer's wife who never left the
upland at all, tending her garden for hours on end.

Harper's was forever prodding her for manuscripts, so they
could bring out a new Millay book every year. If she did not have
enough for a new volume of poetry, they usually thought of something like the *Poems Selected for Young People*, published in
1929. Following the tremendous success of *Fatal Interview*, in
England and to a lesser extent in France as well as America,
Eugene Saxton, Editor-in-chief at Harper's, who handled all of
Millay's work until he died in 1943, decided to publish a gift
edition of *The Princess Marries the Page*. Quite unexpectedly, the

one-act play had received a distinguished revival production in December, 1930.

One weekend when Deems Taylor and Mary Kennedy were visiting Edna and Eugen after the "grand house-party," they made a point of mentioning that they needed a playscript for the annual presentation of the Cosmopolitan Club in Philadelphia and asked if she had any on hand. She could not think of anything suitable immediately, but later, when she was searching through her old papers for something else, she came across the manuscript of *The Princess Marries the Page*. She dusted it off for Deems and Mary, who were delighted to find that it was just what they wanted and started working on the production at once. Though the one-acter had been presented several times previously, in colleges and at the Provincetown, it had never been produced with such elegance or fine casting. Staged by the noted actor, Dudley Digges, who played the part of the King, it was embroidered with music by Deems Taylor who wrote a little tune expressly for the Page's pipe-playing scenes; sets were by Grant La Farge, and costumes were provided by courtesy of the Metropolitan Opera Company. Mary Kennedy took the role of the Princess; and two minor parts, the First and Third Soldiers, were played by a couple of promising young composer-friends of the Taylors: Samuel Barber and Gian-Carlo Menotti.

Now Harper's proposed to bring out a special gift edition of the play to match the Cosmopolitan Club's production in style, with illustrations in color, and a preface by the author. Edna agreed to write a few paragraphs, but she objected strenuously to the publishers' suggestion of woodcuts for the illustrations, which she maintained were much too weighty for so "slight" a play. She thought this printing should be a true Christmas gift book, "as gaudy as a Christmas tree," and had already picked J. Paget-Fredericks as illustrator. And, although Mr. Fredericks' delicate, dotted-line color drawings were almost too frothy, as it turned out, the publishers were so eager to offer another Millay book that they granted her every wish, accepting also her idea that it be "a big, flat book, 14 by 10." Unfortunately, she and Eugen had already gone to Florida and missed the performance in Philadelphia on December 22, 1930. She thought it necessary to talk with one of the principals before writing even a brief preface; but it was another six months before she consulted Mary Kennedy.

Her public career continued to burgeon as a result of *Fatal Interview*. The noted French novelist, Madame Lucie Delarue-Mardrus, whom Edna had met in Paris, translated a number of the love sonnets for French readers, who were most *sympathique* to such a subject. The sequence was the topic of lively discussions in Paris literary circles; and Miss Natalie Clifford Barney, an expatriate whose *salon* was frequented by internationally known celebrities, wished to give a tea in the poet's honor in June, 1932. The invitations read with dignity, "To meet Miss Edna St. Vincent Millay." Hundreds of international notables were invited. Edna discovered that Mary Kennedy was in Paris, and Eugen wanted to visit his family in Holland, so they went abroad early in June. He stayed with the Boissevains while she went on to Paris, writing the publishers that she would send them the preface from there. She had some new poems on her mind and, as usual, had a "pain amidships" plaguing her. Mary had few details of the performance to offer, and Edna stayed up all night writing a preface which was different from the one she had planned; it had been almost easier to write the play, she declared in a letter to Saxton. She was exhausted and the next night drank too many cocktails, making an exhibition of herself before Mary's friends. But when she started to explain or apologize, it seemed pointless, for "who cared what tripped a fallen woman?" she quipped. She gave Mary some cards for Miss Barney's big tea and let it go at that.

The ornamental edition of her little play, which, she admitted in the preface was "very slight . . . but rather pretty," appeared in the late fall of 1932. Significantly, the words, "By the author of *Fatal Interview*," were printed below the title in bold type. But the book had small appeal, either as a gift item or as dramatic literature. Much more successful was the first in the series of radio broadcasts, which finally took place on Christmas Day; it brought an overwhelming response from listeners. Never before had a literary figure appearing on radio been given the acclaim of a stage or concert artist. Edna's subtly-shaded voice, with its undercurrent of excitement, captured the radio audience just as it did the audience in the lecture halls. Letters poured in, bearing requests along with praise; and many a long distance conference took place between Miss Margaret Cuthbert of the WJZ Blue Network and the poet in Austerlitz in arranging the programs. Miss Cuthbert became one of Edna Millay's close friends personally as well as professionally, and the pleasant relationship lasted until the end of the poet's life.

Edna and Eugen had planned to go to Africa by way of England that year, paying a return visit to Llewelyn Powys and Alyse Gregory en route; "Lulu" had insisted that they give him and Alyse a chance to reciprocate the Powys' stay at "Steepletop." However, when the job on the radio came through, Edna immediately dropped all plans for an extensive trip. The visit with Lulu and Alyse would have to wait a year. Instead, she spent her spare time selling little "blue books" to make money for the Stage Relief Fund, which Mary Kennedy had helped to organize. The plight of unemployed actors during the Depression was meaningful to Edna Millay. She had witnessed unemployment in the theater all her adult life, but nothing as widespread or bleak as in the early thirties; and though she had little talent for selling things, she did her best, and she contributed her own money to the fund.

She was working to complete a sonnet sequence, which, though only a third as long as *Fatal Interview,* was to be the most monumental of all her work. In 1920 she had spoken to Edmund Wilson about a long philosophical poem of the same nature as the new work, but using a different technique. Later she decided to cast the work in a sonnet sequence, ten of which had already been printed in a special anniversary edition of the St. Louis *Post Dispatch* in 1928; but the whole was far from complete, and she wanted to have it ready for her next volume. Wrestling inwardly with ideas, as she always did, besides writing prefaces or blurbs for the books of various friends; serving on the Guggenheim Committee, to which she always submitted minute and conscientious reports; going on a short reading tour; and giving eight radio broadcasts amounted to herculean activity, and Edna did not have the physical stamina even of most women. By June, 1933, she was worn out, in spite of a short vacation in Florida late in the winter. On June 4, Esther Adams had invited her and Eugen to hold the annual celebration of her birthday at her house on Bailey's Island in Casco Bay. They arrived on June 3 and awoke to a morning of heavy mist; but when the sun's rays lifted the white bank, they could see a beautiful little island across the bay, gleaming like a mirage on the outermost rim of the deep. Edna and Eugen could not get over it, and when Tess told them that was Ragged Island, once owned by Elijah Kellogg, a Maine minister and writer of a popular series of boys' stories, who had died some time ago, Edna could not contain herself. When she heard that it was uninhabited and that there was nothing on it but the house Kellogg had built, she knew she had found the spot she had been searching for. She cried out that she must have that island; and Eugen, his genial Dutch face glowing in anticipation, said he would find out right away if it was for sale. A few weeks later, they were the sole owners of Ragged Island.

Edna made all sorts of lovely plans: they would spend at least the month of August loafing on their island. It was not far from Brunswick, Maine, and they could stop to see her Aunt Susie, Mrs. Frank L. Ricker, the aunt the Millays had lived with during Edna's tenth year. Her aunts were now the main link with her mother, whose passing was still painful to her. She would wake up in the middle of the night and weep, putting her knuckles to her mouth, as she revealed in the poem, "Childhood Is the Kingdom Where Nobody Dies," one of the series she was writing in memory of her mother at this time. In 1928 she had been instrumental in securing a publisher for Cora Millay's book, *Little Otis*, a collection of comic "runes"—some of them rather a strain—reminiscent of the pranks Vincent used to play, which prompted Cora to make up the rhymes to read to the little girls. Recently Edna had arranged the printing of a song, "The Good Ship Maud," the words and music of which had been written by her mother long ago; and she was going to take a copy of it to her aunt when she and Eugen stopped by in Brunswick on their way to Ragged Island.

But just as they were getting ready to load up with provisions and look around for a few pieces of second-hand furniture for the island house, Edna came down with a severe case of flu, which lasted almost all summer. She had been feeling all right, but very tired, in June, right after they had decided to buy Ragged Island. Then she made a short trip to receive honorary degrees of Doctor of Literature from the University of Wisconsin and Russell Sage College. Though she made light of it, she could not help feeling great satisfaction in the growing string of colleges she could add to the "Litt. D." after her name. And Eugen was always so proud of the honors conferred upon her that it heightened her own pleasure. As soon as they returned, both plunged into work: Eugen had to look after the berry crop and see that it was harvested before they could go away; and Edna wanted to complete the new sequence, and other poems much freer in form, in preparation for her next volume. At night she spent hours watching the stars through a telescope, often with Eugen, and Arthur and Gladys, who frequently came over from "Hardhack" to join them. But sometimes she stayed out alone, lying on the ground, gazing at the sky with purposeful intent. Her sonnet sequence involved the theme of man in relation to the universe, and she had to be absolutely sure of the courses taken by certain constellations or planets, Vega; Aldebaran; Capella and her golden kids, so that her poetic images could not be faulted.

Perhaps from exposure or perhaps from overwork she caught the flu. When the fever subsided, she would get up, but was so weak she would have to go back to bed. Yet through the weeks of illness, which lasted until early winter, she kept writing poetry, "about twenty-four hours a day," and would not have eaten if Eugen had not insisted, bringing her meals on a tray most of the time. Finally, the day after Christmas, they left for the south of France, where Eugen's brother had a house at Cap d'Antibes, way out on the peninsula that juts into the Mediterranean. Hitler, who had just come into power, was already threatening Holland with annexation; the Boissevain family did not want to leave the country at such a crucial time, so Edna and Eugen rented his brother's house at the Cape. Antibes was usually warm and sunny, and Edna, who was "working like fury," needed to save her strength for poetry. If she grew too tired, she could relax, or "get tired in a different way," by playing tennis or swimming in the

Mediterranean. Her mind was heavy with personal emotional trouble in the wake of her affair, and sore with the cares of the world. They had heard terrible stories about Hitler's persecution of Jews; she believed his relentless hounding of a people because of their religion was a kind of mental sickness that might infect all nations. Her mood was reflected in a strange little poem, "Cap d'Antibes," which was inspired by the aftermath of a storm one morning, when, in spite of the calm, the "disturbed Mediterranean" beat against the "bird-twittering shore."

In April, they went to Chaldon Down in Dorset, making the postponed visit to the beloved "Lulu" and Alyse, where the four talked of many things, including the terrible treatment of her charges by one Mrs. Nincom, headmistress of a home for delinquent girls located nearby. The Powys family and their neighbors, the well-known writers Sylvia Townsend Warner and Valentine Ackland, who shared a house across the Down, were all more upset by this manifestation of crime than the possible effect Hitler might have on the fate of England. But if there was sad, angry, and sober talk, there was also wit and laughter, and poetry read aloud and discussed, probably over a cup of mead and more. Edna enjoyed herself so much that only when she and Eugen were homeward bound on the S.S. *Roosevelt* from Southampton did she realize that she had forgotten to have a duplicate made of the manuscript for her new book to leave with Lulu and Alyse in case anything happened during the crossing. Here she was, at the mercy of the capricious ocean for eight days, with the sole copies of many new poems tucked under her arm in her "Black Note-Book"! Luckily, the ship put in at Cobh, where she had copies made, even of some unfinished works, and mailed them to the Powys with "lots of love to her darlings."

At home, the country was still floundering in the Depression, although Roosevelt had worked miracles in the "hundred days" after he became President. Much machinery was silent, and many men were idle, standing sulkily in soup lines in the cities, hanging around pool halls in small towns and villages, or wandering across country, hitching a ride westward in hopes of finding work. Organized labor was beginning to assert itself: there was a dairy strike in upstate New York and in Pennsylvania, but for the most part men were helpless and the futility could be seen in the faces of the jobless. The lack of work was uppermost in everyone's mind, whether they were personally affected by the Depression or not.

One night shortly after Edna and Eugen's return, they went over to "Hardhack" to visit Arthur and Gladys. As usual, Arthur, delighted to see them, brought out some of the stock he had put in soon after Repeal, declaring that a celebration was in order. Before long they were discussing the human condition in relation to the times. Arthur, with his usual ingenuity, suddenly said, "Let's have a game," and passed paper and pencils around. "Name five requisites for the happiness of the human race."

Gladys demurred; she was always afraid to speak her mind in front of Vincent, although she had no difficulty expressing her ideas when she was alone with Arthur. For her part, Edna decreed that Arthur had given them too large an order. But the men cried her down, and the three were soon jotting down their immediate reactions. After twenty minutes Arthur announced that time was up, and they should all read what they had written.

The results were rather curious. Arthur, who as ringleader, recited his requisites first, showed the most organization. The list included, "Work to be provided for every human being, at a fair living wage, for the whole of his or her life; Complete freedom in sexual matters, (so far as the state is concerned); Elimination of national boundaries, and the teaching of history as 'the story of the common adventure of mankind'; Devotion of one-half of the world's income to medical investigation and relief; A very small but living wage for all people who care to register themselves as 'artists.' (Yellow ticket.)" It was like Arthur to end with a sly jab at himself and all professional creative people! Eugen, at Vincent's behest, came next, with a fanciful recipe revealing his Dutch-Irish background: "Freedom from economic worries; love of beauty by education: literature, music, nature, etc.; development of intelligence, not hampered by religion, patriotism, etc.; . . . . a love for romanticism, fairies, sagas, mythological stories, etc.; freedom about all matters of love, (love in the best sense, meaning both heart and penus,[1]) i.e., a worship of passion,

---

[1] Eugen's English spelling was not always accurate.

voloptuism [1], and everything pertaining to the body; and further, all other things understood by love, such as friendship, understanding, kindness, etc." Edna, preoccupied with the last of the sequence she was writing, had scribbled in her sprawling backhand five succinct directives for human happiness: "A job,—something at which you must work for a few hours every day; An assurance that you will have at least one meal a day for at least the next week; An opportunity to visit all the countries of the world, to acquaint yourself with their customs and their culture; Freedom in religion, or freedom from all religions, as you prefer; An assurance that no door is closed to you,—that you may climb as high as you can build your ladder."

In view of the Depression, it is not surprising that all three should list some kind of work as the prime requisite for man's happiness, though none of them lacked work or economic security. It is rather astonishing, however, that both Arthur and Eugen should emphasize freedom in love and sex, while Edna, the staunch advocate of free love in her poetry, and presumably in practice, should fail to mention it. Her emphasis on freedom of religion was doubtless due to the plight of those who were suffering in Europe because of their religion. The language of her list was matter-of-fact, hardly what one would expect from a lyric poet. Nevertheless, after the little impromptu "party" was over, Arthur gathered up the three scraps of paper and put them among the writings he wished to preserve.[2]

During the next few weeks, Edna continued to "work like fury" completing and polishing the poems for her new book. And then, in August, they finally went to Ragged Island. Eugen had seen to it that some renovating and repair work was done on the small, rough stone house Kellogg had built, but neither he nor Edna cared much about having the usual "facilities." There was no electricity or running water on the island and no house but theirs. A pump was installed to bring well water into the kitchen, but otherwise very little was done before they moved in that first year. Furniture was kept to a bare minimum, as it had been at Truro. Loading up the car with provisions, pots, and a big iron

[1] See footnote on page 218.
[2] Now in the Ficke Collection, Beinecke Rare Book Library, Yale University.

kettle to boil lobsters in, they set off one day early in August, after Edna had sent in the manuscript for her new book.

Ragged Island proved to be the kind of retreat both had hoped for; the salt air and sea were the best tonic the poet could have found to revive her exhausted body and spirit. A quiet cove on the bay side of the island provided a perfect swimming area. They decided at once that it would be indecent to wear any sort of bathing suit or dress in such a spot; the waves and the seagulls and the wind would certainly object. From the day of their first dip, neither Edna nor Eugen, nor any of a few intimate friends they invited ever thought of bothering with a bathing suit. Edna, like the sea creature she had always been, seemed to be as much at home in the water as out of it. She would stay in a whole morning sometimes, after the first vigorous swim just paddling or lying on her back, floating, dreaming, motionless as a pond-lily on the sea-green surface. Eugen was concerned that first summer, fearing she might get a cramp, for Casco Bay was not the Mediterranean; but she laughed and reminded him that she had been born and brought up on the coast of Maine. And after a long time she would climb out of the water onto the rocks, dripping and shining like a mermaid, her body and spirit refreshed by the salt water and air.

After drying, she would pull on a pair of blue jeans and a shirt, and she would sit on the rocks and read. She had brought a whole armload of detective stories, her favorite recreational reading. Then she and Eugen would gather driftwood and haul in the lobster traps they had set. If they were lucky and the haul included lobster, they would boil it outdoors in the iron kettle, and enjoy it hot or cold, either way with their favorite white wine, which was always an essential part of their provisions. Eugen loved to sail, and they would go up and down the coast in the boat they kept tied up at the little wooden pier on the harbor side of the island. By the second year they were familiar with the entire stretch of neighboring waters, and considered it all part of their domain. Eugen knew all the hazards of the coast line, and neither he nor Edna worried if the breeze blew them farther out than usual when the sails were full.

Except for the wind, the sound of the sea, and the cries of the ever-circling and diving seagulls, the island was perfectly quiet. Sometimes the gulls, in their frenzy for food or blown by stormy winds, would career against the rocks, wounding their wings or legs, or falling stunned from the impact. Edna began to care for the stricken birds right away. She and Eugen would pick them up and take them to a sheltered place near the house, revive them with water and food, and keep them until they were healed and able to fly with the flock again. The "patients" even had names, and it was a sad moment if one of them died. As at "Steepletop," the wild birds here soon recognized a friend in Edna Millay, and would circle around her unafraid as she went down to the shore from the house.

On Ragged Island the poet found peace, if only for short interludes: they usually went there early, during the month of April, before the spring planting and pruning had to be done at "Steepletop," or in late summer, after the berry crop had been harvested. If a reading tour was scheduled for late fall or early winter, as was usually the case, the late summer stay on the island gave her a chance to fortify herself against the weeks of strain. Or if, as now, she had just sent off a manuscript after months of furious writing, she could relax completely, her mind free of commitment. In this island retreat, as she wrote much later, thought could "unbraid itself," and the tangle of personal problems, of worldly strife, faded into the distance, if only temporarily. This year she had the double pleasure of discovering the island, and enjoying the deep gratification that only a poem could bring her. For no matter what the critics might say, she was fully aware of the scope and significance of her latest sonnet sequence.

Enduring Epitaph

O N NOVEMBER 1, 1934, little more than three years after *Fatal Interview,* while the tongues were still wagging about the love affairs of Edna St. Vincent Millay, her new volume appeared. It was a work that should have silenced the gossip and deprecation once and for all, for it proved that she was indeed "a whole poet," not merely the facile writer of bittersweet love lyrics. She borrowed the title of this book from *The Buck in the Snow,* taking one of the commemorative poems inspired by the Sacco and Vanzetti case, "Wine from These Grapes." This in itself was a bold, individualistic gesture. Some considered it conceited and others found it confusing, but most readers applauded the author's temerity.

Wine from These Grapes, like her other volumes, was divided into several parts, the sonnets separate from the lyrics. Here, however, the sonnets were a single work, and in the first "gift" edition were bound separately, the two volumes offered together in a slipcase. The slimmer one contained the sonnet sequence that had been occupying most of her conscious and subconscious attention, the extraordinary "Epitaph for the Race of Man." In later editions, the poem was included as Part V of *Wine,* in a single volume. Although much has been written about the work, few critics have fully recognized the stature of the sequence in relation to the rest of her poetry, or its contribution to American poetry as a whole.

222

"Epitaph" had been brewing in the poet's brain for almost fifteen years. Doubtless in 1920, when she was caught up in the antiwar fervor which brought forth *Aria da Capo,* she began thinking of man's tendency toward self-destruction. At first she chose the same form in which she had composed "Renascence," iambic tetrameter, for a long poem, which she called then, as now, "Epitaph for the Race of Man." From the beginning, the theme was evolutionary, beginning with the earliest stirrings of man. At that time she started with the monkey and traced the development of man through his rise and fall by his own doing and undoing, and regarding him as a species capable of climbing to great heights only to be felled by the weapon of his brother's hand. The poem surprised her friend Wilson, "in being purely philosophical, and gave him a new idea of her range." That the frail but electrically vibrant Edna was absorbed by broad, abstract ideas as well as by objective study of her own emotional experiences had not occurred to him until then. He had seen *Aria da Capo* and found in it an inkling of her "peculiar power" and of her acute sense of life's cruelty. But her true intellectuality—what he termed her "tough intellectual side"—did not strike him until a year later, when she sat in his apartment reading parts of the original version of her long epitaph for the human race.

She had put the poem aside for several years; but when she took it out again, she decided that the form in which she had written "Renascence" was not stringent enough for a poem designed to record the inevitable doom of the human race as she envisioned it. For "Epitaph" like "Renascence," must have stemmed from a vision encompassing not only the world but the entire universe. Ever since the move to "Steepletop," she had been studying the stars, and as her amateur astronomy increased, her concept of this particular study of man altered; and she began writing the series of sonnets which eventually became the sequence of eighteen now published together under the title of the earlier poem.

Viewing the Earth as an infinitesmal planet in the cosmos, the sequence starts with the prediction that long before the core is cold Earth will be utterly still, and man and his engines will be gone. From there the sonnets look backward in time to the age of dinosaurs, and proceed slowly forward past other prehistoric creatures, "through fifty million years of jostling time," to man, "crawling out of ooze and climbing up the shore." Man, destined to stride across the sky like the sun, the strange, brilliant creature capable of laughter and "droll tears," music and art, and engines, is gone without a trace, and the silent Earth cannot tell the story of his demise. It is the poet who, with an eloquence and economy of phrasing camparable to the classic lines of the Latin poets she knew so well, reveals the tragic reason for man's eradication. Taking him through the trials of the ages—surviving the jungle, fire, flood, and earthquake—the sonneteer tears away the veil of mystery to show him receiving destruction "at his brother's hand." Only for a brief moment in history, when "his neighbor was his friend," was loss "sweeter than silver coins to spend"; otherwise he goes his way alone, "flinging a ribald stone/At all endeavour alien to his own." It is the bad cell within, "obsequious Greed," that betrays him, so that in the end he is "split along the vein by his own kind." Throughout the narrative, the action on Earth is correlated with the movement of the stars, the other planets, and the appropriate constellations, across the vast reaches of outer space.

Seen in this larger perspective, the Earth, "unhappy planet born to die," and Man, her fairest creature though to her anonymous like the rest, appear in new dimensions: smaller, to the point of becoming microscopic, but not necessarily less important. In sonnet number twelve, with a composer's change of mood, the sense of doom is momentarily lifted as the poet depicts two of Earth's inhabitants: the farmer with his milk buckets and the black ant "hurrying to milk the aphis pastured on the rose." They pass without so much as a "good-morrow," if, indeed, they see each other at all. And it is the same in autumn when they meet again, "two herdsmen driving their flocks to stall"; the closing measures observe quietly that "on the quaint abode of each, the evening and the first snow fall!" This sonnet and the next, the thirteenth, pointing up the contrast between the awesome sight of the stars moving through the night past the turning sphere of Earth, and "industrious man," going about his business "unamazed," provide an intermezzo before the crashing chords of the climax.

The last five sonnets, the fourteenth through the eighteenth, are key poems of the sequence and belong to the strong Millay canon of antiwar poetry. The play on words is inadvertent but not inappropriate, for she waged a war of words against the violence and destruction of the military until events in Europe caused her to become an interventionist. The theme of man's inhumanity to man, of his cancerous greed, is sounded in eloquent, powerful passages, until, in the seventeenth sonnet, with a sense of horror the reader sees man "set in brass on the swart thumb of Doom." In the closing sonnet, she sings with melodic phrasing, a heartbreaking lament for "most various Man, cut down to spring no more," "and all the clamour that was he, silenced, and all the riveted pride he wore." Then, with a masterful stroke, in answer to the wracking question, "What power has brought you low? whose the heavy blade? . . . ," the poem ends with the tender admonition, "Strive not to speak, poor scattered mouth; I know."

At the time of publication, "Epitaph" was more or less overlooked, in that it was lumped with the rest of the poetry concerned with social problems contained in *Wine from These Grapes.* Included among these, actually the lesser portion of the volume, which had many lyric poems, such as "The Fawn," several reflective poems on the season of autumn, and the elegiac series to her mother, was the acrimonious "Apostrophe to Man," a withering denunciation of war. Readers who were shocked and dismayed by the opening line, "Detestable race, continue to expunge yourself, die out," and critics who cited the poem as evidence that the optimistic author of "Renascence," reaffirmer of the human spirit, had become a cynical pessimist, apparently neglected to note the explanatory subtitle, "On reflecting that the world is ready to go to war again." These lines, with phrases like, "Commercialize/Bacteria harmful to human tissue,/Put death on the market," even more applicable today than in 1934, were written in anger and represent a momentary mood of disillusion if not despair. The "Epitaph for the Race of Man," on the other hand, was created after long periods of gestation, during which the poet reflected and, as in *Fatal Interview*, evaluated in tranquility her turbulent emotions, to which she now added feelings evoked by events of her time. The element that sets the work apart from other poetry about social problems is its broad perspective and poetic excellence which enables "Epitaph," while maintaining its value as social commentary, to reach the realm of art.

Elizabeth Atkins, the prime eulogist of Edna Millay, was among the first to recognize the stature of the work. As with *Fatal Interview*, she discussed the contemporary and classical background of "Epitaph"; but in her ardor for Latin references, makes a comparison which is misleading when she states that "in its finished simplicity and purity of expression, Millay's 'Epitaph' might make another chapter of Ovid's *Metamorphosis*." The subject of Millay's sonnet sequence is far removed from Ovid's tales of transformation of the gods; and even from the standpoint of style, there is nothing about "Epitaph" to suggest the *Metamorphosis*. More accurate is Atkins' comparison of the work with "the graver and larger style of the *Aeneid*." Closer still is Max Eastman's statement of some twenty-five years later (1959), which in another context declared of "Epitaph": "Brief as it is, it is the only poem in the language since Milton that can be compared in mental boldness with Dante and Lucretius."

Eastman was taking issue with John Crowe Ransom, who in a 1937 article dismissed Edna Millay's poetry as did John Ciardi after her death with a small rosemary bouquet of nostalgic praise for her love poems of the twenties, her spirit of "flaming youth." Ransom went further, declaiming that Millay lacked intellectuality, and that "the modern intellectual field of reference is too wide to be commanded by the innocent female mind." This is a laughable statement in view of Edna's personal life, and nothing short of ridiculous in the light of her astonishing intellectual achievement in "Epitaph for the Race of Man."

There are various peace poems in *Wine from These Grapes*, notably the free-form "Conscientious Objector," the first line of which might well be adopted by present-day draft protestors: "I shall die, but that is all I shall do for Death." The figure of Death as the Black Rider preparing to mount his steed in haste to go about "his busy day in the Balkans, in Cuba" is not original; but the concept of refusing to help or cooperate with Death in any way is a bold and different approach to the antiwar theme. Here also is the lyric of the disillusioned seeker of justice, "My Spirit, Sore from Marching," with its self-counsel to "cleave henceforth to Beauty;/Expect no more from man." These eight stanzas of rhyming quatrains have an eighteenth-century air in counterpoint to the modern idea of "cool and aimless Beauty . . . that made no promise,/And has no word to break"; who offers "hope for priest and laymen; . . . heresy for all." Again, inspired by the Sacco and Vanzetti case, Edna expressed her sense of futility by warning against future involvement in "Causes"; yet, given her particular makeup, she could not cut herself off from humanity and its cares, any more than she could stop writing poetry about it, or about anything that, like an intaglio, made a deep impress on her mind.

One of her later critics, Jean Morris Petitt, points out in a doctoral thesis that when Millay became consciously aware of the times in which she lived and tried to write poetry on such subjects as Sacco and Vanzetti (there were two sonnets in memory of these men in the new volume) and other social problems, her verse lost its singing quality: "for she was then out of her essential nature." But who is to say what Edna Millay's "essential nature" was? Certainly it was not limited to the cry of all-for-love-or-the-world-well-lost, except in the sense that love embraces all of mankind and his suffering. There was something in her that could not keep silent when she was moved by an event or circumstance that outraged her sense of justice. As far back as 1914, fired by the outbreak of World War I, she had written a sonnet identifying herself as "the child of all mothers," a poem she called "the blueprint of her social consciousness." And although it is true that in another five or six years she was to speak out on issues to the detriment of her poetry, she definitely had not lost "the singing quality" in *Wine from These Grapes*, or the lyric passion in "Epitaph for the Race of Man."

Those who deplored the pessimism of the sequence failed to grasp its underlying mysticism. Like O'Neill, Edna Millay at this time and later was darkly pessimistic but deeply compassionate toward mankind. She proclaimed man's weakness and the tragedy of his doom, but her vision of self-destruction was accompanied by sympathy, sorrow, and a feeling of oneness with man and the universe. To accomplish her aim in a cycle of eighteen sonnets, with a distillation of language equal to Emily Dickinson and the philosophic magnitude of Milton, is nothing short of poetic genius. Yet the significance of "Epitaph" is rarely recognized. In fact, it is seldom mentioned by chroniclers or anthologists.

Most glaring was the omission of both of Millay's major sonnet sequences, *Fatal Interview* and "Epitaph," from the *History of American Poetry, 1900–1940* by Horace Gregory and his wife, Marya Zaturenska, published in 1946. Gregory, whose taste is usually impeccable, may have let a personal grudge override his good judgment in this instance: Edna had refused to recommend him for a Guggenheim fellowship on the grounds that his translation of Latin poetry was inaccurate. The refusal was quixotic on her part, but she was obsessive on the subject of Latin poetry, and her loyalty to her first academic love would not allow her to permit what she considered a slipshod translation go unnoticed. Though his annoyance may have been jusified, it is hardly an explanation for ignoring two such important contributions to American poetry; or for summing up a figure like Edna St. Vincent Millay in a brief patronizing sentence. After a routine recognition of "Renascence," the *Fig* poems, and some of the love lyrics in *Second April*, the *History* concludes: "Her virtues are those of an effortless, seemingly artless charm of youth and of lightly touched and quickly dispelled sorrow, and voices prophetically that her poetry will probably introduce other generations of girls and young women to the phenomena of an adolescent self-discovery in terms of poetry."

In one of the later revisions of Louis Untermeyer's *Modern American Poets*, the perennial anthologist adopts an avuncular attitude toward Edna Millay, appraising her with the surface fondness he might feel toward a talented but wayward niece. He ends the biographical critical sketch with an affectionate pat on the head; and although his selections include one sonnet, number six, from "Epitaph," he does not identify it, or make any mention of the sequence as such. Moreover, he changed the punctuation at the end of the second line, replacing a colon with a question mark, thereby altering the tone from the imperative to one of superficial inquiry, reducing it to banality. The Millay correspondence is replete with admonitions to publishers, editors, even to translators that not one change be made in her work, no matter how minor it might seem. In a letter to Rolfe Humphries concerning her translation of a Spanish poem into English, she warned him to "make sure that no change whatever, not even so much as the change of a comma" be made in the poem by anyone except herself. She was especially adamant in regard to the sonnets in "Epitaph" when Cass Canfield approached her with some suggestions made by an associate involving a meaning different from that she intended. She would have been outraged by Untermeyer's arbitrary alteration if she had been alive.

Most anthologies, besides "Renascence" and "God's World," include only the lighter verse, and the more easily understood love poetry of Edna Millay. They leave out many sonnets in the major sequences. Fortunately a few eminent critics and literati like Edmund Wilson, Robert Hillyer, Max Eastman, and a handful of discriminating admirers have been unafraid to place Edna Millay's mastery of the sonnet in its proper perspective. And although it is true that she has always been "overplayed or underplayed," [1] lauded beyond all bounds or dismissed as a youthful exponent of free love expressed in old-fashioned, conventional forms, the sequence constituting "Epitaph for the Race of Man" has been generally neglected in either case. However, the fact remains that the timelessness of the theme, ironically more applicable today than it was in 1934, the flawlessness of the technique, and the depth of feeling combine to make this eighteen-sonnet poem a profound and enduring work of art.

[1] Pointed out in a doctoral dissertation by Jean Morris Petitt, dealing with Millay's poetry in its "Social and Literary Milieu" (1956).

CHAPTER XV

"The Masonry of Art"

REGARDLESS of the critical response to the meaningful and artistic merits of the major poetry in *Wine from These Grapes,* the volume was an immediate sellout, and went into multiple printings soon after publication. Four months later, Edna, writing to "Lulu" from Florida, informed him that "the new book had sold already more than forty thousand copies." She gave the figures to reassure him and Alyse that she could well afford the thousand dollars which she had just cabled, and would arrive in about ten days to help them out of a legal jam. As she and Eugen had feared, the Powys and their neighbors in Dorset had been sued for libel because they circulated petitions against the treatment of the inmates at the Home for Delinquent Girls. The headmistress, Mrs. Nincom, wearing what Edna called a "Two-Hundred-Pound-Look," had convinced the jury that the accusations were false and the petitioners were all fined one hundred pounds and court costs. Together with the staggering amounts the Powys had to pay their solicitors, the fine was a terrible blow; and the ordeal was so disturbing to the British writer that it aggravated his tubercular trouble.

As soon as Edna heard the distressing news, she mailed the thousand dollars, offering to send another if necessary. But the Powys were reluctant to accept, so she wrote a forceful but fond letter, telling them that they would "hurt her beyond healing" if they refused her gift. With the proceeds from the new book she could easily afford it, and even if she could not, she added, what else could she buy with the money that would be so precious to her as the thought that she was helping him. Her attitude was so typical that her English friends, touched, could not help smiling as they gratefully accepted her generous help. However, it was true that she did not have to deprive herself at this particular time. She and Eugen had just spent the winter in the Virgin Islands on St. Thomas and were slowly making their way back north, stopping in Puerto Rico, Haiti, and Santiago de Cuba as well as Havana and Islamorado, Florida, where she wrote the Powys. From there, they visited Mr. Brann, their neighbor in the Berkshires, who had a place at Boynton Beach; then they went to see the great magnolia gardens outside Charleston, South Carolina, at the invitation of the owners, Mr. and Mrs. Norwood Hastie, who were admirers of Edna Millay. They looked in at "Steepletop" just long enough to "say hello to the dogs and pick up the car," and went on to Ragged Island, where they spent the month of April before returning to the farm in time for the spring planting. Eugen would have said, teasingly, "Yes, it's a hard life." But this was one of the few periods when the poet and her husband seem to have been truly relaxed, in relatively good health, free of commitments and economic worries.

In fact, the years from 1930 to 1936 represent the peak of Edna Millay's career professionally and financially as well as creatively. Her popularity was at its height. Everywhere she went she was met by requests for readings. More than once she stopped for an appearance at the University of Florida in Tallahassee on the way down or going back to "Steepletop" and always created a stir among students and professors. Her regular reading tours continued to be fabulously successful in spite of the Depression and her frequent outbursts of temperament. A Providence schoolteacher, then a student in Boston, tells of saving her pennies for weeks during one Depression year in order to buy a seat in the top balcony for one of Edna Millay's readings. And when the poet appeared onstage in a flowing Fortuny gown of sea-green chiffon, a scarf across her throat, she announced in a hoarse whisper that she had laryngitis; but if the audience would bear with her and be very quiet she would read her poems anyway.

The audience cheered; and although the student-teacher had to strain her eyes and ears, she found Millay's performance "unforgettable—thrilling in some mysterious manner, though you could hardly catch her words."

This was a typical reaction. No one ever dreamed that Edna Millay dreaded these appearances beforehand, that she was sometimes forced to go to bed with a severe headache, and that she often had to have a few gulps from the flask Eugen always brought along to brace her before she went onstage. But, like many poets, including Robert Frost, who read to packed halls up to the year before he died (1963) and never quite overcame the trauma preceeding a performance, Edna felt entirely at ease as soon as she was in front of the audience, acknowledging the warm applause. She had the trick of Frost and Carl Sandburg of being able to make spontaneous quips and confidential asides, as if she were speaking to an intimate and sympathetic friend. And, unlike either of her older colleagues, who read their verses in rasping tones, she had her extraordinary clear, melodic voice and an acting ability that enabled her to project her lines. In addition, she possessed an indefinable quality akin to the incandescence of Sarah Bernhardt that thrilled her audiences, allowing them to accept her occasional displays of temperament as part of her performance. If the microphone was not working properly, she would angrily demand that it be fixed at once. If the buzzing that usually accompanied her entrance did not die down soon after her bows, she would wait for what seemed an unconscionably long time; she would not begin until the hall was totally quiet. And although she expected her listeners to allow for her laryngitis, she was annoyed if some of them coughed. More than once she stopped reading in the middle of a poem to announce that unless "those people who could not restrain their coughing left the hall, *she* was leaving!"

But for all that, the people loved her, and she put on a good show for them. Her interpretation of her poetry, like her personality, was many-faceted, according to the content of the selections. Her reading of "Renascence" was as varied as the moods of the poem, all the way from the awed innocence of an adolescent girl to the cynical sadness of the world's sins and sufferings, to the somber tones of the entombment, the terror and excitement of the releasing storm, the exultation, and the final oracular chords of the closing stanza. When she read any of the short pieces in *From a Very Little Sphinx,* particularly the one about the boy "born in Paris, France," she would take on the demeanor and tone of a freckle-faced twelve-year-old, standing with feet apart and hands behind her back. Then she might recite some meditative poems sitting in a chair, which was the only prop she ever used, and after a brief pause, rise, with a regal air seeming taller than her five foot height, and recite some of her Elizabethan sonnets with the directness and nobility of their classic form.

For a time during the late twenties she had assumed an aspect of rather severe simplicity, cutting her hair in a short, neat bob, wearing navy dresses with demure white collars and cuffs, or man-tailored dark suits and even a man's shirt and four-in-hand tie. One custom-made tweed outfit she ordered included a pair of "plus-four" knickers, a popular fashion among men engendered by the golf craze at the time. Edna's game was tennis, but she had the suit designed for country wear, and was photographed in it at "Steepletop" during an interview with a reporter for a Sunday magazine feature story in a New York newspaper. Many photo studies were made of her during this brief period, some of them still favorites for reproduction, but they are not "typical" Millay likenesses. In the thirties, when the hemlines of women's skirts dropped, she returned to the long, "floaty" gowns that had helped to create her legend, and she let her red hair grow to almost shoulder length. During her readings, she would fling back her slightly unruly locks with a toss of her head or smooth them down dramatically with one hand; and when she stood to recite her sonnets, she always allowed her flowing skirt to fall into graceful folds before she began to speak.

The gestures were instinctive with her, attuned to the tempo and mood of the lines she happened to be reading; if her poetry had not been of such high caliber they might have seemed absurd; and indeed, a number of her colleagues criticized her "theatricalities" or "histrionics" as being a bit too obvious and old-hat staginess. But the people who flocked to the halls expected a professional dramatic performance when they came to hear Edna St. Vincent Millay, and she did not disappoint them. She was not yet at the point of some years later, when she had to force herself to accept these engagements; and she could not deny that she derived a certain amount of pleasure from being so much in demand.

However, in spite of the fact that outwardly things were going well in the early spring of 1935, Edna was still a prey to inner doubts and neurotic fears, one of which she mentioned for the first time in a note to Hal Bynner on May 2: she simply could not write letters any more. She, who had been such a copious correspondent while her mother was alive, now had so great a dread of letter-writing that it was like suffering from a disease, for which she had coined a new term: "Epistophobia." She would make use of the word or a variant of it, "epistolaphobia," whenever she tired to excuse herself for not writing letters in the future, even to old friends like him or "Bunny" Wilson. Her state of mind was further revealed in her half-joking remark that she "was going to die in a few days and had no time left except for people she was crazy about": she wanted Hal to come to "Steepletop" for a visit, but without his mother if possible.[1] Finally, she berated her friend for getting *her* headache, on which she felt she had exclusive rights.

Her plaintive mood may have been due to the let-down she usually experienced when she was between books, but it was not long before, quite by accident, she became involved in a new project. She received a request from George Dillon, the poet and editor, whom she had known for several years, asking if she would write the introduction to his translations of Baudelaire. They had often discussed and argued about the French poet's *Les Fleurs du mal*, from a literary point of view, and Edna consented at once to write the foreward. He sent a few translations for her to look over. She got out a copy of Baudelaire to compare his version of one of the poems with the original. A line from another poem caught her eye, and "to her horror," before she realized what she was letting herself in for, she had translated it.

[1] Bynner lived with his mother in New Hampshire until her death at the age of ninety when he moved to Santa Fe. He died there on June 1, 1968.

She was drawn to do more, and although she struggled against the impulse, she suddenly found herself a full-fledged collaborator of Dillon's book.

She plunged into the project like a veteran translator, trying different metrics, seeking the advice of Herbert Lipscomb, Professor of Latin at Randolph Macon College, and Miss Margaret Gilman, Professor of French at Bryn Mawr, on some of the fine points in regard to rhythm, as well as French professors at Vassar, Barnard, Harvard, and Yale on other obscure points. She did all the biographical research she could in this country, for little had been written about Baudelaire at the time. She and George Dillon, for all their reading and dissecting of French poetry, had never delved into the unorthodox "domestic arrangements" of Baudelaire, which included living with a mistress for many years, and the habits of a confirmed opium eater. The poems themselves, not the practices, evil or otherwise, that served as their source fascinated both American poets. Now, however, Edna Millay felt that she should find out more about Baudelaire's personal life as background for the Introduction to the book, which was her responsibility. She made a trip to Europe to visit the village of Honfleur, in Normandy, Baudelaire's birthplace. A few of the old native families remembered him as a boy and were able to give her some useful information. She worked industriously on the translations, sometimes with Dillon, but they worked separately for the most part; each took a specific number of poems to translate and then read each other's results for possible errors, suggestions, or changes. He spent most of August at "Steepletop," and then accompanied Edna and Eugen to Maine for a week's rest at Ragged Island, after which she went to Europe for the special biographical research on Baudelaire, returning in October.

It was a busy summer, a long period of sustained effort, and would have been free from worry except that Arthur Ficke suddenly became ill again, and was rushed to the hospital for an operation. Through a surgical error, he nearly lost his life, and had to stay in the hospital much longer than he otherwise would have. When Edna and Eugen visited him, he was so weak he could scarcely speak to them, and seemed drained of all his life force; Gladys was almost sick from anxiety, though she tried valiantly to hide it. And even after Arthur came home, his face was blanched and bleak; the old, fun-loving spark of gaiety seemed to have gone out of him. His recovery was slow; as soon as he was able, he started writing poetry that dealt with his traumatic experience. In "Hospital," a long free-verse poem, he related his sensations throughout the ordeal, including the thoughts that came to him while he was in a half-conscious state, not yet completely under the anesthetic; one remarkable passage quoted part of Eugen's philosophical outlook, mentioning him by name: "the voice of Eugen Boissevain, as if directly inside my ear, said, 'You see now that there are many modes of being, and that all you have to do is choose which level you prefer and stay there.' I realized that this was true. . . ."

The poem, published the following year in *The Secret and Other Poems,* represented the rambling, conversational style to which Arthur had inclined more and more, in spite of his loyalty to the sonnet, and his satire of the free-verse cultists in *Spectra.* As always, he read his latest offerings to "Vincie" and Eugen; and while she preferred some poems to others, she was deeply impressed with the work as a whole. Moreover, the fact that Ficke had adopted the modern trend undoubtedly influenced her change of style in her next book.

She worked with her customary concentration during the fall and early winter of 1935, polishing her translations. And she wrote, with innumerable additions and revisions, a long introduction to the Baudelaire book in which she revealed for the first and only time in her career some of her ideas on the creation and composition of poetry. She began by speaking of the initial, barely defined form in the creative process, pointing out that "when the image of the poem first rises before the . . . suddenly agitated person who is to write it, its shadowy bulk is already dimly outlined. . . ." She went on, listing various features a poem might take on, and one cannot help feeling that she must have already had in mind her next work, which was to contain a sampling of most of the varieties she mentioned in regard to the incipient poem, which possibly is "rhymed or unrhymed; it is trimeter, tetrameter, and pentameter; it is free verse, a sonnet, an epic, an ode, a five-act play." As she continued, her eye turned increasingly in the direction of contemporary experimentation: "To many poets, the physical character of a poem, its rhythm, its music, the way it looks on a page, is quite as important as the thing they wish to say; to some, vastly more important." The last was certainly true of e. e. cummings, whose work she had recently recommended for a Guggenheim award in an exhaustive three-thousand word analysis. Yet Cummings was the antithesis of Millay: up to this point, she had put original ideas into conventional forms, while he had put conventional ideas into original, or distorted, disfigured forms. In the Introduction, she employed the vocabulary of her profession, speaking technically of syllables, dactyls, and such various unusual meters as the heptameter, before treating of translations in general, and those she and George Dillon had made of Baudelaire's poetry in particular.

She was worn out by the time she finished, shortly after Thanksgiving. Eugen had gone down to Florida to locate a restful place for the winter, admonishing her to follow him as soon as she got the manuscript off to Harper's. But before she left, she made a point of selecting a whole suitcase of books for "darling Artie" to divert him during his convalescence. She sent them to "Hardhack" with a note for "Gladdie," advising her to read *BUtterfield 8* "before letting Arthur see it." She must have felt that John O'Hara's recently published novel concerning abortion, describing the tragic consequences of surgery, would be disturbing to Arthur, who was far from well. Other books in the lot were just as interesting, and some of them were gay. He and Gladys were also leaving for Mexico or another warm climate where he could recuperate faster. Edna would look forward to seeing them the next summer when they would all have "lots of fun" together, because Arthur would be well again, and more like his "cute, gay old self," and she would not be working so hard, so perhaps she would be more like *her* "cute, gay old self!" Her affectionate tone toward Gladys was slightly patronizing, a feeling the latter resented, though she rarely showed it. Whatever the interplay of emotions, the ties between these four distinctive personalities were extremely close; and the effect of Arthur Ficke's writing on the poetry of Edna Millay is easily discernible in reading the works of both.

Just now she had to spend the last months of 1935 and the first two months of 1936 in a muddle of proofreading and making last-minute arrangements for the book. She was in a constant fever of combined energy and exasperation, especially since she was in Delray Beach, Florida, Dillon was in Virginia, and the publishers were in New York. Her letters to both her co-author and Eugene Saxton at Harper's crackle with barbed humor; her wit sometimes barely covered her irritation. One important change she demanded was that the title, instead of the scholarly but "unattractive," "Selected Poems of Charles Baudelaire," be simply a translation of the French poet's own title, *Flowers of Evil*, which she felt would be "extremely attractive, arresting to the eye, and exciting to the imagination." The others agreed, and the publication date was set for spring: any date but April 1, Edna warned, for she would not be published on April Fool's Day, and the book came out on April 2.

After a period of "absolute rest," during which she reread all of Vergil, she began concentrating on the completion of a long philosophical verse drama, a series of dialogues, on a wide variety of subjects. It was an experimental piece, written in a variety of styles. The previous fall *Harper's* Magazine had published a few of the poems, dissimiliar in style, ranging from a formal sonnet, "Lucas, Romantic Love Is on the rocks," to free verse, "If you do not believe in God it is a good thing to believe in Communism." In February, after returning the corrected proofs of *Flowers of Evil* to Harper's, she wrote an answer to a recent letter from Arthur, sympathizing with him for having had to go to a sanitarium in the southwest by himself before he and Gladys could go to Mexico; he had "plenty of pluck," she felt. She was "happy and excited" with his news that his new volume [2] would soon be published by Doubleday-Doran, but she hoped he had not cut out any of her "pets," and she warned him not to be too clever. This was the time when they all got "so clever and cynical" they were "capable of doing more harm to their own book than the Commissioner of Police could do. . . ."

Without realizing it, she may have put her finger on her own problem in the manuscript she was striving to complete. If any-

[2] *The Secret and Other Poems,* including "Hospital."

thing, this new work, which she planned to dedicate to Arthur, suffered from being "too clever"; and, while not exactly cynical, it was agnostic and analytical to the point of being coldly hyper-critical of human nature. Stimulated by the disturbing events of the times at home and abroad, the alarming trend toward mech-anization and military conflict in the world, and favorably dis-posed toward the freedom of Arthur's latest work, Edna had set out to write a running commentary on life on earth at that particular moment in history, treating of man's struggle for sur-vival, his beliefs and doubts, his mental and moral shortcomings, and his one saving grace, humor.

The device she chose for presenting her observations was a dramatic exchange of ideas and opinions among seven men, seated with the host after a dinner party, in the drawing room of his "fine old house in Tenth Street, just west of Fifth Avenue." The setting was similar to that of Arthur Ficke's five-act verse play, *Mr. Faust,* which takes place in the home of a wealthy man, and deals with a discussion among a number of characters. Arthur's play was published by Kennerly in 1913; and in 1922, a new version for stage production was brought out by Frank Shay, right after *Aria da Capo,* so Edna undoubtedly knew Arthur's play; but the resemblance between *Mr. Faust* and *Conversation at Midnight* ends with the locale, for the latter is entirely different in content. The guests are stereotypes, each serving as a mouth-piece for his particular segment of civilization: a stockbroker, a capitalist-Republican; a painter; a writer of short stories; a poet, the Communist of the group; a cynical young advertising executive; a Roman Catholic priest; and a wealthy liberal, the agnostic and host of the gathering. The last, Ricardo, seems to have been created with the combined virtues of Eugen and Arthur in mind; he has "a gentle and affectionate nature, a striking physical beauty, and an aristocratic and subtle mind," in addition to a liberal, questioning outlook. One detail of the stage directions—a "small fire of pinon wood from New Mexico" burning in the grate of his marble fireplace on Fifth Avenue probably came from Edna's recollections of the aromatic pinon-wood fires they had enjoyed at the Fickes' in Santa Fe. It was just the touch she needed to indicate Ricardo's finesse and discriminating tastes.

As the men start talking while having an after-dinner drink, it is evident that the main conflict lies between Merton, the sportsman-hunter-capitalist, and Carl, the poet-Communist; but there are minor arguments among the others on the topics of religion, love, women, modern conveniences and their nuisance value, even the motive of a surgeon performing an operation. Edna had the manuscript nearly completed early in May when she and Eugen began to think of going back to "Steepletop." She had not had much rest during the winter and wanted some recreation before they returned. She had heard that the islands of Sanibel and Captiva off the Florida coast were ideal for discovering rare seashells on the beaches, a collector's interest from Camden days that she still retained. They decided to try the Palms Hotel on Sanibel, and arrived one late afternoon with a full hour left before sunset; Edna was eager to get out on the beach and start gathering shells, so they had the luggage sent up to the room, one suitcase of which contained the manuscript for her new book.

Some impulse made her turn and look back up the beach a few minutes later, and, to her horrified, unbelieving eyes, she saw the hotel engulfed in flames! In what must have been a flash fire, the building was burnt to the ground, and all their belongings, including the manuscript, burned with it. The sight must have been sickening, especially since she knew there was no hope of saving the *only copy* of her manuscript. Everything was lost: their wraps, their clothes, a favorite emerald ring of Edna's, and her cherished seventeenth-century copy of Catullus, a "tiny, shabby brown leather one" that Eugen had given her before they were married. She took stern comfort from a line of Catullus, which she kept repeating to herself: "Cease this folly . . . and what you see is lost, set down as lost."

They drove miserably back to "Steepletop," Edna wrapped in a steamer rug over her wrinkled, once-white linen suit. The car developed a loose bearing and they had to creep along at thirty-five miles an hour. By the time they reached Charleston they were so unpresentable they could not possibly stop to see the magnolia gardens and their friends, the Hasties, as they had promised the previous year. According to her account, they "slunk into hotels late at night with their arms over their faces, and sneaked out before daybreak."

When they finally got back to Austerlitz, she went to work at once, trying to recall the lost poems. But unfortunately, her usually reliable memory failed her when she needed it most, probably, as she explained in her foreword, because she was acutely conscious that, except for the few poems published in the magazine, "no line of the book existed anywhere except in her memory. . . ." Ordinarily she would have been able to recollect the whole work, line for line. But the fire was an unforeseen hazard, though she realized ruefully that any author must take it into account in safeguarding a manuscript. In such moments she had to repeat again the words of Catullus,[3] and remind herself sternly to stick to the job of reconstructing her play. She wrote under constant strain.

It was an ill-fated summer. A few weeks after their return, another accident occurred; she and Eugen were driving home one night after having been out for the evening. Edna was leaning against the door of the station wagon, which suddenly flew open as they took a sharp turn, and she was "hurled out into the pitch darkness"—"a very strange sensation." She rolled down a rocky gully until she "was able to grab at some alders and come to a halt." Eugen, who rushed to rescue her as soon as he could stop the car, found that she had "a big bump on her little red-head," as he wrote to Alyse Gregory, "bruises and scratches all over, and her right arm was all bunged up. . . ." Several nerves were injured by the strange mishap, and for a time, and again two years later, she had to wear a sling, and could not play the piano or use the typewriter. When it got better, toward the end of the summer, she tried to play tennis, but "had to stop because it hurt," she wrote to Dante Bergonzi, one of the two music students who stayed at "Steepletop" in the early part of the season. She might have been able to type again, but her typewriter chose just that time to "crack up under her." The first

---

[3] Luckily she had left at home a beautiful copy of Catullus given to her by Professor Lipscomb, without which she would have been "lost indeed." On a previous trip she had taken along both copies.

draft of poems was always done in pencil in her black-bound note-books, but when she prepared the final draft for the publishers, she used the typewriter consistently. In December, while in New York to replenish her wardrobe, she caught the flu, and was ill there all winter long.

The pain and misfortunes only added to the strain of trying to reconstruct her manuscript; but eventually she managed to piece together a verse play made up of poems "remembered word for word" from the original, others partly remembered and rewritten, and new ones, composed during her illness in New York. By the middle of April and through most of May, she was consulting with Eugene Saxton of Harper's and correcting proofs for the new work.

Just before leaving the city, she was notified that New York University wished to confer on her the honorary degree of Doctor of Humane Letters during the commencement exercises in June. Mrs. Chase, wife of the Chancellor invited her to be the guest of honor at a dinner "for a small group of ladies" the evening before commencement. She "answered at once, accepting the award of the degree with happiness and pride, and the invitation to dinner with pleasure." But a week or so later, when she heard from the secretary of the university that a separate dinner was being given at the Waldorf in honor of the male recipients of honorary degrees, she was incensed against the discrimination toward her sex and registered a heated objection to the secretary when she submitted a request for tickets for Eugen, Norma, and Charles at the commencement exercises. She ended her protest by begging of the secretary, in the interests of all women, that she might be "the last woman so honoured, to be required to swallow from the very cup of this honour, the gall of this humiliation."

The new book, aptly entitled, *Conversation at Midnight*, appeared in early autumn approximately a year after it was originally scheduled. The rather puzzling dedication read, "To Arthur Davison Ficke and 42 Commerce Street." The address, a reference to the apartment Arthur and Gladys moved into right after their marriage at Edna and Eugen's house on Bedford Street, was Edna's way of indirectly including Gladys, and of recalling fond memories of the months the four had spent living in Greenwich Village, back yards touching, fifteen years before. No one except those involved realized that this was an intimate, affectionate note, but Edna knew that the Fickes would surely understand its significance. She had been in the habit of giving Arthur an inscribed author's copy every time a new work was published; yet this book, dedicated to him, was the only one in which she did not write some tender inscription. Perhaps she thought that the dedication implied all she felt. It is more likely, however, that at publication time she and Arthur were temporarily estranged from each other because of a curious circumstance.

In September, the LaBranches, one of the neighbors who had joined in giving the "grand house-party" in 1930, and were still most hospitable, invited a large gathering for cocktails one evening, and the overflow, Edna and Arthur among them, drifted into the "gun-room" George LaBranche had fixed up at one end of the house. As usual, the two old friends were deep in conversation, when Arthur, who had a "devil's trick" of catching people off guard, suddenly came out with what seemed to her an utterly irrelevant question. Murmuring the first line from one of the poems in *Second April,* he asked casually but pointedly: "To whom did you write that sonnet, Vince?"

Edna, who was "at least six cocktails off her guard," stared at him for a moment, furious. This was the sonnet beginning, "And you as well must die, belovéd dust," one of those written in the heat of her ardor after their extraordinary encounter in 1918. Arthur must have known it was written to him, but even if he did not, it was shockingly indiscreet of him to ask such a question in the crowded party. Of course he spoke so low that nobody could have overheard him, but even so, she had no alternative but to counter quickly with his name and let the matter drop "to keep her loosened tongue from folly."

She could not forget the incident. This was not the first time that Arthur had played such a trick on her. Whether it was because he needed reassurance, or because he still felt some possessive love toward her and was jealous of others, she could not tell; but once, not too long before, he had asked her in the same offhand way, as if it was just a joke: "Vince, was Lulu ever your lover?" Her only reply then was to rebuke him gently, for his indelicacy. Now, the more she thought about his brash behavior, so unlike his angelic disposition in everything else, the more she resented his attitude, and she resolved to put a stop to it.

She knew he would probably feel hurt, but two or three days after the LaBranches' party, she sent him a note flatly denying that the sonnet was written to him. It was a strangely emotional letter, sorrowful and tender rather than angry, reasoning with her "darling Artie" rather than reprimanding him. She pointed out that, knowing how reticent she was about her own private affairs and those of others, it was wrong of him to persist in persecuting her with indiscreet questions. If he loved her as he claimed, it was foolish of him, because it would mean that she could no longer feel at ease with him, and that, eventually, she would have to avoid him. She repeated her regret at having to hurt him, but she knew that it would have been worse to let the matter go: their "two distinct and incompatible memories of that moment in the gun-room" would have contorted "every word either of them ever said to each other again." She signed the letter, with her love, so that Arthur would know her deep feeling for him had not changed in spite of her disapproval and disavowal in regard to his connection with the sonnet.[4]

Since *Conversation at Midnight* was dedicated to him, she probably saw to it that the publishers sent him a copy, intending to write in it when the trouble had blown over, as she was confident it would, though she heard nothing from "Hardhack" for a time. Arthur realized that he had deeply offended her, and after an interval, resumed contact with "Steepletop" as if nothing unpleasant had occurred. He refrained from prying queries, and it was not many weeks before they were back on their old footing as close friends and colleagues, tearing apart the Pulitzer Prize committee for handing out or withholding awards "more for moral than for aesthetic reasons." Oddly enough, Edna never got around to inscribing the one book she dedicated to Arthur, and he evidently felt the omission keenly enough to bring it to Gladys' attention some years later.

Perhaps she was sharply aware, and did not want to call Arthur's

4 The one in question is number VIII in *Second April*.

attention to the fact, that *Conversation at Midnight* was not an unqualified success, either artistically or financially. Most of her colleagues, Arthur included, acknowledged the analytical brilliance and wit of the lines; James Weldon Johnson, another Hillsdale neighbor, sent a note describing it as "magnificent" and "delicious," two adjectives which pleased her. Because the verse play was written by Edna St. Vincent Millay, several directors and producers rushed to bid for its presentation on Broadway, and though she turned them all down, requests urging for production kept coming in. The critics, however, and the general public were much less enthusiastic about her conversation piece. Part of the negative reaction may have been due to her groping reconstruction of the original manuscript. But it is more likely that the basic concept would not strike a responsive chord in most readers anyway.

Revealing as it did Edna Millay's growing social consciousness, her concern for the direction of world events, the work contained too much dialectic to make either good drama or poetry; and the style is diffuse, ranging from the formality of the sonnet through the metrical blank-verse lyric to the frankly formless free verse, only a half-step away from prose. Indeed, the effect of the whole is prosy; and while it is stimulating in some parts and thought-provoking and entertaining in others, the work fails to sustain the reader's interest with anything like the intensity of "Renascence," *Fatal Interview*, or "Epitaph for the Race of Man." The occasional sonnets, like Father Anselmo's, "If you live in a house called Here/ On the street called Now . . . ," cannot approach the level artistically or from a religious-philosophic standpoint of "To Jesus on His Birthday," "On Hearing a Symphony of Beethoven," or "Euclid Alone Has Looked on Beauty Bare." Even the passages of pure entertainment, perhaps put in for comic relief, like the rhymed speeches that parody Ogden Nash, on the subject of the flighty-housewife woman, sound more like Nancy Boyd's "Distressing Dialogues" than the poetry of Edna Millay—a point well taken by her friend Edmund Wilson, who reviewed the volume in the summer of 1937.

Wilson's article, entitled, "Give That Beat Again," has overtones of sorrowful lament for the "old strong beat of English verse" in general, which he felt was then already "so broken, sprung, muted, loosened, that it might as well be abandoned altogether." He had not seen Edna since 1928, and it would be almost another ten years before he saw her again, but he was always objective toward her work. Here, after dealing with the content of the play, in which he agrees with almost everyone else that "the discussion doesn't come to much," goes on to make some cogent remarks about the direction her style was taking, and in the process rapped her sharply for her venture into translation with George Dillon. "Now Edna Millay," Wilson says in part, "one of the sole surviving masters of English verse, seems to be going to pieces, too. She was beginning to indulge a loose hand with her metrics in a volume called *The Buck in the Snow*, in which she was quite successful in some of the lyrics; and she went even farther in this direction in *Wine from These Grapes* (excluding 'Epitaph'). But it was not until her translation from Baudelaire that the ravages of the mischief became alarming."

Like other critics, he speaks of her technique and its underlying error. "Instead of rendering Baudelaire's alexandrines into English meters equally ringing, she fell into what seemed a fallacy entirely uncharacteristic in assuming that the effect of the French could be conveyed by slurring over the English stress and producing a line completely fluid. But the result was not a bit like Baudelaire: it was merely inferior verse for Edna St. Vincent Millay." Strong words, which continued, "Now, in *Conversation at Midnight*, you see metrics in full dissolution." He points out that stress is neglected, lines run on for paragraphs, and so on; but his conclusion is: "I don't complain of this state of affairs. I know that it is all on the cards. And *Conversation at Midnight* is, in any case, a highly entertaining interlude in Edna Millay's work. Miss Millay at her most relaxed is livelier than most of our poets at their brightest. Yet I miss her old imperial line."

His feeling was shared by many readers as well as critics at the time, and again, nearly thirty years later, when the verse play was finally and unfortunately produced on Broadway. Edna Millay, who was a ruthless self-critic, in addition to her repeated refusals to producers, would not even consider publishing the work as a theater piece. Only a few years before she died she wrote to Cass

Canfield, who was trying to persuade her to let Harper's bring out a volume of her "collected plays," telling him firmly that *Conversation at Midnight* was *not* a play, though in the foreword of the 1937 volume she had suggested that the reader think of it as a play, only as opposed to a narrative poem. She liked the work, but she knew its shortcomings, chief among them the fact that it was not stageworthy. When Norma, as the only living relative, gave permission for production at long last, she, perhaps unwittingly, did her sister a grave misservice. As Walter Kerr wrote in the *Tribune* on November 13, 1964, "I won't say an enemy hath done this. But it cannot be called a friendly act, either." His principle objection was that both the lines and the ideas were dated. It was true that in 1937, the threat of dictatorship under Hitler and Mussolini was alarming; that communism, although it seemed a worse threat to capitalists, was considered the ideal solution to the Depression by young poets and liberals; but most of the arguments pro and con had been debated hundreds of times in the intervening years and "to display old heat as old hat," Mr. Kerr felt, was "no favor to Miss Millay."

The late Howard Lindsay, in putting together the vehicle of Millay poems for his wife, Dorothy Stickney, to perform in 1961, while omitting the "tough intellectual side" of the poet almost entirely, presented her in "a lovely light." And Miss Stickney's disarmingly delightful reading of the poetry, while again giving too one-sided a picture of Edna Millay, proved at least that her lyric quality and the singing beauty of the sonnets were the immortal mark of a distinguished American poet. But *Conversation at Midnight,* clever as it is, when viewed as a play is little more than a display of ingenious but rather tedious polemics.

The consensus among the critics in 1964 was that "Millay Is for Reading," as John McClain headed his review, which certainly proved her point against any production of the piece. But the salient flaw, even in reading, is that through the contradictions of her "characters" the poet took no stand and arrived at no definite conclusion from her lengthy conversation. As Wilson observed in his 1937 review, the reader would never guess from the variegated lines that Edna herself went much further than the liberal Ricardo in the dialogue. She was an active supporter of the Loyalist cause in Spain; and the winter before, at the request of Rolfe Humphries, had translated a Spanish poem into English for a book entitled *Songs of Spain,* the proceeds of which went to the Loyalist cause.

Just why she was so chary of exposing her true position in this instance is difficult to divine. Part of the indecision, as before-mentioned, was undoubtedly due to the strain under which the work was reconstructed after the original manuscript was lost in the fire. However, it is likely that, though she supported liberal causes, Edna Millay was again in a state of emotional and mental flux, full of doubt and indefinable anxiety: she was physically ill a good deal of the time and sick with worry over the "hopeless muddle" of civilization; and she did not feel free to state a definite point of view. But before another year was out, events occurred which caused her to become more and more involved in world problems; and she was to take a stand so strong that it all but obliterated her art.

CHAPTER XVI

Vincent, the Valiant: Crusader Poet

THE SIGNS of the poet's feverish concern were hardly perceptible
in 1937, in spite of the controversial political sentiments aired
in *Conversation*, which were largely leisurely and often poetic
armchair discussions during an after-dinner drinking session. That
year Harper's published a comprehensive Millay bibliography,
compiled by Karl Yost, with a fifty-page biography by the young
poet, Harold Lewis Cook, and a Foreword by Edna herself. It
was hailed as a scholarly contribution to the Millay canon. *Conversation*, which was a disappointment to some critics and not as
successful as her volumes earlier in the decade, nevertheless went
into eight or nine printings, and was far from an artistic failure.
It did not suffer from lack of attention, like Arthur's *The Secret*,
which had been dismissed as too analytical and intellectual.

Edna was affected by the alarming episodes in Europe that led
to World War II. The fall of Czechoslovakia, and the terrible
mounting turmoil in Spain all evoked strong poems in which she
expressed her anguish and despair as indicated by the title poem
of her next book, *Huntsman, What Quarry?*, published in 1939.
The metaphor of the lead lyric, the hunter on horseback, hovering
with indecision between the warm-hearted offer of a "one-night's
bride" and the "pointed mask of the red fox" but is lured on by
the streaking flame of the fox, whose freedom the hunter would
destroy, unmistakably refers to the human quarry being hunted
down in Europe. Again, in the moving sonnet, "Czecho-Slovakia,"

with its unorthodox rhyme scheme suggesting broken sobs, the poet says she would seek a balm in Gilead for the unhappy land, but "the oils and herbs of mercy are so few;/ Honour's for sale" and "the barking of a fox has bought us all," she employs the same figure but in a different context. Once more, in "The Rabbit," a tense and startling lyric, she warns the mother rabbit to take cover from the hawk squealing in the sky just before the kill, but to no avail: the last of the three stanzas gives a picture of the dying and dead "interrupted grazer" that is unforgettable and unequivocal in its implication. "Say That We Saw Spain Die" and "Underground System," though less successful as poetry because the figure in each is rather confused, reveal no less anxiety over the disturbing events of the times. The latter poem, which refers not to the resistance movement abroad but to the undermining forces like the Bundists in the United States is indicative of the direction Millay's work was to take during the next few years.

The "Three Sonnets in Tetrameter," while fraught with message in such lines as, "We could keep this planet warm/ By friction, if the sun should fail" and "does the rose regret the day she did her armour on?" are carefully formed and full of melody. The third and last is deeply compassionate toward the strife-torn countries of the Orient: China that she "loved so well"; but, "Love does not help to understand/The logic of the bursting shell." She can only "wake in fear, and weep and sweat/ Weep for Yoshida, for Japan." It is sorrowful news that love is laid by, and logic alone "must calm this crazed and plunging star": she had hoped that men, "just as they are,/Sinful and loving," could "secure/A human peace that might endure."

Huntsman also contains many lyrics and sonnets that are not concerned with world problems. Beginning with "The Ballad of Chaldon Down," which opens the volume, there are half a dozen or more poems of a fanciful nature that are the product of Edna and Eugen's visits in Dorset [1] with the Powys. They must have given pleasure and cheer to Edna's beloved "Lulu," whose tubercular condition had become so serious in 1938 that he had to go to a sanitarium in Switzerland. He died on December 2, 1939,

[1] One of them bearing the place name in the title, "Impression: Fog Off the Coast of Dorset."

to Edna's profound grief. He had disapproved of her Introduction to the Baudelaire translations, though he consented to write a paragraph for the jacket of the book; and the Dorset poems must have restored his faith in Edna's rare gift, particularly the lovely, melodic Ballad, with its mention of Lulworth Cove, Diffey's Farm, the place names that formed the route of "the lady who came from over the sea, All for to say good-bye to me." Who "found a track without a name/ That led to Chaldon, and so came/Over the downs to Chydyok," the tiny Dorset village where "Lulu" and Alyse lived.

Here, at long last, Edna included the six elegiac poems to Elinor Wylie, beginning with the 1927 "Song for a Lute" and ending with the beautiful lyric, "Over the Hollow Land," in which she hears the song of the nightingale "in the full moonlight . . . across the tulip-scented air," and thinks of her poet-friend, "Shaken from the bough, and the pure song half-way through." The single phrase, "the tulip-scented air," was perhaps the image that evoked the formal elegance and subtle beauty of Elinor Wylie most perfectly. The passage of time had enabled her to write more objectively about Elinor; she recalled with tender pathos in an almost playful tone except for the heart-broken, "Oh, answer!" at the end in one lyric the Keats versus Shelley arguments of the two poets.

Nor was sexual love neglected in this volume. In the eight poems of "Theme and Variations" which deal with Edna Millay's dominant motif, she remarks for the first time that she regrets, "Not that this blow be dealt to me:/ But by thick hands, and clumsily." Part II opens with a sonnet addressed to "almighty Sex." In both of these poems, and in "Rendezvous," with its revealing last line, "I wish I did not feel like your mother," the reader glimpses some of the sordid details connected with the "sly, unspoken pact," of an illicit love affair, and the more matter-of-fact outlook on love imposed by passing years. The poet admits that though her "lofty tower" was "reared To Beauty, it was wrought from the human mortar of honest bone, anguish, pride, and burning thought." As if in postscript, she adds that "lust was there, and nights not spent alone," thereby emphasizing, with the restraint of quiet statement, the most important factor in the

towering emotion of sexual love. But for all that, in the third
sonnet of Part II, she reaffirms her belief in the genuiness of love,
no matter how fleeting, or how clandestine the meeting; and she
utters, with God as her judge, the cry of "holy, holy/Upon the
name of love however brief."

Huntsman also contained poems describing the joy of marital
companionship as the autumn of life nears, and depicting a relationship that obviously paralleled hers with Eugen. "Thanksgiving
Dinner," a loosely woven lyric of great charm, discloses a hidden
"pride in her love" through the metaphor of the frost-bitten
"broken garden." The ripe fruits are all frozen, but the poet can
live on the "woody fibres of the overgrown kohl-rabi, on the
spongy radish, coarse and hot." She "will cook for her love a
banquet of beets and cabbages,/ Leeks, potatoes, turnips, all
such fruits . . ." and they will "laugh like spring above the steam-
ing, stolid winter roots."

The monologue, "Menses," which contains the stage direction,
"He speaks, but to himself, being aware how it is with her," is
an objective portrait of herself and Eugen. This was another poem
begun in 1928, among those she discussed with Wilson on one
of her trips into New York; its delayed appearance in 1939 indicates that it bares an experience which is the sum of many such
moments during the intervening years. In the narrated scene between the man and the woman, which begins with his calm reaction to a venomous barb she has just delivered in a sudden fit of
antagonism, the chronic moodiness and quixotic behavior of Edna
Millay is perceived through the patient, understanding eyes of
her husband with a minimum of dialogue. The reader is allowed
to view the various changes in her chameleon-like makeup. She
is visibly cheered by means of a mere mention of the meadowlark, about which he cleverly asks her a question, and is almost
as suddenly saddened by her observation, "Some people shoot
them." She leans against him and weeps, more for the vagaries
of time than the meadowlarks, "for all the lovely things that are
not and have been." The poem ends with a woman's sorrow and her
annoyance at her "silly" moods, of which she is only too conscious.
The man, who at one point has said to himself, "Go to. You are
unwell," repeats her words of penitence and irritation, her blas-

phemy against her body "with its muddy feet in her mind." The last lines might be considered a perverse plea for understanding, not only of her own irrational vapors, but those of womanhood so mysteriously bound by the orbiting of the moon. It is, perhaps, a weak apology for her easily aroused anger and quickly induced depressions, the uncalled-for sting in words often flung at an innocent victim; but the remarkable fact about this monologue is that Edna Millay was able to see herself and Eugen so clearly to present the picture through his eyes in poetic form. It is obviously a tribute to his devotion and forbearance, and was perhaps written to atone for her increasingly fretful and trying temper displays.

The trenchant poem of self-accusation which follows it in the same volume seems to bear out such a theory. The intense personal conflict, the petty sins and selfishness, and the deep inner guilts from which the poet evidently suffered are all woven into "The Plaid Dress" with dexterity. She is sorely troubled by the hidden garment she has to wear, never seen, but always there, "lining the subtle gown." Beginning with a plea to the sun to bleach if possible the "violent plaid of purple angers and red shames, the yellow stripe of thin but valid treacheries," and so on through the gamut of emotional guilts, the eighteen-line free-flowing poetic fabric represents the culmination of Edna Millay's symbolic interpretation of clothes. Some may criticize the device as being too obvious, but the poem is nevertheless a powerful and exciting piece of self-castigation contained in a valid figure of speech.

Unfortunately, her neurotic state was aggravated by a prolonged attack of the bursitis she had suffered after the strange automobile accident. It was brought on by strain in trying to rid the lawn at "Steepletop" of plantain weeds; the spinal nerves leading to her shoulder and right arm, which had been injured in the accident now flared up in continuous pain that was at times sheer agony. She was severely handicapped again and could hardly lift her arm to eat, let alone type or play the piano. She bore her arm in a sling and tried to make the best of it, hoping the bursitis would run its course; she even made jokes about it with friends. When she heard that Blanche Bloch, of the Hillsdale

Music College was also wearing her arm in a sling, Edna suggested that the students make an occasion of their dress rehearsal for a Mozart recital and have a preview at "Steepletop." Music was her greatest solace when she was out of sorts, and if she could not practice it herself, she loved hearing her favorite composers, especially when performed with the earnestness and ardor of young students.

However, when the painful condition had not subsided by the end of summer, Eugen insisted that "Vincie" consult a doctor, and a long series of medical treatments ensued, in the course of which she was in the hospital three times in one year for nerve surgery, in addition to innumerable X-rays, infrared ray treatments, and medication including morphine, which did not take effect for hours. Eugen, who looked after her with loving care, learned how to give her the injections. He was gray with concern and almost ill himself with worry about her and their suddenly weakened finances, diminished not only by the enormous doctor bills but by tragic world events. His income was abruptly cut off with Hitler's entry into Holland, which brought Edna and him the additional anxiety over the safety of his relatives. The Boissevains, as a prominent family, were stripped of their fortune and position, and though Eugen's parents were safe, one of his cousins was tortured by the Nazis and others were in continual danger.

Ill as she was, Edna tried to awaken the people to the dangers of the mad dictatorship that was rapidly devouring Europe and trying to devastate England. Like Robert Sherwood and others who were ardent pacifists long after World War I, she began to change her attitude in the face of the evil of Nazism. Taking her theme from Hitler's brash assumption that militarily there were no more islands, she pounded out a long series of rhymed stanzas, through which the couplet, "The tidal wave devours the shore,/ There are no islands any more," ran like a distraught refrain. The latter served as title for the piece, with the word "are" underlined; and, in parenthesis by way of explanation, "Lines written in passion, and in deep concern for England, France, and my own country," as if she were pleading with her readers to understand why she was throwing her poetic spirit headlong

into the defense without stopping to mold, perfect, and polish
her creative efforts. After it appeared in newspapers and several
literary journals, Harper's published her "lines written in passion"
in pamphlet form in the spring of 1940. Though she and Eugen
were hard-pressed for money, Edna announced that the proceeds
of the booklet would go to the British War Relief.

The doctor bills were piling up. Her books earned royalties but
not enough to take care of the extra expenses; "Steepletop" had
to be mortgaged, and, wretched as Edna felt, she made several
reading tours, one in California during the summer of 1940. Some
of her old friends there got in touch with her, among them Upton
Sinclair, who came to the Community Theater at Pasadena when
she was scheduled to read. She had known "Uppy" years before,
but had seen little of him since her Village days, and greeted
him warmly when he came to the dressing room. Eugen was with
her of course, and the three visited briefly. When it was time for
her to go onstage, Sinclair was astonished to see Eugen draw
a flask out of his hip pocket and hand it to Edna. She took "a
heavy swig" and handed it back as a matter of routine; evidently
neither thought it necessary to make any comment. Then she left
the dressing room to go into the wings, and "Uppy" went out
front to hear her read her poetry. After the performance he returned backstage, and when Edna came off following numerous
bows and repeated applause, Eugen brought out the flask again
without a word and she drained it. If she had not had the alcohol
before and after these readings she probably could not have stood
the pain and tension of the tour, which at one point included four
appearances in five days.

Upton Sinclair, however, in his little book, *Cup of Fury,* dealing with the effect of alcoholism on the lives and careers of noted
literary figures, including Jack London, Ambrose Bierce, Stephen
Crane, and F. Scott Fitzgerald, fails to mention the fact that his
old friend Edna Millay, whom everyone in the twenties had loved
for her "vivid, charming personality," was in a state of great
physical and mental strain at this time. He does concede that
he knows people "use alcohol to relieve their tensions," but he
implies that in this instance it was not necessary. He deprecates
the Pasadena performance by dismissing it with the cursory de-

scription, "she read a dozen or more of her poems to an audience of ladies"; apparently he believed the task did not warrant the alcoholic stimulation beforehand and certainly not afterward. It is possible, though hardly likely, that Edna did not mention her bursitis to him, since most of her letters over a period of several years, some of them to less intimate acquaintances than he, are full of complaints about the whole siege. One would assume that he inquired after her health, and she would certainly have not been backward about telling him. Moreover, he does not even comment on her drawn, haggard bearing, as Vincent Sheean did in relating that she was in her "smallest, most frightened mood" at a China War Relief dinner later in 1940; and photographs of the period give ample evidence of her painful illness. In his brief discussion of her case, Sinclair seems to have made no effort to find out why Edna drank, but offers this one incident as conclusive proof that she was a confirmed alcoholic by this time.

Edna, unaware of her friend's disapproval and future indictment, pushed ahead with her schedule. Through all her trials she continued to sound the warning bell for American people to arm themselves against the threat of Nazi aggression. In *Make Bright the Arrows*, published in the autumn of 1940, she summons the ghost of Joan of Arc in one of the volume's few valid poems, "To the Maid of Orleans." She was acutely conscious of the fact that there was very little poetry of artistic merit in *Make Bright the Arrows*, which took its title from the biblical words of the prophet Jeremiah, and included, besides the title poem with its thematic statement that "the bowman feared/Need never fight," the long poetic diatribe which had been published in pamphlet form. Edna wanted this to be issued the same way, but Harper's was not interested in publishing a Millay work which could be thrown away after the message had been absorbed.

When she consulted Arthur about the matter, he advised her strongly not to publish the book at all. Privately he felt, as he stated the following summer in his notes and comments on the preparation of Edna's *Collected Sonnets*, that the trouble with the poetry in *Make Bright the Arrows* was not so much "that it was propaganda as that it was *bad* propaganda." It was bad, he felt, because of being "so largely hysterical and vituperative." The poems neither gave "a clear picture of the issues of the hour for readers of posterity or had "the power to move those of the present." Her egocentricity, he felt, "repelled the very people she wished to attract;" but he could not very well voice his harsh opinion in counselling her not to publish. He did, however, persuade her to omit "at least half a dozen of the most blatant and crude" poems in the original manuscript, thereby saving her even more pain and embarrassment than she eventually suffered from this book. For in the end, she gave in to Harpers. Somehow Eugene Saxton convinced her that it should be in hard-cover, but she insisted that at least the volume should carry the subtitle, "1940 Notebook," to indicate that this was "a book of impassioned propaganda rather than a book of verse." She knew well that her writing was faulty and unpolished, but she felt that time was too important.

She was perhaps too subtle in her signs, and might have done better to write a lengthy foreword, as Robert Sherwood did for his play, *There Shall Be No Night*, in which he explained exactly why he had done a complete turnabout, making it very clear beforehand that he had written a propaganda play. As it was, Edna Millay's critics paid no attention to the succinct subtitle. By the line on the book's jacket, calling it a "collection on which the ink is hardly dry"; and by the sonnet beginning "Peace was my earliest love, and I presume/ Will be my latest," the poet hoped to convince her readers that her preparedness-interventionist point of view was a matter of expediency, not a permanent philosophy. Almost without exception, however, the reviewers criticized her for her polemics; one of them labeled the book "nothing but fancy doggerel"; others were "insolent to the point of actionable," she wrote later. Some granted that the poet was so profoundly disturbed by the human capacity for evil, manifested in hatred, greed, and bigotry, that she had been driven to "a noble fury," dashing off lines of "quick and passionate loathing." But in the main they all scolded her, consigning the worthwhile poems in the book to oblivion along with the rest.

In her weakened condition following the nerve operations, Edna Millay felt the sting of the barbs tenfold, but she stuck to her position. One of the strongest defenses she made was contained in a letter to her old friend and roommate at Vassar, Charlotte Babcock Sills, who now had three grown sons, all eligible for military service. Edna had sent her an inscribed copy of *Arrows*, confident that "Charlie" would understand what she was trying to do, and would join the support for the Aid-to-Britain and lend-lease program. To her dismay and deep distress, Charlotte wrote a very chilly letter which showed clearly that she had misunderstood the purpose of the book. She pointed out that Vincent did not seem to be aware of the fact that the Sills had three sons who would be rushed off to war immediately if their country took the course the poet had advocated. Deeply hurt as well as annoyed with her friend, Edna Millay sent back a long letter expressing her keen disappointment and clarifying her position. Although she had no sons to give, she admitted pointedly, she was giving her cherished reputation as a poet, a reputation she had built up practically with her life's blood over a period of twenty-five years. She closed by repeating with emphasis that "the dearest thing in life" she possessed which might help her country had "already gone over the top," in the hope that Charlotte's sons would never need to go to war.

Her letter was firm, clear-headed, and unshaken, but she felt so miserable physically and emotionally that at the United China Relief dinner at the end of the year she was trembling all over at the mere idea of reading one of her poems, as she had promised to do at the affair. It was then that Vincent Sheean, Chairman of the United China Relief for aid to Chinese resistance against Japan, and Master of Ceremonies on this occasion, noticed how frightened the poet appeared, and went over to her after she was seated at the speakers' table on the dais. She was visibly shaking, and told him that if Eugen could only sit beside her she would be all right. Eugen was at one of the tables on the floor. Sheean, after consulting with Pearl Buck and others on the committee, located Eugen and had him seated next to Edna.

As it turned out, the program was so full that, through an oversight, Edna Millay's name was not on Sheean's memo list, and he did not even call on her to read. Edna, tense from waiting, must have been vastly relieved, though she may have thought the omission odd; but Sheean was greatly chagrined when he discovered the oversight. He did not know what he could do by way of tactful apology until the lady in charge of fund-raising suggested that he send Miss Millay some roses. Edna appreciated the gesture, but felt too sick to acknowledge it at the time. However, she did not forget the exceptional beauty of the bouquet, which stayed fresh for days; and five years later, when he had forgotten the incident, she was to startle him with a simple expression of thanks.

Shortly after the first of the year Edna decided to try another sort of treatment for persistant neuritis, this one recommended by a specialist, Dr. Timmey of the New York Neurological Institute, who loaded her down with vitamins of all kinds. At first she saw little improvement; but she persisted so that she could be strong enough to carry on the battle of alerting her country against encroaching dictatorship. As she had written in one of the sonnets in *Arrows*, she dared not "die of pity but must live; grow strong . . . eat, digest her food" that it may build her body and so broaden her perception. Carrying the theme further, the sonnet concludes that if she "would help the weak, she must be fed in wit and purpose, pour away despair/And rinse the cup. . . ." She put the theory into practice and adhered to the regimen of vitamin pills; miraculously, it seemed, as if they had all had a cumulative effect at the same moment, she had one whole day in March almost completely free of pain. She held her breath for fear the improvement would not last, but toward the end of the year she wrote to Hal Bynner that she thought she was cured of her terrible two-year siege.

That spring and summer of 1941 must have been a respite for the poet not only from physical pain, but for a brief period from worry over the ever increasing fires which led to World War II. She made recordings of her poems, an album of four sides, beginning with "Renascence" and selections from her other early volumes, through the Harp-Weaver ballad, which she read with great feeling, and proceeding with selections down through her most recent work. When she read "Maid of Orleans," a note of doom was in her voice.

She also compiled the selections to be included in twin volumes of her *Collected Lyrics* and *Collected Sonnets,* which Harper's had suggested, and planned to bring out as soon as the manuscripts were ready. For some reason, Edna omitted most of the elegiac series of poems to Elinor Wylie in these collections, leaving out all of the lyrics.[2] Perhaps she felt that they were too revealing of her love and grief for her friend; but that is unlikely, since she selected one of the two sonnets among the elegies, entitled, "To Elinor Wylie (In answer to a question about her)," with its ecstatic first line, "Oh, she was beautiful in every part!" for inclusion in the prospective volume of sonnets.

For advice on the latter she consulted "the Sage on the hill," as she called Arthur. He came over from "Hardhack," taking time off from his own work on a new volume of poems, *Tumultuous Shore,* to be published the following year by Knopf, in order to assist her, with the selections and with a foreword she was writing. It was during one of these sessions that "Vincent" startled him by quoting the first line of his sonnet, "Sea Midnight," written on shipboard right after their 1918 encounter: "Wakeful I pace the deck and watch the stars." She cited it in connection with a point she was trying to make about sonnet-writing in general, but when he expressed surprise, she astonished him still more by quoting the entire poem, and going on to others. She knew most of his sonnets by heart, many more than he knew of hers, or of his own, for that matter. She had memorized them when he first sent them to her.

Arthur agreed with her selections. They both decided it would be well to omit the short sequence, "From a Town in a State of Siege," published in *Huntsman, What Quarry?* and all but two of the sonnets in *Make Bright the Arrows.* An early and a recent sonnet, both of which had appeared in magazines but never in any of Millay's books, were to be included in the collection, the former as the first sonnet in the group of *A Few Figs from Thistles;* and the latter placed among the *Huntsman* group. He had grave reservations, however, about the lengthy academic preface she was writing, involving the mechanics and history of the sonnet form, in the course of which she pointed to some of

---

2 They were all included in the posthumously published *Collected Poems,* Harper's, 1956, however.

John Milton's glaring faults when he took liberties with the form. Arthur admitted that the "old boy" had been guilty of some looseness in his structures, but the end result justified the means and was no less enduring as poetry. Moreover, Edna Millay, who often switched the octet and sestet around at will and used unorthodox rhyme schemes, was not in a position to object to Milton's occasional poetic license.

However, Arthur did not object so much to her "giving Milton hell" as he did to the fact that she had revamped Milton's lines, and "was actually going to publish her own re-written and improved versions of some of his most famous sonnets." Arthur had to admit that her versions "were indeed a very good trimming off of the Miltonic thorns," which made it difficult for him to persuade her of "the impropriety of printing them in quite such a 'know-it-all' way."

The two poets at "Steepletop" had quite a heated discussion on the subject, and Arthur did not know whether or not Vincent would accept his suggestion to omit mention of Milton entirely and to shorten her essay on the technique of the sonnet. She told him when he left that day she would have to think about his criticism of the preface. He was surprised, therefore, when he returned to find that she had scrapped the technical discussion, and had decided to write a simple foreword, stating the omissions and additions; and, as an "object of possible curiosity" to Millay readers, quoting the first sonnet she had ever written. It had been composed at about the age of fifteen and was entitled "Old Letters"; it concerned the burning of a packet "yellow with age" in the author's "lonely grate." From her remarks about the composition, it was evident that Edna Millay's sense of humor had reasserted itself. The final foreword was not only more ingratiating, but much more appropriate than the original rather heavy-handed dissertation. Arthur, who was an inveterate notetaker, commented on her literary aboutface in recording his impressions at the time.

It was he who wrote the final wording of the first paragraph of the short preface, merely an explanatory note concerning the omissions. He had been greatly relieved when Vincent told him of her decision to remove the entire "elaborate . . . . treatise" on the sonnet, even though it "meant cutting out parts of the preface

in which she said that it was his sonnets and Meredith's that had
been the origin of her own use of the sonnet, and had quoted his
'Wakeful I pace the decks' as one of the great achievements of all
time." He gladly took over the task of correcting the proofs as well
as writing the first paragraph. He spent twenty-four hours correcting the galleys, and the next afternoon "drove over to Steepletop and explained all his suggestions and changes to her and she
accepted them." That night he transferred the changes to the
publisher's copy of the proofs so they could be sent off right
away: she had had them since the middle of May, and it was now
September 4! (1941)

The explanatory note, which she asked him to take over for
her, had been much longer and involved, because she had been
making excuses, offering "page after page of argument and defense of the things she left out." He felt that "she knew subconsciously that they were very bad, and could not bear the thought
that the reader should agree with her." This may very well have
been the case, except that she must have known *consciously* that
these hastily-written sonnets were not material for a collected
volume, or she would not have agreed to delete them. Edna
Millay was too good a craftsman not to be fully aware of her
mistakes.

Arthur was struck at this time by the sharp cleavage in her
personality. She was the "oddest mixture of genius and childish
vanity . . ." that he had ever known. In three closely-written pages
he analysed her character and work and their friendship. He had
undertaken three months of intensive psychotherapy with Dr.
Karl Menninger in the winter of 1939, and could see Edna Millay
more clearly than before, but it is unfortunate that he did not
complete his analysis, for then he might have delved deeper into
her cross currents to discover the true mainstream of her being.
Nevertheless, his notes contained some penetrating observations,
and after scoring the "self-consciousness" in both her personality
and parts of her poetry, he praised the beauty and fearlessness of
her convictions regarding sexual love, especially in the sonnets
written during their extraordinary exchange of creativity in the
1918-1922 period of their relationship.

All too soon those summer sessions were over, and the stresses of a strife-torn world supplanted the poetic accents of the *Collected Sonnets* and *Lyrics*. Before the end of the year the Japanese attack on Pearl Harbor proved that Edna's fears were well-founded. In spite of the poor reception of her latest poetry, she wrote verses on behalf of her "poor, foolish, bewildered, beloved country," as she called it in her letter to Bynner on Christmas Eve. One of these, "Not to Be Spattered by His Blood (St. George Goes Forth to Slay the Dragon)" was to be published in the Sunday New York *Times* of December 28, 1941; at that time word came that her cousin, George Ricker, son of her Aunt Susie and an Air Force officer, was "missing." She wrote a long letter, trying to comfort her aunt, saying among other things that this poem might well have been written for him. Two weeks later he was declared dead in a plane accident. After New Year's Day Edna doubled her efforts and worked with many of her colleagues on the Writers War Board and the Red Cross. She took part in symposiums and conferences concerning the war effort.

Her service to the country was without pay; reading tours were stopped during the war years; and while the two volumes of collected verse and the record album brought in some royalties, the earnings were scarcely enought to keep them going. Before long she was writing Harper's that she and Eugen were "stone broke"; she asked if another advance or "loan" could be arranged. She and Eugen observed the rationing laws to the letter; at "Steepletop" they used the horse and buggy for the marketing and errands in order to save gasoline. Spiritually, she drove herself with the fury of the fanatic who is powerless to act otherwise, even though repelled by the state of the world she was trying to save, and by her own lack of artistic integrity. When she heard that Arthur and Gladys were spending the winter of 1942 in New York where he was taking a course in ancient Chinese art at Columbia, she sent him a note of awed admiration. It seemed wonderful to her that at that turbulent, anguished moment in history somebody should be studying ancient Chinese art, and that somebody was he. Wistfully she longed to take a course in something that would take her mind off the brutality of war, the "ugliness and greed that was like a stench in her nostrils," yet she was too deeply involved in the war effort to remove herself.

On June 10, 1942, word came of the atrocity of Lidice: the Nazis had totally destroyed the little Czech village suspected of sheltering underground patriots who had killed the hated Nazi "hangman," Reinhard Heydrich. As an object lesson, the Nazis rounded up all the men in Lidice and executed them in the village square; women and children were sent to concentration camps; houses, churches, and other public buildings were systematically burned to the ground. The world was shocked by the heinous act, and the Writers War Board called on Edna Millay to write a memorial poem suitable for an international shortwave broadcast. She wrote all summer at fever pitch and was able to turn out a dramatic piece entitled "Murder at Lidice," which was broadcast over NBC on October 19, 1942, as the featured work on a special program with Alexander Woollcott and Clifton Fadiman presiding. Paul Muni read the lines and hastily written scenes of "Murder at Lidice" with deep sincerity and subdued passion, a performance shortwaved to England, with Spanish and Portuguese translations beamed to South America. At the close, the author was escorted to the platform to assist in auctioning the bound manuscript of the broadcast. Edna, frail and skeleton-like in a long, red-velvet dress, scarcely knew what was being bid, but was glad when it was over and the final figure was $1,000 for Czech War Relief.

Afterward, as she moved slowly back to where Eugen was waiting, she was stopped by wellwishers in the invited studio audience, most of them colleagues and professionals in New York literary circles. Among those present was Jean Starr Untermeyer, who, stunned by Edna's altered appearance, has remarked in a recent book of memoirs that the latter's face resembled a winter apple that had wizened but not ripened. In her description, Mrs. Untermeyer, who deplores the fact that Edna Millay had become "a travesty" of her former self, apparently had not heard of the poet's devastating illness; she simply assumed that Edna's ghastly, emaciated aspect was the result of burning the candle at both ends. This may well have been a factor in Edna Millay's ultimate breakdown, but it was more a matter of overwork than dissipation. Arthur ascribed her "nervous illness" in large measure to the fact that she had lost much of her former vast popularity, and was "no longer the center of the stage." Some of her friends wondered if Edna could be having her menopause; she was fifty years old in 1942. Both of these circumstances may also have contributed to her feverish behavior and frail health. However, the most destructive force was her own inward awareness that she had written and was continuing to write "bad poetry." The compulsion was like a disease from which she could not cure herself.

Nevertheless, since she had been playing the role of "unofficial feminine laureate," as her friend Louise Bogan put it, for so many years, it was inevitable that she was called upon to represent the nation's artistic expression in crucial moments of history; and she continued to receive professional honors as well as public recognition. In 1940 she had been elected to the American Academy of Arts and Letters; and a few months after the broadcast of "Murder at Lidice," the original version of which had been published in pamphlet form by Harper's, the Poetry Society awarded Edna Millay its gold medal "for meritorious work and abiding interest in humanity." Such homage was impossible to ignore, and, as much as she disliked formal occasions, Edna had to attend the ceremonial dinner on January 31, 1943. Luckily, her friend Leonora Speyer made the presentation speech, so Edna did not even try to listen, except to the sound of "Nora's" voice. She just sat gazing at the speaker's radiant face, her beautiful blue eyes, blue as the sea sometimes could be. . . . Although she didn't remember a word Nora said, Edna recalled two lines of Matthew Arnold in praise of expressive eyes.

The year brought a crushing, completely unexpected personal tragedy. Kathleen, who had been working in a war plant and left to join the WACS, suddenly collapsed. Apparently seized by some strange illness, she died within a few days. It was almost impossible to grasp, neither Vincent nor Norma could realize that their "baby sister" was gone. The New York *Times* carried a story of her sudden death and her career as the author of several books of poetry and fiction, accompanied by a photo that caught her Irish beauty; there was no doubt that she had been the prettiest of the three Millay sisters, and probably the least temperamental. The two older sisters often had arguments which had become so frequent that Eugen discouraged Norma from coming to "Steepletop" because Vincent would be so keyed up she could not rest at night. But Kathleen, though not as demonstrative as the others, was always even-tempered. It was a long time before Vincent could bear to speak of "Wumpty-Woons," the sister with the best disposition and the most whimsical nickname, who was no more.

Around the middle of the summer of July, 1943, another blow came with the news that Edna Millay's long-time editor at Harper's, Eugene Saxton, had died of a heart attack. She wrote to Amy Flashner, his assistant, that she felt "utterly lost" without the reassurance of his calm, kind presence at Harper's; somehow he had always been able to smooth out the snarls of publication without undue argument or altercation; and Edna had come to rely on him also for arranging financial assistance from her publishers. Now between her tears she had to plead with Miss Flashner for understanding of her plight, and ask if Harper's could help her.

Recently she had been one of twelve distinguished women invited to serve on a symposium on rebuilding the postwar world, sponsored by the New York *Times;* a rewarding experience in a way, but costly in terms of hours spent far from poetry, and she could ill afford the actual daily expense involved. Small wonder that she felt like writing a note to her "darling Artie" to ask his advice, or just to say hello—she, who never wrote letters any more, who shied away from people more than ever when she did not have to appear in public.

On June 6, 1944, D-day, the National Broadcasting Company planned a continuous twenty-four hour program composed of news bulletins, prayers, and special items. Once more the Writers War Board called on Edna Millay, and she put her whole heart into writing a "Poem and Prayer for an Invading Army," which ended significantly with the plea that returning American soldiers might not find in their own country "the very monster" they had set out to conquer. The piece was read by Ronald Colman, whose diction and feeling brought out the best elements of the work; but just as before, the glaring fact that the poet had had no time for "the masonry of art" stood out in spite of Colman's eloquent delivery. Eventually this poem was published in the *Collected Poems,* but it falls short of the lyric genius that predominates the rest of the posthumous volume. One cannot help feeling that Edna herself would not have included it. In any case, the strain of writing "acres of bad poetry" which she hoped would be ploughed under as soon as its message had taken root in the minds of the people, and the nagging fear that it would be allowed to stand, smothering the rich fields of earlier flowering, proved too great for her highly strung nervous system. Shortly after the broadcast, she broke down completely, and was taken to Doctors Hospital in New York, where she spent several months.

While there she memorized at least a third of the poetry of Gerard Manley Hopkins, Keats' "Eve of St. Agnes," and Shelley's "Ode to the West Wind." But when she came out, she was still weak and trembling; and she suffered from the worst affliction that a writer, particularly a poet, can experience: she could not compose a single line of poetry. The war had ended, so she should have been able to sing for the joy of peace; but the world was too spent with destruction. The peace was confused, and the President who sought to insure it forever with the United Nations was gone before peace was declared. In a letter to Basil O'Connor a year later, Edna Millay paid great tribute to Roosevelt, who in her mind was still "the President," "no matter who was taking his place—not filling it."

In the summer of 1945, however, she felt drained from the war years and from the losses she and Eugen had sustained. If it had not been for Ragged Island she might not have been able to regain the joy of living again. They took off around the usual time, after midsummer, loaded down with provisions as always, and spent the night with Tess Adams on Bailey's Island. Vincent Sheean and his wife, who were spending the summer on the Maine coast, were at Esther's for the weekend; and, although it should have been a happy occasion, Edna was feeling too miserable to contribute much to the conversation. Eugen, knowing her state of terror, was overly merry to make up for it; as Sheean has related, they were all under a strain. For a few minutes at dusk, when the two writers happened to be alone on the terrace, she seemed calm. She sat on a low wooden wall, breathing in the salt air, with which the sweet fragrance of a hedge of Rosa rugosa growing in the sand below mingled faintly, but it was strong enough to serve as a reminder. And after a meditative silence, she astonished him by saying simply, "Thank you for the roses. They lasted a long time." She assumed that he would remember the bouquet he had sent her five years before, following the dinner for Chinese War Relief. He had forgotten the incident, and did not know what to say. So he remained silent as he tried to recall when he had sent her flowers. A small bird whose evening song from the hardy rose bushes suddenly broke the embarrassed silence saved the situation, for Sheean immediately asked what it was; and Edna told him, supplying all the information about habitat, destination, and the meaning of the song as she felt it. She spoke softly, almost as if from another sphere.

It was a different Edna Millay, however, who greeted them about a month later when Tess and the Sheeans went to spend a day on Ragged Island. With three seagulls circling about her, she came down the rocky, winding path almost in a run, waving her arms in gleeful welcome. As she helped unload the fresh provisions Eugen had brought, talking to them all at the same time, her green eyes were shining again, her red hair was windblown and bright with copper lights once more. Dressed in a white shirt, rolled-up blue jeans and old canvas sandals, she had the air of a carefree vagabond. Before anyone realized what she was doing, she had grabbed the handles of a wheelbarrow that was kept at the dock to carry provisions, and had started pushing it up the steep path to the house. The small, frightened creature of a month before seemed to have vanished entirely, though Eugen told their guests that her health was glowing less with vigor than with the simple joy of being on their beloved island.

She cooked the lobster that day in the big pot boiling on a fire outside the kitchen door. They picnicked on the rocks when it was ready; as they lounged on the flat stones afterward, she was moved by a remark Tess made to recite one of the sonnets from "Epitaph for the Race of Man"; and when they begged for more she recited others, her head thrown back, looking out over the water. She had to take a brief nap early in the afternoon, but later, when they all swam naked in the sea, she stayed in longer than anyone, and seemed to gather strength from the salt waves. But for all that, she was far from fully recovered and was still troubled by lack of creativity; at one point during the day she confessed to Vincent Sheean that she sometimes felt it would never return.

The stay on the island might have renewed her poetic powers except for the setback caused by the alarming news that she and Eugen received from Gladys on their return to "Steepletop." Arthur had a malignant cancer and was in almost constant agony. Vincent sent him a note at once, full of tenderness and concern, of rebellion against the gods for torturing her "oh-so-darling" Arthur. She had thought she knew something about physical and mental pain after all she had been through during the past few years; but she realized mournfully that her suffering apparently had been nothing compared to his. She thought about him constantly, wanting to do something that would help him; "she would have given him her love, but she had done that long ago," she told him.

As the weeks passed and the news from "Hardhack" became more discouraging, it seemed futile to try to do anything; but there was one truth that Edna Millay must have felt would bring him some satisfaction or comfort. Or perhaps it was for her own peace of mind that she wrote him one of the most revealing letters of the published correspondence. Confessing at the start that she "*did* write that sonnet to him," the one he had asked her about in the LaBranches' gunroom, she went on to take him to task again for his indiscretion. And then abruptly, she admitted that the reason she denied it at the time might have been that she did not want him to know "how terribly, how sickeningly in love" with him she had been when she composed the sonnet; and she declared perhaps still was in love with him when he asked her about it almost twenty years later at the cocktail party. She identified the sonnet for him, quoting the first line. The letter, which was the last she was to write him, was briefer than the previous note, as if she were steeling herself, purposely adopting a gruff tone to cover up her emotion at the finality of the hour and her confession of her feeling for him throughout the years.

Arthur Ficke died on November 30, 1945; at his burial at "Hard-hack" Edna Millay read, in addition to passages from one of his favorite poems, Milton's "Lycidas," this poignant sonnet of hers, beginning, "And you as well must die, belovéd dust."

CHAPTER XVII

Final Harvest

ARTHUR WAS GONE. His death, thirty-three years after he first entered her life in that fateful Thanksgiving Day letter of 1912, left a void which could not be filled. Now more than ever the poet and her husband confined themselves to their two retreats, "Steepletop" and Ragged Island. Both were the subjects of poems when Edna finally began to emerge from the nervous prostration and the frustration of producing propaganda poetry. For a time after the funeral she remained barren, too heartsick to think of composing new lines of poetry. But slowly, with the passing months and slowly returning health, the creative urge returned, and she was able to bring forth true poetry again.

During this time Eugen watched over his "child" as if she were an infant hovering between life and death, and as if any unnecessary exposure would tip the balance toward the latter. They were still in straitened circumstances, trying to make ends meet without having to appeal to Harper's again. Except for John Pinnie, they did without hired help, Eugen being "chief cook and bottle washer," as well as nurse to "Vincie." He guarded her against unexpected callers or any interruptions like some huge, benevolent St. Bernard, gentle beneath his bark, but warding off unwelcome intruders. Even close friends were discouraged from coming to "Steepletop" without a special invitation, and few were invited.

Dorothy Thompson, who at that time had a place not far from

"Steepletop," once told mutual friends that she had come there late one afternoon on a more or less informal invitation from Edna, who said she should stop in some day since she was living in the neighborhood. Eugen, who was in shorts pruning some bushes when she arrived, asked whether she had an appointment with "Aidna" and was reluctant to let her come in. He finally consented to see whether Edna felt up to company.

After what seemed an intolerably long time he returned bringing Edna by the hand, as if she were a recently invalided small child. She was wearing a Chinese Mandarin coat of once-brilliant blue, slightly faded though still handsome; it was one of the treasures they had brought back from the Orient. Eugen fussed over her, speaking in language just short of baby talk; and she answered him like a little girl getting over a mild case of the measles and wanting to be babied. When he saw that she was properly settled, Eugen went out and closed the door. As soon as he was gone, Edna's whole manner changed; she began talking in the customary hearty way Dorothy remembered, and the two friends gossiped like a pair of old cronies about the weeks they had spent together in Budapest, and all that had happened to the gay literary circles of the twenties. An hour later they were still going strong; the sun had set and the light was fading. Dorothy was thinking about leaving when the door opened and Eugen entered carrying a table tray, which he set on the floor by the fireplace, arranging a large pillow beside it, and announcing that his child must have her supper now. Edna instantly reverted to her earlier role, allowing herself to be docilely led over to the low table and seated cross-legged on the pillow, Japanese style, while Eugen spread a napkin across her knees, murmuring over her like a fond nurse. Dorothy was all but dismissed, but she was leaving anyway, she said.

As she was going out, Edna called after her to say that they would invite her to dinner soon; later in the summer the invitation came. It was a small party, and a simple one; the Boissevains could not afford to entertain lavishly any more. Eugen usually prepared a dish that he enjoyed fixing; afterwards they sat a long time over coffee. The talk turned to Russian novelists, and someone mentioned Tolstoi. On hearing the name, Edna said, "Oh,

Tolstoi—he was my downfall." It was an enigmatic statement, and Dorothy Thompson exclaimed spontaneously, "Why, *Edna!*"

She was about to ask for an explanation, but Edna had jumped as if she had been struck, and the others turned on Dorothy with disapproval. It was obvious, Eugen seemed to say, that she did not understand the poet's fragile state of nerves. There was a long pause, followed by a change of subject in a chilly atmosphere which made Miss Thompson so uncomfortable that she soon left, and never went back.

These stories were probably exaggerated in the second telling, but there has been ample testimony from other sources, most notably Edmund Wilson, that Eugen was overly solicitous of Edna following her breakdown in 1944. When Wilson and his wife attended the Berkshire Festival in the summer of 1948, they dropped in at "Steepletop." Though they had begun to correspond again after an interval of fifteen years, "Bunny" had not seen Edna for nineteen years, and was shocked at the change in her. Eugen again seemed reluctant to fetch his "child," but finally did, and when she came in Wilson hardly recognized her. She was extremely nervous and seemed on the verge of tears several times, at the slightest emotion, the slightest frustration: for example, when she could not find a poem she wanted to show Wilson, Eugen tried to soothe her as he might an infant. The impression was so strong that Wilson's wife later remarked that there were moments when Eugen seemed to be shaking "Bunny" at Edna as if he had been "a new toy with which to divert her" from her neurotic, nameless terror.

On the other hand, two months earlier, when Vincent Sheean came to "Steepletop" with Tess Adams for the annual June 4 birthday celebration with Edna and Eugen, the poet had been full of good spirits. She dressed for dinner in an aquamarine satin gown, and she had brushed her red hair so that it fluffed out around her face, recalling her "spritelike" look in early years. Tess observed later to Sheean that Edna had been "just like the old days" that night; and the mood remained with her all during the weekend, in spite of the chill, rainy weather that lasted for three or four days. Perhaps this was because she had looked forward to the duets she and Tess played on the pianos, earnestly going at the Brahms-Haydn variations as they did every year. Perhaps also it was because both Vincent Sheean and Tess had seen her at her worst in recent years, during her most frightened, desolate moments and, unlike Wilson, would understand if she suddenly went weak and trembling (though she did not); and they would not look sad or shocked by her altered appearance.

Indeed, it is interesting to note that Sheean, who did not meet Edna Millay until the latter years of her life, when she was supposed to have lost much of her unique spirit and charm, found in her the same qualities that Wilson had ascribed to her early years: her "own peculiar magic"; the sound of her extraordinary voice reading her own poetry or someone else's; her pantheistic joy in nature; her affinity for wild, bright birds; her sense of other-worldliness "somewhere near the gates of wonder." Sheean speaks of her beauty, as variable as her moods, and Wilson admits that, as Edna relaxed after a drink or two, his feeling of strangeness about her wore off and he could see glimpses of the girl, the great poet he had known. So she must always have retained the core of physical and spiritual beauty that formerly cast a spell on so many who came within her sphere; and for intimate friends who saw her consistently throughout the years, she never lost the power to enchant.

Actually, Edna Millay had been severely hurt by her "crack-up" in 1944, and during the long period of convalescence after she came out of the hospital, she had many intervals of depression and nervousness. When Edna was in regressive intervals, Eugen hovered over her with the tenderness of a fond parent, and she no doubt came to depend on his paternal solicitude to see her through her bad days.

However, this was by no means a constant physical or psychological condition. There was nothing of the child or even the helpless woman in the long diatribe she sent to Cass Canfield at Harper's on January 8, 1946, castigating him severely for suggesting, on the advice of a friend, that certain changes be made in sonnet XIV of "Epitaph for the Race of Man." Moreover, the change that Canfield's friend, about whose mentality she makes some scathing remarks, had recommended would have rendered the sonnet meaningless. She cited two other sonnets in the sequence, numbers VI and XV, in which the planets she named had also been questioned, to show that she always says exactly what she means; then she went on to explain why sonnet XIV must remain intact. The whole is a comprehensive statement of her unswerving attitude of disapproval toward *any* changes made or even suggested in her poems by anyone but herself. And it is proof that the "tough intellectual side" of Edna Millay was not weakened by her breakdown or impaired by Eugen's pampering. In fact, most of her correspondence with her publishers during the next few years indicates that although she might let him baby her, and babied herself to some extent, she was a hard-headed, mature woman where her poetry was concerned. The objectivity of her discussion in analyzing the value of her verse plays when Harper's wished to bring out a volume of her "collected plays," and her scornful refusal to compile a volume of love poems with a "mellow foreword revealing under what impulsions" they were inspired, could never have been made by a pampered poet, or one gone sodden with self-pity and alcohol, as some writers have implied.

By August, 1946, she had regained her health and her creative power so that she was able to include three new poems in a long, rather melancholy but objective letter to her old friend "Bunny" Wilson. It was in answer to the one he had sent her in 1944, breaking a fifteen-year silence between them. He wrote in part to let her know that John Peale Bishop had just died, and more because he had been alarmed by her propaganda poetry; he thought she was suffering from it and from the "scolding" she had received from so many critics. When he wrote, therefore, he merely told her about John, and went on to praise her reading of the poem in the album of recordings, which he had just heard. It was then that he related his reactions to the incomparable sound of her vocal phrasing, her mystical interpretation of the *Harp-Weaver*, which lifted the ballad out of the sentimentality into which he had been about to consign it twenty years before. His letter had reached her while she was at her lowest ebb in Doctors Hospital, and had rescued her parched spirits from the disintegrating effects of her nervous breakdown. It had taken two years, however, until she felt strong enough to combat her "epistolaphobia," equal only to that of Gerard Manley Hopkins; she forced herself to explain her silence and expressed her gratitude to Wilson for his perceptive "verdict" of the album. She told him with Dickinsonian intensity that the latter had been like an imprimatur to her. Once she had "flogged" herself into writing a letter, she rather enjoyed it, especially to a tried and cherished friend like "Bunny." [1] The singular sign of her most recent neurotic illness and continuing state of anxiety came in her postscript in regard to the three new poems: she hoped he would like them, but begged him in God's name not to feel he *had* to comment on them!

Edna Millay was understandably quite sensitive toward these initial postwar efforts to regain her poetic powers, as if the newborn poems, the product of a late conception, had to be shielded from prying eyes and the harsh handling of outsiders. She had to relearn the true creative process. Now as never before she had to go at her own pace, in her own way. For this reason she kept warding off her publishers' commercial schemes, and pleading with them to be patient: if she could only convince them that she *was* writing poetry again, slowly, and there would be a book, then they might stop harassing her and she could work in peace. Yet funds were low, and money was necessary to live. It was in one of these tirades to Harper's concerning the suggested biographical volume of love poems that the poet, in a brilliant play on words to the everlasting delight of all writers, remarked that although she "rejected their proposals, she welcomed their advances."

Though she needed financial help, Edna Millay refused to compromise her principles in regard to either the writing or the publication of her poetry. She turned down an invitation to serve on the Board of Chancellors of the Academy of American Poets, an organization set up to promote new poetry in the United States offering an annual fellowship of five thousand dollars to qualified poets, because she felt the restrictions imposed by the award were humiliating, and would only hamper the creative spirit. To her, the idea of progress reports to the award committee several times a year was repugnant as well as terrifying; and the

---

[1] She evidently had written two versions of this letter, the earlier of which was sent to Wilson after her death by Norma Millay Ellis.

restriction concerning the limits set on outside income during the fellowship year aroused the temper in her. Her final barb was to the effect that a Chancellor was supposed to decide whether a poet was worthy of the fellowship; but, in view of the stipulations, she decided the fellowship was not worthy of any poet.

Such vehemance was effective, and the articles of the prospectus were amended by striking out all the offensive clauses. Few if any restrictions remained; but the following year, when Edna herself received the award, and it came at a time when she desperately needed the money, she stubbornly refused to accept the fellowship. Max Eastman, who was instrumental as a Chancellor in the selection of Edna Millay as a recipient, was disturbed and nettled; he tried to persuade her to come to the award dinner and receive her fellowship, but she would not. Neither he nor Leonora Speyer, who again was presiding and exclaimed, "She's a goose!" when she heard of Edna's refusal, could understand her obstinacy. But it is probable that apart from her staunch stand on principle, she feared she would be unable to produce under the pressure the grant would cause her. She had had her fill of writing under feelings of compulsion; her returning creative powers were too precious to her to jeopardize them in any way.

Tentatively at first, and then with more and more assurance, Edna was able to add to the small sheaf of poems until it began imperceptibly to build into a book. The long periods of solitude with Eugen, particularly on Ragged Island, somehow nourished her sense of well-being. She was strengthened physically and mentally. She came to appreciate his many kindnesses and subtle talents with increasing tenderness.

Both of them were so fond of the island that in 1947 they decided to stay on through September.

One day there was a great wind just after Eugen had gone down to the harbor to take the boat out for supplies. As the surf rose high and the wind howled around the house, Edna grew worried. She hoped he would not risk going out, but there was no way to call him back except by some message of the mind. Before going to take her nap, she wrote him a note warning him of the danger and pleading with her "Darling" to come up from the harbor. Then, as a heartfelt afterthought, she added a little poem in her limited, laughable Dutch to her Love (Mien Liefe).[2] *That* might bring him back. They survived the September storm and they lingered on, charmed by the magnificent surf. It was almost Thanksgiving before they returned to "Steepletop."

The prolonged stay, which may have inspired the poem, "Ragged Island," around this time, seems to have tapped new freshets within Edna Millay, for the poems continued to flow steadily, at an even pace. By June of 1949, when she wrote to Cass Canfield to offer her overwhelming gratitude for Harper's arrangement by which she received a monthly payment of royalties, she was able to tell him that she would soon have a new volume ready for publication. She had been working hard for the past seven months. She had so far recovered that she was also writing a satire in verse against T. S. Eliot, inspired by Lewis Gannett's review of Eliot's *Notes Toward a Definition of Culture*, which had recently been published. In it, Eliot attempted to lay down arbitrary rules for literature with such pomposity and lack of humor that she could not resist ridiculing him. She had already written about twenty such satiric verses, which, she claimed, could not be construed as abusive; they were "merely murderous." And she had enjoyed Robert Hillyer's brilliant, witty article in the *Saturday Review*, "Poetry's New Priesthood," berating the Bollingen Award to Ezra Pound that year. Edna had nothing but scorn for the latter's politics and his anti-Semitism. She once remarked that Ezra was "such a short-weight Pound," and she could not feel differently now.

Such comment could not come from any but an alert mind, one aware of the cross-currents in the literary atmosphere and unafraid to assert her individuality. Her poetic senses continued on the *qui-vive;* her lyric gift began to revive; though only the year before Wilson had thought most of the fragments she showed him "of an almost unrelieved blackness," the light was beginning to return. She wrote of her childhood—her wild delight at the first sight of a fawn, a joy she still experienced each spring with dizzying intensity; of her girlhood in Camden, the wonder of a

2 The *Letters* translates this loosely as "Dearest."

romantic dawn alone on the top of Mount Megunticook. She wrote of "Steepletop," and of her garden, in lines that sang again. In August, when "Bunny" wanted to come there again, she was working too hard to see him, as much as she would have loved talking to him. She was packing in every moment with poetry-writing, and she didn't dare risk being "deflected" from the forward-going direction in which her work was moving rapidly with the old "beat."

Then, just as she was regaining the rhythm of her creative activity, Eugen was taken to the hospital for surgery following an examination for suspected lung disease. He had had a persistent cough all summer and the doctor advised going into Boston Hospital immediately. The trouble proved to be malignant; the operation was performed at once. For a day or two he appeared to be recovering, but he suddenly suffered a relapse and died on August 30, 1949. Edna, stunned by the swiftness and the blackness of the final blow, managed somehow to remain composed during the funeral for her sixty-nine-year-old husband, but collapsed afterward. She had to spend weeks in Doctors Hospital again; and when she came out, late in October, she felt desolate in grief, by the loss of the one man who had cared for her so tenderly.

She must have wondered at first not only how she was going to bear the sorrow of her loss, but how she was going to cope with the myriad details of daily living. For more than twenty-five years Eugen had assumed the entire responsibility of the household as well as the office of business manager for Edna Millay. For years he took care of her correspondence after the accident had disabled her right arm. Edna certainly could not afford a secretary. Perhaps she might not have felt so forsaken if Eugen had been less ubiquitous. He had been all things to her and there was no one who could possibly fill his place. She did not want anyone to live with her, and she stoically refused to leave "Steepletop." John Pinnie would take care of the chores, and she would manage somehow. She remained firm in her decision to live there alone, despite the offers of relatives and friends, and would not hear of anyone staying with her, even Norma and Charles. She was not willing to have the telephone connected again because she was afraid she would hear Eugen's footsteps running to answer it. If she remembered those habitual acts of servitude he performed she would break down in tears.

Whether her stern stoicism arose from a feeling of guilt because she did not fully appreciate Eugen until after his death, is difficult to say. Yet her dogged determination to remain alone in the face of her frail health and weak finances, forfending all company in living arrangements, including the sister who had once been her closest companion, is rather odd. It seems that her reaction came from a belated loyalty to the man who, in Sheean's words, "had served and guarded her like the priest of a temple." She had always taken him for granted. Though there is no doubt that she loved him, she was never in love with Eugen as she was with the unattainable Arthur, or with love itself, as manifested from time to time in her poems. Her feeling for Eugen is revealed in one sentence of a note to Mrs. Mary Herron, a neighbor and postmistress at Austerlitz, who had helped her like a sister in answering the many sympathy letters she received. After thanking her friend, she added that it must indeed seem impossible to the postmistress that Eugen would not be coming down the hill for the mail on such a beautiful autumn day. But then "he never came up the hill either, any more." It must have been all but impossible for Edna to grasp that inexplorable fact for some time.

However, the inner fortitude which she had inherited from her mother, and the bravery she herself had built up as a child stood her in good stead now. Although in "The Solid Sprite Who Stands Alone," and in a recent poem beginning, "The courage that my mother had," Edna Millay claims that she lacked the powers she admired in her mother, she in fact personified them when events called for strength. In any case, she was able to adjust her life and begin to complete the new volume of poetry.

In November, about nine weeks after Eugen's death, she was able to send Cass Canfield a clear-headed, logical piece of criticism in regard to an introduction that her old friend William Rose Benét had written to a Modern Classics edition of *Second April* and *The Buck in the Snow*, which Harper's planned to bring out. She objected primarily to Benét's overly familiar tone, to his use of the name "Vincent," for one thing. Though he and

Elinor, like most of her close friends, had always called her that, she felt it was too intimate for a formal introduction. Nor was this the place for the "bit of gossip" that Bill had implied by saying, "I think I know whom," in referring to the subject of one of the sonnets: the reader would be more interested in wishing to squeeze this morsel that might be juicy than in reading the remarks on the poetry. Then she outlined the various revisions necessary to whip the piece into shape and generally clean up the sloppy writing. She had four pages of critical notes by the time she finished, all so well stated that Benét, far from being annoyed, felt that "Vincent" had vastly improved his introduction. Whatever private sorrow she might be suffering, she was not so grief-stricken that she could not write a clear and even hard-headed letter where her professional reputation was at stake.

With publication of a new volume as her goal, she kept close to the track, hardly allowing herself to be diverted for a moment. On the first Thanksgiving Day she ever spent alone she was working so hard at the "masonery" of her art, that the holiday passed painlessly. Early in December, she sent a busy letter, almost too bright and breezy, to Margaret Cuthbert of NBC and Alice Blum, an editor at the *Ladies Home Journal*, telling them that all she wanted for Christmas was a practical present of three Remington portable typewriter ribbons; six composition books with stiff covers; and some "who-dun-its" or Westerns. But at times she would break down, bursting into tears unexpectedly. Her state of being is probably best summed up in a brief note to Professor Manuel Mischoulon, an Argentine poet who had translated seven sonnets from *Fatal Interview* into Spanish for publication in a South American literary journal. Edna had written a long letter to him just before Eugen's illness, discussing the translations in detail. Mischoulon had answered her right after the funeral, and of course had received no reply. He wrote again, wondering whether he had not heard because she was ill. Her succinct explanation—that she was far worse than ill: her husband had died—was poignant testimony of the emotional upheaval caused by the infinite void that Eugen's sudden death had left in her life.

Alone again on Christmas Eve, she courageously played and

sang some Christmas Carols; and on New Year's Eve, she made a Transatlantic call to Eugen's family in Holland; she had not sent them any word following the fateful, stark message of the "shocking cablegram," and she was sure they would be thinking of him on that night, which the Dutch observed with solemnity. They were probably worrying about her, too, for although they rarely spoke of it, the bonds of family love had always been strong between them.

By steady writing, and, as if she were both nurse and patient, making herself take the full quota of vitamin pills and orange juice, she was able to weather the winter. But she dreaded the thought of spring without Eugen; she was fearful of being hurt by the tender green shoots that had always meant so much to both of them. In April, the sight of the first dandelion one warm sunny day brought her abruptly to a standstill; she stared at it in horror. A moment later she felt ashamed and "sorry for the dandelion"; all of a sudden, involuntarily, her face "just crumpled up and cried." She confessed her mixed emotions in a touching note to Mary Herron and related the incident recalling a host of heartbreaking memories: Eugen's excitement at discovering the early dandelions, his digging a fine mess for greens long before the rabbits found them, his half-serious plea not to scold him for saying "pick" instead of "dig" the dandelions. She ended with the repeated sigh of "Alas" like a rueful refrain of sorrow and regret.

In the same telling note she informed the postmistress in no uncertain terms that she wanted to give *fifty*—not five—dollars to the Cancer Society. And in outlining her reasons, she crystallized her feelings toward Eugen and Arthur when she stated that her "own wonderful darling" and their "beloved friend, Arthur Ficke, *that fine poet*" [3] had both died of cancer.[4] However complicated her feelings for Arthur may have been, she always admired his gifts as a poet, although his last book, *Tumultuous Shore and Other Poems*, had been either ignored by the critics or dismissed as too intellectual. Her fierce professional loyalty indicates that friendship predominated in her attitude toward Arthur; and

[3] Italics mine.
[4] As well as members of Eugen's family.

Eugen over the years, she now realized, had become so close to her it was as if he had been part of herself.

Yet Edna Millay steadfastly maintained her individuality. In a brief letter to Tess later in the summer, after saying that Ragged Island was not for sale because as soon as she could bear it she was going back there, she asked her friend to see to it that the tax invoice for the property was sent under her own name: "Miss" was her correct and legal title; she had never used Eugen's name and did not intend to start now that he was gone. It was both annoying and painful to read the tax on Ragged Island listed in his surname with only a "Mrs." in front of it.[5] He had loved the island, more if possible than she; it would be at least a year before she could trust herself to return, and she would not stop off at Bailey's Island to visit Tess, the way she and Eugen often did.

The lyrical impulse continued to throb within her, evoking new poems. In many of these, soon to voice the title of the promised volume, *Mine the Harvest,* Edna Millay took stock of her portion of life's bounty and found it fulsome, despite the tragedy of her recent loss and the trials of the past. Here once again was a re-affirmation of life's richness, joy in the gifts of the good earth, and the essential value of the human spirit, as in the great title poem of her first volume, *Renascence,* but presented in a more reflective mood. Other poems repeated the theme: it was as if she had come round full circle, and, with her uncanny prescience, probably sensed that she was completing the cycle of her life as well as her work. She wrote furiously, not feverishly, as in the war years, but with her former joy in a beloved labor. A letter to her agent, begun in June, was not finished until the middle of August because she was too deeply involved in poetry, and had not a moment to continue. Her genius for song was returning in a surge of free-line lyrics; the book was taking shape at last. This was the volume of which Robert Hillyer was to decree happily, "Here is Edna Millay at her finest." And other critics would agree that her lyric quality had come back in full voice if in more flexible form.

Part of her time was spent on the research and writing of a

[5] When traveling, Edna Millay always registered at hotels under her own name, whether on tour or not.

Thanksgiving Day poem she had been commissioned to write for the *Saturday Evening Post*. In July she wrote to the library in Lenox, asking for factual material on the Pilgrims. As the summer progressed and the situation in Korea grew worse, she realized that a poem dealing with nothing more lethal than a "neighborly scalping party" would mean little to a "nation waiting in dread for a possible atom bomb" attack. Though she had only ten days left until her deadline, she scrapped the whole poem, on which she had worked very hard, and started again. She forced herself to relax, and almost immediately a new poem started to form in her mind. She would never stoop to propaganda again, but neither could she ignore the problems of a doubtful peace. Peace was still her first love and her last. There is little doubt of the position Edna Millay would have taken on the war in Southeast Asia had she lived.

She passed the summer alone, working. Early in October she allowed Tess to drop in for a visit, but asked if her old friend would "come after lunch and leave before dinner"; she could not take time to explain; and she did not want Tess to bring her any lobster or any seaweed.

She had almost enough poems for a book, and she was determined to have no unnecessary delays. However, when Rolfe Humphries wrote requesting her to read a set of proofs and give an opinion on his translation of Catullus, she consented gladly. She admired Humphries' ability as a translator who was also a creator: his Latin versions of some of her *Fatal Interview* sonnets several years earlier were in themselves Latin poems rather than translations. She went to work on the proofs of his latest achievement with her usual thoroughness, reading and jotting down marginal notes or corrections for hours one chill October night. She sat in the living room, which she had redecorated during the summer, partly for relaxation, partly as a memorial to Eugen, because he had remarked on its shabbiness the summer before. It was bright and polished—the walls fresh, the floors waxed, the sofas and chairs newly covered—it was the most cheerful room in the house. She had been stationed in her wing chair beside the bird-window until dark, and then moved next to the fire John Pinnie had set in the fireplace. Sliding her legs under her, she settled down on the hearth, one elbow resting on the couch, and began to read.

When she was deep in a task that fascinated and absorbed her, she lost track of the hour. By the time she finished, a pale streak of light glowed in the sky; another day was dawning: October 19, 1950. The galleys were strewn around on the floor, but she was too tired to pick them up. She had been sipping some Alsatian wine now and then as she read. Taking her wine glass and the partly empty bottle, she went into the kitchen to leave a note for Lena Reusch, a neighbor who occasionally came in to do the ironing and help with the heavy cleaning. Edna wanted to warn her not to set the iron too high or it would scorch, and to be careful not to burn her fingers in shifting from one heat to another. The kitchen clock said five-thirty. Explaining that she had been working all night and was going to bed, she ended her note as if she were sounding a reveille to some new dawn, with "Good-morning—." Then she picked up the bottle and wine glass, went into the hall and up the few steps to the landing, where the stairs turned sharply in a full flight leading to the library–poetry room at the top. Just as she was about to go up, she must have felt faint, or possibly a stab of pain, and instead, she sat down on the first step above the landing; at the same time, she carefully placed the wine on the next step above. There on the stair, like a wand in the wind, she swayed forward and died.

Shortly after eight o'clock, John Pinnie came in the back door to deliver the milk as he had been doing for years. He looked into the hall, saw nothing unusual, and left. It was not until three in the afternoon, when he came to place the wood for the evening fire that he went farther into the hall and saw her. She was still sitting, bowed over, on the first step above the landing. And, perhaps because of the inherent spirit of her patron St. Vincent, protector of wine growers, the bottle and wine glass were standing unbroken.

She had vowed in "Moriturus" that she would put up a fierce fight against Death no matter how decrepit she might be: that only by dragging her forth, "Shrieking to the south/ And clutching at the north" would he succeed in forcing her to surrender. And she repeated the theme many times in her poetry; but in the end she seemed to have gone quietly with Death, her spirit easing away without disturbing her body. She had predicted more correctly in "Midnight Oil," a variant of the candle quatrain, that the years Time took off *her* life would be from the other end: far from decrepit with age, Edna St. Vincent Millay was only fifty-eight years old, and, in spite of all her woes, once again singing the praises of life—"the phrase in air"—when her heart stopped beating. Perhaps she had her own inscription in mind when she advised the world to "forget the epitaph" and "take up the song."

Epilogue: 1969

I T IS AN unfortunate fact that poetry, perhaps the most abstract of the literary arts, is subject to the shifting winds of fashion. One would expect that poetry, once it has been accepted, would hold a permanent place, but it is constantly buffeted by changing currents; and too often the work of an individual poet is nearly blown into oblivion before it is recovered.

Such has been the case with Edna St. Vincent Millay.

It is true that she precipitated her fall from grace by continuing to write propaganda poetry even after her public had turned the cold shoulder of disapproval on her exhortations; and that her nervous breakdown caused her to go into seclusion after the war in 1945. It is also true that after Eugen's death Edna Millay's insistence on solitude was almost obsessive, following the period of reckless drinking that sent her back to Doctors Hospital. Her behavior toward old friends was unduly harsh at times, as intimated in two letters written by Margaret Cuthbert in late September of 1949. Moreover, when her emotional balance had been partially restored and she started writing again, she clung to solitude as a rampart against any interruption of her work. If she alienated people, it was because she could not help herself.

The funeral was in keeping with those last years. Only Norma and Charles, together with a few other relatives and close friends, perhaps twenty-five people in all, gathered at "Steepletop" to hold a simple service. Norma read some of her sister's poetry, including "The Poet and His Book," and Allan Ross MacDougall followed with the poet's distinctive "Dirge Without Music." Her friend Tess played one of her favorite pieces, Beethoven's "Appassionata" to end the service. At Vincent's request, her body was cremated at Chatham, New York, as Eugen's had been only a little over a year before, and the ashes of both were buried in the laurel grove at "Steepletop" at the same time.

The newspapers, although duly respectful in reporting her death, were hardly expansive in recognition of her place in American literature, and spent little space in recounting her life or mourning the loss of a remarkable poet and personality. *The New York Times* headline read, ʹEdna St. Vincent Millay Found Dead at 58;ʹ Noted Poet Succumbs to Heart Attack in Upstate Home . . .ʺfollowed by a sub-head, "Won Pulitzer Prize in 1922," and the pertinent details of her death. An editorial the following day, entitled "A Stilled Voice," was more in keeping with Edna Millay's creative career, describing her as "one of this country's most eminent personages in the arts," and containing one telling line, "Her stature was beyond cavil."

The *Herald-Tribune* began its story on the funeral, "Non-religious services were held here for Edna St. Vincent Millay in the same atmosphere of poetry and privacy in which she had lived for the past twenty years." Such a statement is indicative of the short memory of the public; while "Steepletop" afforded the privacy she needed to write poetry, Edna Millay actually had lived in seclusion for about only five years, from 1945 to 1950. Various periodicals carried brief stories, among them *Life* Magazine and the *Saturday Review* with its patronizing account of her life and work by John Ciardi, discussed previously. Within a few days, the articles dwindled down. There was a memorial service at Camden, Maine, honoring the poet on "her native heath," and a memorial week there in 1953, when the Music Room at Whitehall Inn (where she first read "Renascence" in 1912) was dedicated to her, and five performances of "The King's Henchman" were given.

But the general attitude was certainly not as eulogistic as one would have expected; no memorial volumes were suggested, no poetry prizes or awards established in her name, no foundations

set up in her memory. Such tributes as were paid her were mere
trifles compared to some of those she had received at the height
of her popularity. Among her colleagues, Rolfe Humphries alone
recorded a succinct protest in the *Nation* (December 30, 1950)
against the apathy of the press; he pointed to her qualities of
enduring value including her wit and clarity, and her elemental
language that had universal appeal. It was not until Vincent
Sheean's slim book of memoirs, *The Indigo Bunting,* was published in 1951 that the eminent critic, Edmund Wilson, decided
to append an "Epilogue, 1952: Edna St. Vincent Millay," to his
literary chronicle of the nineteen-twenties and thirties, an objective and meaningful account of his friendship with the poet
who had died two years before. His piece begins with an apologetic note that so far no full tribute had been paid to "this great
writer." He gave voice to the "unfashionable opinion" that Millay
seemed to him one of the few poets in a predominantly prose
age who had "attained to anything like the stature of great
literary figures." He went on to explain his statement, citing her
as "a spokesman for the human spirit."

The appearance of the *Letters of Edna St. Vincent Millay* in
1952, and of her final volume, *Mine the Harvest,* in 1954, brought
favorable reviews from such sources as Lewis Gannett (whose
enthusiasm for the "triumphant revelation" of her personal correspondence is refreshing, and reflects Gannett's appreciation of
Edna Millay both as poet and personage), Irwin Edman, Robert
Hillyer, and Louise Townsend Nicholl. Their estimates, along
with those of Wilson took the first steps toward restoring critical
esteem following the decline of Millay's reputation with *Conversation at Midnight,* and the denigration resulting from the
propaganda poetry; but the progress was slow.

Publication of her *Collected Poems* in 1956 brought a tribute
to her greatness in Francis Hackett's review of the book in *The
New Republic* (December 24, 1956). He emphasized her quest
for freedom from the bondage of outworn, nineteenth-century
mores, her quest for justice, her feeling for America in the broad-
est sense, her intense love of life and her anger at man's misuse
of its gift, the tragedy of his tendency to destroy it, all as contained in her poetry. With few exceptions, he found the body of

her work equal to its objectives, a legacy bequeathed to American literature from a poet who was both artist and humanist. The collected volume also brought to light a wide following of devoted readers who wrote commemorative verses, based on Millay themes, the best of which were published in the book-review section of *The New York Times*. Michel Ferano's "Autumn Elegy," for example, which catches the essence of her reflective mood, making use of some of her classical references and metaphoric language in such lines as, ". . . Death caught you unaware,/ And seized you like Persephone—/ The song usurped, 'the phrase in air.'" could have been written only by one well-schooled in her poetry.

The Millay revival, however, was brief as far as critical appraisal was concerned; reviews of the volume in the spring of 1957 were typical of the unfavorable attitude of the forties and early fifties. The late Bette Richart, who in her own early poetry had been an ardent Millay disciple, later switched her allegiance to Marianne Moore, and writing in *Commonweal* ("Poet of Our Youth," May 10, 1957), found Millay for the most part a shrill, neurotic and immature poet, except for the sonnets. Other critics of that year relegated Edna Millay to the limited realm of youthful lyricism and subjective sorrow. Here, save for a juvenile biography by Toby Shafter, she was allowed to languish for the remainder of the fifties.

With the sixties, there was the advent of the "new left" among the young, and the rise of the liberals concerned with civil rights, against a background of loss of individualism in an age of mass production and potential atomic destruction. These characteristics of the times brought an increasing audience for the qualities of human warmth and hard-core realism that were combined in Millay's poetry with a beauty of expression. There is not so much difference between the Greenwich Village Peace Center today and the Liberal Club or the Provincetown Players of an earlier time that the young cannot "relate" to the involvement in public issues as well as the personal feelings they find in Millay. They are constantly discovering her with delight, while older readers have remained steadfast in their admiration for much of her work.

The truth is that Edna Millay has never lacked an audience. Her books are not out of print, as are those by many of her colleagues, and they enjoy a wide circulation from library shelves. The recordings she made of her poetry are currently advertised in leading magazines along with those of Robert Frost, Carl Sandburg, e.e. cummings, Dylan Thomas, and W. H. Auden, listed as "the great poets of our age." A prominent folk-singer recently performed her "Ballad of the Harp-Weaver" on television with great success.

Clearly the edicts of earlier critics—that her sonnets are so derived from another century and her work in general so plainly marked with the stamp of the twenties that she is "dated"—is in itself an outmoded attitude. Fresh critical appraisal has already begun with Norman Brittin's study, *Edna St. Vincent Millay*, published in 1967, which concludes that much of her writing, although it typifies the twenties, also transcends that era and well withstands the test of time. A projected bibliography, entitled, *A Comprehensive Bibliography of Millay Criticism* by John Joseph Patton is scheduled to appear in the near future. A book on Millay's life, written for young adults, *Restless Spirit* by Miriam Gurko, was published in 1962, and several biographies are in process, one of them by Norma Millay Ellis.

A definitive biography of Edna St. Vincent Millay has yet to be written, and cannot be written until all the material is available. Every writer of biography is entitled to his own interpretation of an artist's work. I have tried to give my interpretation of Edna Millay's work through this story of her life and her relationship to those who touched her. Some of the material was given to me by people who wished to remain anonymous, but most of it has been derived from reading the poetry and the personal correspondence of my subject, the latter always a primary source in any biography. For all of its shortcomings, hers was a remarkable personality, one I hope I have brought alive in these pages.

A Selected Bibliography
Including Sources of Background Material

Works by Edna St. Vincent Millay (Listed chronologically):

I. VOLUMES OF POETRY:

Renascence and Other Poems. New York: Mitchell Kennerly, 1917.
A Few Figs from Thistles. Poems and Four Sonnets. Salvo One. New York: Frank Shay, 1920. Enlarged editions, 1921, 1922.
Second April. New York: Mitchell Kennerly, 1921.

> (All three of the above were reissued by Harper & Brothers directly after 1923, the year that the firm became Millay's permanent publishers.)

The Harp-Weaver and Other Poems. New York and London: Harper & Brothers, 1923.

> The following works by Edna St. Vincent Millay were all published by Harper & Brothers, which became Harper & Row in 1962, unless otherwise stated:

The Buck in the Snow. New York and London: 1928.
Edna St. Vincent Millay's Poems Selected for Young People. New York and London: 1929.
Fatal Interview. New York and London: 1931.
Wine from These Grapes. New York and London: 1934.
Conversation at Midnight. New York and London: 1937.
Huntsman, What Quarry? New York and London: 1939.
Make Bright the Arrows; 1940 Notebook. New York and London: 1940.

Invocation to the Muses. New York and London: 1941.

Collected Sonnets. New York and London: 1941.

The Murder of Ludice. New York and London: 1942.

Collected Lyrics. New York and London:1943.

Poem and Prayer for an Invading Army. New York: National Broadcasting Company, 1944.

Mine the Harvest (Post.) New York and London: 1954.

Collected Poems (Post.) New York and London: 1956.

II. VERSE PLAYS:

Aria da Capo. First published, *Reedy's Mirror,* March 18, 1920; then in *The Chapbook (A Monthly Miscellany)* Vol. 3, No. 14; London: Poetry Bookshop, August 1920; then by Mitchell Kennerly, 1921; then in *Twenty-five Best Plays of the Modern American Theatre,* ed. by John Gassner. New York: Crown, 1949.

The Lamp and the Bell. New York: Frank Shay, 1921.

Two Slatterns and a King. Cincinnati: Stewart Kidd, 1921.

Three Plays (contains the above three titles in one volume). New York: Harper & Brothers, 1926.

The King's Henchman. New York and London: 1927.

The Princess Marries the Page. New York and London: 1932.

III. TRANSLATIONS:

"Heavenly and Earthly Love," in *All the Plays of Molnar.* New York: Vanguard Press, 1929.

Flowers of Evil, from the French of Charles Baudelaire, with George Dillon. New York and London: 1936.

"The Arrival," (translation of "Llegada," by Emilio Prados) in *And Spain Sings,* pp. 57-61; edited by Rolfe Humphries. New York: Vanguard Press, 1937.

IV. LETTERS:

Letters to Charlotte Babcock Sills, October 12, 1917 and December, 1917. Vassar College Library, Special Collections.

Letter to the *New York World,* October 6, 1927.

Letters of Edna St. Vincent Millay. Edited by Allan Ross Macdougall. New York and London: Harper & Brothers, 1952.

Burden, Jean, "With Love from Vincent," *Yankee,* XXII, May, 1958, pp. 40-43, 92-95. Contains letters to the poet's Aunt Susan, Mrs. Frank L. Ricker.

Carpenter, Margaret H., *Sara Teasdale.* New York: Schulte Publishing

Company, 1960, pp. 166, 231-232. Contains letters to and from Millay.

V. UNCOLLECTED POETRY:

"Sonnet" ("You men and women all of British birth,") *The New York Times Magazine,* February 16, 1941, p. 2.
"Not to Be Spotted by His Blood," *The New York Times Magazine,* December 28, 1941, p. 5.
"Thanksgiving, 1942," *The New York Times Magazine,* November 22, 1942, pp. 5-6.
"For My Brother Han and My Sisters, in Holland," *The New York Times Magazine,* January 7, 1945, p. 24.
"To the Leaders of the Allied Nations," *The New York Times Magazine,* January 21, 1945.
"Thanksgiving . . . 1950," *Saturday Evening Post,* November 25, 1950, p. 31.
Untitled poem ("Let me not shout . . .") Yost, Karl, *A Bibliography of the Works of Edna St. Vincent Millay.* New York: Harper & Brothers, 1937, p. 60.

VI. PROSE:

The Wall of Dominoes (prose play). *Vassar Miscellany Monthly,* May, 1917.
Distressing Dialogues. (pseud., Nancy Boyd) New York: Harper & Brothers, 1924.
"Fear," an essay in *Outlook* Magazine, November 9, 1927.
Preface to *Flowers of Evil* (on the translation of poetry).

Works about Edna St. Vincent Millay and Her Work:

I. BIBLIOGRAPHICAL MATERIAL:

Kohn, John S. van E. "Some Undergraduate Printings of Edna St. Vincent Millay," *Publishers' Weekly,* November 30, 1940, pp. 2026-2029.
Yost, Karl, *A Bibliography of the Works of Edna St. Vincent Millay.* New York: Harper & Brothers, 1937.

II. BIOGRAPHICAL AND CRITICAL MATERIAL:

Adams, Franklin P., *The Diary of Our Own Samuel Pepys.* New York: Simon & Schuster, 1935.
Atkins, Elizabeth, *Edna St. Vincent Millay and Her Times.* Chicago:

University of Chicago Press, 1936. Reissued by Russell & Russell, 1963.

Bogan, Louise, *Achievements in American Poetry*. Henry Regnery Company, 1951.

——— *Selected Criticism*. New York: Noonday Press, 1955.

Brenner, Rica, *Ten Modern Poets*. New York: Harcourt, Brace & Co., 1930.

Brittin, Norman A., *Edna St. Vincent Millay*. New York: Twayne Publishers, Inc., U.S. Authors Series, No. 116, 1967.

Churchill, Allen, *The Improper Bohemians*. New York: E. P. Dutton Company, 1959.

Cook, Harold Lewis, "Edna St. Vincent Millay—An Essay" (precedes text in the Yost bibliography).

Cowley, Malcolm, *After the Genteel Tradition*. New York: W. W. Norton, 1937.

——— *Exile's Return*. New York: W. W. Norton, 1934.

Dell, Floyd, *Homecoming: An Autobiography*. New York: Farrar & Rinehart Company, 1933.

——— *King Arthur's Socks and other Village Plays*. New York: Alfred A. Knopf, 1922.

——— *Love in Greenwich Village*. New York: George H. Doran & Co., 1926.

Eastman, Max, *Enjoyment of Living*. New York: Harper & Brothers, 1948.

——— *Great Companions: Critical Memoirs of Some Famous Friends*. New York: Farrar, Strauss & Cudahy, 1959.

Ficke, Arthur Davison, *Out of Silence*. New York: Alfred A. Knopf, 1924.

——— *The Secret and Other Poems*. New York: Doubleday-Doran Co., 1936.

——— *Selected Poems*. New York: George H. Doran Co., 1926.

——— *Sonnets of a Portrait Painter*, Revised Edition. New York: Mitchell Kennerly, 1922. "Epitaph for the Poet V (Hymn to Intellectual Beauty) To Edna St. Vincent Millay."

Glaspell, Susan, *The Road to the Temple*. New York: Frederick A. Stokes Company, 1927.

Gould, Jean, *Modern American Playwrights*. New York: Dodd, Mead & Company, 1966.

Gregory, Horace, and Zaturenska, Maria, *History of American Poetry from 1900 to 1940*. New York: Harcourt, Brace & Co., 1947.

Gurko, Miriam, *Restless Spirit: The Life of Edna St. Vincent Millay*. New York: Thomas Y. Crowell Company, 1962.

Hanau, Stella, and Deutsch, Helen, *The Provincetown: A Story of the Theatre*. New York: Farrar & Rinehart Company, 1931.

Kreymborg, Alfred, *Our Singing Strength*. New York: Coward-McCann, 1925.

Langner, Lawrence, *The Magic Curtain*. New York: E. P. Dutton Company, 1951.

Loggins, Vernon, *I Hear America*. New York: Thomas Y. Crowell Company, 1937.

MacCracken, Henry Noble, *The Hickory Limb*. New York: Charles Scribner's Sons, 1950.

Mearns, Hughes (ed.) *Edna St. Vincent Millay*. New York: Simon & Schuster, 1927.

Munson, Gorham, *Penobscot, Down East Paradise* ("Edna St. Vincent Millay and the Town of Camden"). Philadelphia: J. B. Lippincott Co., 1959.

Powys, Llewellyn, *Dorset Essays*. London: John Lane Company, 1935.
——— *Impassioned Clay*. New York: Longmans, Green Co., 1931.
——— *Letters* (with a Preface by Alyse Gregory, his wife). London: John Lane Company, 1943.
——— *The Verdict of Bridlegoose*. New York: Harcourt, Brace & Company, 1926.

Rittenhouse, Jesse B., *My House of Life*. Boston: Houghton Mifflin Company, 1934.

Shafter, Toby, *Edna St. Vincent Millay, America's Best-Loved Poet*. New York: Julian Messner, 1957.

Sheean, Vincent, *The Indigo Bunting: A Memoir of Edna St. Vincent Millay*. New York: Harper & Brothers, 1951.

Simonson, Lee, *Minor Prophecies*. New York: Harcourt, Brace & Company, 1927.

Sinclair, Upton, *A Cup of Fury*. New York: Channel Press, 1956.

Smith, William Jay, *The Spectra Hoax*. Middletown: Wesleyan University Press, 1961.

Untermeyer, Jean Starr, *Private Collection*. New York: Alfred A. Knopf, 1965.

Untermeyer, Louis, *American Poetry Since 1900*, Revised Edition. New York: Harcourt, Brace & Company, 1953.
——— *Anthology of Modern American Poetry* (New and Enlarged). New York: Harcourt, Brace & Company, 1953.

Valenti, Michael, *Question of Guilt*. New York: Paperback Library, 1966.

Van Doren, Carl C., *Many Minds: Critical Essays on American Writers*. New York: Alfred A. Knopf, 1924.

Ware, Caroline F., *Greenwich Village, 1920-1930*. Boston: Houghton Mifflin Company, 1935.

Wilson, Edmund, *I Thought of Daisy*. New York: Charles Scribner's Sons, 1929.

———— *The Shores of Light: A Literary Chronicle of the Twenties and Thirties*. New York: Farrar, Strauss & Young, 1952 (principally, "Epilogue, 1952: Edna St. Vincent Millay," and "Give That Beat Again").

III. PRIVATELY PRINTED:

Haight, Elizabeth Hazelton, *Vincent at Vassar*. Poughkeepsie: Vassar College, 1951.

Pillinger, Douglass, A *Golden Vessel of Great Song*. Chicago: Chicago Literary Club, 1964.

IV. UNPUBLISHED PAPERS:

Ficke, Arthur Davison, Notes on the preparation (with Millay) of several volumes for publication, including *The Harp-Weaver, Make Bright the Arrows*, and *Collected Sonnets* (particularly Paragraph One of the Foreword to *Collected Sonnets*).

King, Grace Hamilton, "The Development of the Social Consciousness of Edna St. Vincent Millay as Manifested in Her Poetry." Dissertation, New York University, 1943.

Pettit, Jean Morris, "Edna St. Vincent Millay: A Critical Study of Her Poetry in its Social and Literary Milieu." Dissertation, Vanderbilt University, 1955.

Roberts, W. Adolphe, "Tiger Lily." Personal Memoir of Edna St. Vincent Millay. Vassar College Library, Special Collections.

V. ARTICLES AND REVIEWS (PARTIAL LISTING):

Barnes, Djuna, "The Days of Jig Cook." *Theatre Guild* Magazine, Vol. VI, January, 1929, pp. 31-32.

Benet, William Rose, "Round About Parnassus." *Saturday Review of Literature*, Vol. XI, November 10, 1934.

———— Introduction to Modern Classics Edition of Millay poetry. Harper & Brothers, c. 1949.

Breuer, Elizabeth, "Edna St. Vincent Millay." *Pictorial Review*, Vol. No. XXXIII, November, 1931.

———— "Mother of Poets." *Pictorial Review*, March, 1930.

Bynner, Witter, "Edna St. Vincent Millay." *New Republic*, December 10, 1924, pp. 14-15.

Chotzinoff, Samuel, "Miss Millay's Part in *The King's Henchman*," *New York World*. c. February, 1927.

Ciardi, John, "Edna St. Vincent Millay: A Figure of Passionate Living." *Saturday Review*, November 11, 1950.

Colum, Padraic, "Miss Millay's Poems." *The Freeman,* November 2, 1921.

Dabbs, James McBride, "Edna St. Vincent Millay: Not Resigned." *South Atlantic Quarterly,* XXXVII, January, 1938, pp. 54-66.

Dell, Floyd (not signed), "Edna St. Vincent Millay: The Literary Spotlight." *The Bookman.* Vol. 56. 1922, pp. 272-78.

Dubois, Arthur E., "Edna St. Vincent Millay." *Sewanee Review,* Vol. XLIII January-March, 1935, pp. 80-104.

Flanner, Hildegarde, "Two Poets: Jeffers and Millay." *New Republic,* January 27, 1937.

Gannett, Lewis, "Letters of Edna St. Vincent Millay." (Review.) *New York Times,* October 29, 1952.

Hackett, Francis, "Edna St. Vincent Millay." *New Republic,* CXXXV, December 24, 1956, pp. 21-22.

Haight, Elizabeth Hazelton, "Vincent at Steepletop." *Vassar Alumnae Magazine,* February, 1957, pp. 11-14.

Hay, Sara Henderson, "The Unpersuadable V." *Saturday Review,* XXXVII, June 5, 1954, p. 20.

Hillyer, Robert, Review of *Mine the Harvest. New York Times,* April 25, 1954.

———— "A Lively, Lonely Spirit," Review of *Letters. New York Times,* November 2, 1952.

Holden, Ray, Review of *The Indigo Bunting. The New York Times,* October 21, 1951.

Humphries, Rolfe, "Miss Millay As Artist." *Nation,* December 20, 1941.

———— "Edna St. Vincent Millay." *Nation,* December 30, 1950.

Macdougall, Allan Ross, "Husband of a Genius." *Delineator,* October, 1934.

Monroe, Harriet, "Advance or Retreat?" *Poetry,* XXXVIII, July, 1931, pp. 216-21.

———— "Edna St. Vincent Millay." *Poetry,* XXIV, August, 1924, pp. 260-66.

Nicholl, Louise Townsend, "A Late, Rich Harvest." *New York Herald-Tribune,* May 23, 1954.

Ransom, John Crowe, "The Poet As Woman." *Southern Review,* II, Spring, 1937, pp. 783-806.

Richart, Bette, "Poet of Our Youth." *Commonweal,* LXVI, May 10, 1957, pp. 150-51.

Rosenfeld, Paul, "Under Angry Constellations." *Poetry,* October, 1939.

Schwartz, Delmore, "Poetry of Millay." *Nation,* CLVII, December 19, 1943, pp. 735-36.

Scott, Winfield Townley, "Millay Collected." *Poetry,* March, 1944, pp. 334-42.

Sills, Charlotte Babcock, "Letter to the Editor." *Vassar Alumnae Magazine,* December, 1960, pp. 25-26.

Taggard, Genevieve, "A Woman's Anatomy of Love." *New York Herald-Tribune, Review of Books.* April 19, 1931.

Tate, Allen, "Miss Millay's Sonnets." *New Republic,* XLVI, May 6, 1931, pp. 335-36.

Taylor, Deems, "Edna St. Vincent Millay, 1892-1950." Commemorative Tributes, American Academy of Arts and Letters. New York, 1951, pp. 103-108.

Watkins, Mary F., "Operatic Events of the Past Month." *The Musical Observer,* XXVI, April, 1927, pp. 12, 38-39.

Index

300

LEE COUNTY LIBRARY
SANFORD, N. C.

LEE COUNTY LIBRARY
SANFORD, N. C.

47

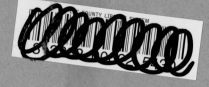

B
Millay
Gould
The poet and her book

Dziengelelki

LEE COUNTY LIBRARY
SANFORD, N. C.